To Carl and Sugy,
I am very grateful for
your support,

Fr. Martin

# Dawn at Last

Dawn at Last

# Dawn at Last

Rev. L. C. M. Ibeh

Library of Congress Control Number:      2017913848
ISBN:                Hardcover           978-1-5434-5028-6
                     Softcover           978-1-5434-5027-9
                     eBook               978-1-5434-5026-2

Rev. date: 09/15/2017

**To order additional copies of this book, contact:**
Xlibris
1-888-795-4274
www.Xlibris.com
Orders@Xlibris.com
764084

This book is dedicated to my loving dad, who lives in my heart and who lives on resting eternally with the Redeemer.

*Whenever the vessel of clay he was making turned out badly in his hand, he tried again, making another vessel of whatever sort he pleased. Then the word of the LORD came to me: Can I not do to you, house of Israel, as this potter has done?—oracle of the LORD. Indeed, like clay in the hand of the potter, so are you in my hand, house of Israel* (Jer. 18:4–6, *NAB*).

# Contents

# Contents

# Acknowledgments

Blessed be the name of my Lord Jesus Christ who "has done all things well" (Mark 7:37).

I'm grateful to my bishop, Most Reverend Felipe Estevez, who has given me his strongest spiritual and moral support and shown me the spirit of a true shepherd. I owe a deep gratitude to Father John Horn, whom the Holy Spirit used as a tool to point me in the right direction; he confidently recommended me to the diocese of St. Augustine, where the Lord calls me to serve His people in priestly ministry. I thank our vocation director, Fr. David Ruchinski and his administrative assistant, Kathy Martens, who always give generously of their time to serve, direct, and support all the seminarians. I'm indebted to the brothers and sisters of the Society of Our Mother of Peace, for all the many ways they have made a lasting impression in my life. Their religious community was my first faith family in the States, and their Solitude served as a "training camp" where the Holy Spirit groomed me for eight years to become a vibrant and brave soldier of Christ. I appreciate the seminary faculty of Kenrick-Glennon Seminary, St. Louis, and St. Vincent de Paul Regional Seminary, Florida, for giving me quality formation and excellent guidance. My sincere thanks to Fr. Harry Voelker, who shows me great fatherly affection and encourages me to write. I'm grateful to Fr. James Boddie and Fr. Jason Trull for showing me much kindness during my internship in their parishes. I appreciate our seminarians and priests who have touched my life with their characteristic fraternal spirit.

I heartily appreciate Dr. Mary and Dr. Michael Soha who opened their hearts and their doors, giving me a key to their home since I arrived in the diocese. I can't thank enough Clifford and Rose Lewis who generously gave me great support and sponsored my pilgrimage to Mexico. I appreciate my big "sister," Amaka Egomonu, for her thoughtfulness and generosity.

I remain ever grateful to Joseph Edden who painstakingly went through my manuscript and made necessary editorial corrections. I'm indebted to Connie Cooley and Mary Ann Sullivan for taking their time to skillfully edit my manuscript. I can't express my gratitude enough to Whit Hansell for his great kindness to me. Many thanks to Carol-Ann Black, managing editor of the *Courier* newspaper, for helping me in the best possible way. I won't forget the parishioners of Christ the King Catholic Church, Jacksonville, for being prayerfully supportive throughout the years of my seminary formation in the diocese. The parish community of St. Elizabeth Ann Seton Parish was a great inspiration to me during my pastoral year in the parish.

I wish this paper would be enough to mention the names of all the people who have inspired, encouraged, and generously supported me in many ways throughout this journey. Their names are written in my heart and above all, God, our just Rewarder, will not forget all their service of charity: "For God is not unjust so as to overlook your work and the love you have demonstrated for his name by having served and continuing to serve the holy ones" (Heb 6:10).

# Part One

## Prelude, Introducing Clay's Life Story

One thing I ask of the LORD; this I seek: To dwell in the LORD's house all the days of my life, to gaze on the LORD's beauty, to visit his temple.
—Psalm 27:4

### Firm Faith

The evening was breezy and refreshingly cool. Clay had just returned from Mass. He joyfully ate his fill of delicious fufu and vegetable soup. Sitting at the corridor, Clay began to read a spiritual book which his friend gave him. It was a book on the meaning of suffering. Clay was very interested in reading the book for some reason. His heart's desire had been to dedicate his entire life in priestly ministry to help those who were hurting to experience the Lord's abiding presence and saving love.

However, Clay's journey of life was like riding through deep ruts. He went through some tough times. Amidst the storms, Clay trusted that he was sheltered in the Lord's arms. In the obscurity and bleakness of his journey, Clay could see with the eyes of faith, the light of victory that Christ radiates in times of gloom and desolation. He likened himself to a lump of clay in the hand of the Divine Master Potter (God). He believed that the Lord was using his struggles and difficulties in molding and shaping him into a vessel of love and grace. In unstoppable zeal and firm faith,

Clay pressed ahead toward the perceived sacred calling, patiently and peacefully awaiting the appointed time.

How did life turn out for Clay? The exciting story is better read than heard.

## The Faithful Father

Clay read the book on suffering and was only through half of it when his friend showed up early one morning. Occasionally, Clay and his friend took some weekends out to pray at a local monastery situated about thirty-two kilometers away from their school. They had scheduled to take a spiritual retreat that weekend. Clay quickly bathed and dressed. He and his friend left for retreat that morning. They arrived at the monastery around 2:00 p.m.

It was a sunny day. In the property of the monastery was a large mango tree that provided a good shade. Clay and his friend sat on a large log under the mango tree to rest and cool off from the sweltering heat. They continued their spiritual conversation which they had started while aboard the commuter bus. Clay was sharing about new insights that he got from the spiritual book. Soon, Father Serene, one of the monks in the monastery, ambled along the narrow path. Drawing close at the place where Clay and his friend were sitting, Father Serene glanced at them, smiled and nodded to acknowledge their presence. Clay felt a fire in his heart moving him to speak to the monk. But he did not do so because he reasoned that the monk was having a quiet time. "Who is this monk?" Clay's friend inquired. "I'm not sure. It is sometimes difficult to identify monks when they wear their hoods. He walks like Father Serene though," Clay responded.

Clay did not think more about the monk until a couple of hours later that day. It happened that Father Serene was the celebrant and homilist for the Mass that evening. It was then that Clay recognized that the monk was Father Serene. By God's grace, Father Serene gave a moving homily. Clay felt touched, believing that God had spoken to him through the monk. "His homily hit home; it cut me to the heart," Clay remarked.

After the Mass, Clay wanted to speak with the monk. He had heard good things about Father Serene. The priest was well loved. His goodness, humility, devoutness, his joyful personality, and deep spiritual wisdom in directing souls had endeared him to many who visited the monastery.

## The Mount of Encounter

Clay was very eager to speak with Father Serene. As it was their tradition, Father Serene and some other priests of the community heard confession after Mass. He was getting ready to go to the confessional when Clay drew close to the sacristy door. He waited for Father Serene to come out. He saw Clay from the sacristy and beckoned: "Hello, my dear brother, if you are waiting to go to confession, please give me a second and I'll be right there." Clay stood there silently, cracking his knuckles. Father sensed that Clay might be looking for something else. And so he asked, "Do you need some help?"

The opportunity Clay had been looking for had come! "Yes, Father," Clay replied, "I would like to speak with you briefly about a personal matter." "Sure, come on in and feel free to speak to me about anything. Hold on a moment, let me place back my chasuble in the wardrobe." Clay and Father Serene sat at the prayer room near the sacristy. Clay spoke with the priest, who listened to him with utmost concern and warmness. Clay was greatly pleased that after that brief conversation Father Serene accepted Clay's request to be his spiritual director. Their spiritual relationship sparked off that evening.

## Soul-Stirring

Father Serene had directed Clay in spiritual life for a while. Clay described his meeting with Father Serene as a soul-stirring moment. After each spiritual direction, Clay would look forward excitedly to his next visit with Father Serene. He had really made great progress in his spiritual life. The saintly priest had helped him to learn the value of meditative prayer and silence. He had encouraged Clay to cultivate a daily habit of solitary prayer and Bible reading. In quiet, Clay began to see and taste more clearly the beauty and sweetness of the Lord. He could hear the whispering of the Spirit, feel his divine presence, and enjoy the peace of mind that the Lord offers to those who love him.

## The Tough Spot

On one occasion, Clay's meeting with Father Serene turned out differently. On that very day, Clay was full of joy, as usual, to meet with Father Serene. They had concluded their meeting that evening. Clay was just stepping out of the conference room when Father Serene called him back. "Clay, wait a minute. I almost forgot what I wanted to tell you. I would like you to start writing the story of your life. Take some time to write about your experiences, the challenges and events in your life that you think are significant to you. I thought your life story would make an interesting testimony of God's abiding grace and faithfulness."

Clay stood puzzled, casting his head down. Then he looked up and struggled out his response: "Yes, Father." Clay felt that Father Serene had placed him in a tough spot. He thought it would be a difficult task for him to write his whole life story. Clay considered his lack of literary skill. He mused over it as he walked the path to the park. His joy of meeting Father Serene was somewhat interrupted by a twinge of melancholic sentiment. Clay had earlier resolved not to think about the trials, the bitter experiences that he had passed through in his life. He felt that writing down the story of his life would be like reliving those grim experiences of his life. With all this in mind, Clay wished Father Serene would change his mind in regard to that. So he made up some excuses to present to the priest.

On the subsequent meeting, Clay and Father Serene were seated in the conference room. Clay lowered his gaze, as though he felt abashed. He scratched his neck and said, "Father, I am concerned about what you asked me to write." "What about it, my dear brother?" asked Father Serene. "I have thought about that seriously. I doubt whether I could remember much about my childhood. I don't even have any idea of how and where to begin. If you wouldn't mind, I can relate the story orally, as much as I have within my memory."

Father Serene was not a sort of person to be taken in easily. Folding his arms, Father Serene blinked his sharp big eyes and looked fully into Clay's face and smiled. Then he cleared his voice and said in a mild voice, "Oh my dear Clay, it is exactly what you can remember that I ask that you put in writing. I'm not in a hurry. Take your time. Each day, try to write down whatever you can recall. Do this each day until you have nothing else to write. No, you will always have something to write down, insofar as you are alive and have the mental and physical capacity to do so. Each day, you will surely have some new remarkable experiences and inspirations to update your story. The passing of time brings with it new experiences and events that you need to update your life story.

"I see a brilliant light around you. Don't let the flame go out. Don't relent in your zeal for the mission. Know that the Lord is with you. I hope to be alive to witness the realization of your aspiration. God's plan for your life will be fulfilled. Keep walking with him. Keep trusting in him. Even when your dream seems unpromising, be consoled and remain firm in faith, for the Lord is with you."

With toothless grin, Clay looked at Father Serene and said, "Father, um . . . I'm afraid, I'm not a good writer." "Oh no!" Father Serene cut in. "That shouldn't bother you, my dear. I'm not testing you for writing skill. We are here for a spiritual business, okay? Rely on God's grace and do whatever is within your limit. I'm primarily interested in the content of your writing and not how you write it. Remember that not all great people of God were great writers. The saints were great not because of their great talents but precisely because of their great love. To become a disciple of Christ, one must not necessarily possess the astounding literary skill of Shakespeare, nor the penetrating theological insight of Thomas Aquinas, nor the illuminating philosophical wisdom of Socrates.

"God does not consider how successful or influential we are, but how much love we have in every seemingly little thing we do. We should desire to deepen our love for the Lord, rather than seek to accomplish great things for him. God wants us to come to him as weak as we are, with a thrust of faith. All good gifts come from the Lord. Each person is uniquely created and gifted. No matter how humble one's gift is, one must strive to put one's gift into work, not for one's glory but for the glory of God. Keep in mind, though, that the Lord assures us that if we have faith in him, nothing will be impossible for us (cf. Mt 17:20). With faith and love, we can touch lives and bring them to an encounter with Christ; we can work with the Lord to build his kingdom in the world, in the heart of humanity. Does it make sense?"

"Yes, Father," Clay responded, with his eyes wide open as though he was piercing into the realm of wisdom. Father Serene's words had uplifted Clay's spirit. Having gained confidence, he promised Father Serene that he would begin writing his story as soon as possible. "I shall endeavor to turn in the first draft of my story after the Pentecost. As you suggested, I shall try to keep up with the update. In my story, I'd like to recount how the Lord, Divine Master Potter, has been working in me, fashioning me like a piece of clay. The Lord is still at work in my life. I believe that God has a plan for bringing me to you."

Father Serene grinned and gazed at Clay with admiration. Then he nodded. "Well, who am I? I am a mere tool in the hand of God. I pray for the gift of the Holy Spirit so that I can direct you to the right path. I pray that the Spirit of the Lord may be upon me so as to lead you to him rather than to myself. Let me say this, I'm really very impressed by your spirituality. You seem to be on fire for God." Clay responded, "I am striving daily to grow in my relationship with the Lord. I need your prayer and blessing to overcome my weaknesses and shortcomings. How true are the words of Christ in my life: my spirit is willing to follow him with undivided heart but sometimes my flesh stands on the way."

Father Serene continued, "This is why heaven is a tough journey, and only the tough ones will attain it. It is not by our own power, but by the Spirit. Christ wants us to be open to breathe in the breath of life and power. He has given us his Spirit, a life-giving breath, our strengthener and sanctifier.

It is sad to say that some of our today's youth have lost spiritual fervor. They do not want to strive to grow in the spirit. They do not care to see the daily events of their lives in a heavenly perspective. They want to live only for the present. Instead of seeking the eternal interest for their souls, they are interested to live at the level of the flesh, rejecting Christ's invitation to life and pursuing recklessly every whim and fancy, all forms of gratification that their hearts desire. We have to pray for conversion of hearts. For some of us who are striving to live for Christ as St. Paul exhorts us, we should fan into flame the gift of faith that we have received. We have to beg the Lord for the grace to persevere in faith in God in times of prosperity or in adversity. The Lord is always with us at all times, even in adverse situations, in the tempest of temptation, in the sting of sorrow, in the deluge of disappointment, in the fuss of failure, in the jolt of rejection, in the hole of humiliation, and in the waves of weakness. Jesus is pleased to see hearts that are on fire with love for him. He longs to see our passionate zeal grow in holiness.

Without Christ in us, our life loses its meaning and purpose; without him, we miss true freedom and peace. Yes, we need this life-transforming relationship with the Lord.

"My dear Clay, I'm interested to learn how your name is significant to you. When I first heard about your name, Clay, what came to my mind was the words of the prophet Isaiah. As the prophet rightly says, we are the clay and God is the potter. We are the work of his hands (cf. Isa 64:8). I also thought of the words of Sirach: 'Like clay in the hands of a potter, to be molded according to his pleasure, so are people in the hands of their Maker, to be dealt with as he decides' (Sir 33:13).

"The image of clay reminds me of my neediness for God in our lives. We are formed out of clay (dust) but through Christ, we have been raised above clay. We have been sealed with the life of Christ, even though we still carry 'this treasure in earthen vessels' (2 Cor 4:7). Because many of us have not realized that Christ is in us, we lose heart in the midst of storms of life. The Lord knows our weaknesses, yet he wills to use the frail, wretched clay as a vessel of his grace. Shouldn't we rejoice always, as St. Paul did, even in our weaknesses, so that Christ's strength and glory may be made manifest through us to the world? Christ in us is our strength. God is our Potter, who works in us, with us, and for us."

## Essential Pencils

After a short silence, Father Serene continued his long sermon: "As you know, one holy woman once referred to herself as a pencil in the hand of God. She was right. We are pencils in the hand of the Creator. However, we are not only pencil. We also bear in us a penciled engraving, a seal made with God's 'pencil.' God uses us to write in the lives of others. On the other hand, God also uses others to write in our lives. When my life influences someone to true conversion of heart, to an intentional decision for Christ, then God has used me as his pencil to write in the life of the person. St. Paul might have had this in mind when he wrote to the Corinthians: 'You are our letter . . . known and read by all' (2 Cor 3:2). Before St. Paul preached to them, some of the Corinthians wallowed in all forms of ungodly lifestyle. They were given up to drunkenness, lusts, gluttony, sexual immorality, and other forms of ungodly attitudes. God used St. Paul to imprint a new culture of life in them. They had experienced an interior transformation. Through the ministry of the fiery apostle, God inscribed in the hearts of the

Corinthians the virtue of chaste life in place of their lustful spirit, temperance rather than sensual indulgence, and faith in Christ instead of their idolatry and superstitions. Like St. Paul, our lives should leave an impression on someone's life. It is written in the Scripture, 'Iron is sharpened by iron; one person sharpens another' (Prov 27:17). God uses me to write on others when I, as a teacher, dedicatedly teach my students in truth and in love; when I, as a pastor, tend the flock of the Lord, feeding them with true spiritual food; when I, as a parent raise my children in the discipline that comes from the fear of the Lord.

"True, it is God's will to use each of us as his instrument for his ongoing work of renewing the face of the world. From generation to generation, God has used countless individuals and groups as his instruments to save the human race. To cite a few examples, Moses was used as God's tool to lead Israelites out of slavery. St. Peter preached on Pentecost and about three thousand souls asked for baptism (cf. Acts 2:41). God used St. Patrick to transform lives in Ireland and beyond. St. Francis Xavier's devoted life helped many to encounter Christ. We need to surrender ourselves to the Lord.

We need to be concerned for our salvation and the salvation of others. Sometimes, God refines us through our neighbor, both those who are nice to us and also those who oppose us, those who hurt us, those who think and behave differently than we do. When we believe and open ourselves to him, the Holy Spirit fills us with the virtues we need for the mission. He gives us the grace to love, to serve, and to remain faithful in good times and in bad times. It is in the challenges of life that our faith is made manifest. How would I know that my faith is strong if I had not suffered any trials? How would I claim to have patience if I had not faced any roadblock? How would I claim to have humility if I did not respect and serve my subjects, especially those who give me a hard time? How could I think I am growing in the virtue of forgiveness if I had no one who broke my heart? How could I say that I have a charitable heart if I did not share my resources with my needy neighbor?"

## Refining Resting

The sky was heavy with rain and seemed to give no promise of lull in the storm.

At some point, Father Serene looked at his timepiece and found that it was getting late. Darkness was closing in fast and the sky seemed to be pregnant with rain. Father Serene said to Clay, "I'm sorry for having talked for so long. Get ready to leave for home, for the day is ending. The road is rough, bow down to receive a blessing before you go." Clay swiftly knelt on the marble floor. "No, you can stand for the prayer," Father Serene said to him. "Please, Father, I'm accustomed to kneeling while receiving a blessing from the hand of a priest. Permit me to kneel as you pray over me." "Take any posture you wish. I have no problem with that." (Before that meeting with Father Serene, Clay had two consecutive nights of vigils, fasting, and prayer for the Life in Spirit Seminar. The rigorous spiritual exercises had taken a great deal of flesh out of him; he was conspicuously emaciated. He had no bodily strength left for he did not eat anything that very day).

As Father Serene prayed over him, Clay prostrated himself. Intermittently, he responded "Amen." His voice gradually began to fade away. It was not long before he became still and his voice was not heard any longer. What actually happened to him? Father Serene went ahead with his long prayer. At last, he concluded with a loud "Alleluia." Gazing at Clay lying still on the floor, Father Serene understood what had happened at that moment. The lad was resting in the spirit.

After some time, he held Clay's arm and called him in a soft voice, "My dear Clay, you can now get up. The Spirit is in control." Clay stayed on the floor for some time and then got up and dusted himself off. He said to Father Serene, "Ah, Father, your prayer penetrated me like a gentle wind. It was as though a powerful breath surged into my veins. I could not withstand it. I was slain in the spirit! God is really at work. Thank you so much, Father Serene." Clay affectionately threw his arms around the saintly priest. Father Serene reminded Clay to save the date for their next meeting. Bidding Father Serene goodbye, Clay quickly set off for home. He left Father Serene's community house at about 5:00 p.m.

## The Sobering Storm

The bus was nearly set to depart when Clay arrived at the bus station. Providentially, two seats were still vacant. Clay made haste to secure a seat, as the passengers jostled each other in the overcrowded bus station. Clay's home was about eleven kilometers away. He thought that any further delay would result in his late arrival to his home. By the time the bus was set to depart, the sky was overcast. The road was not good. It was even worse whenever it rained heavily. Clay feared flood would cause heavy traffic along the way. He was praying his rosary, asking for clement weather. As he prayed his rosary, Clay rolled the beads between his thumb and index fingers. For several times, Clay interrupted his prayer to gaze anxiously at the sky. Unfortunately, the weather conditions did not turn out as he wished. Even so, Clay believed that God always answered his prayer, whether things went his way or not. At 5:20 p.m., exactly five minutes after Clay went aboard, the bus departed. It was moving slowly because the road was in bad shape. Some of the passengers were having conversation; some were making phones calls. Some were reading. Still some were either praying or resting with their eyes closed. Perhaps, they were worried about the threatening rainstorm. Clay was completing his third decade of the rosary when it started drizzling. It did not take long before the sky let loose with a heavy downpour.

Soon the road was flooded. It was so muddy that the bus got stuck in the mud. Cars and trucks could not move; their tires were spinning in the muddy road, causing a great deal of traffic. There was little hope that the traffic would end that evening. He realized the bus was stuck for the night. By that time, nightfall was deepening into intense gloom. The sky was still heavy with rain and seemed to give no promise of lull in the storm. The passengers who were strong enough to walk the road, those who were not impeded by their luggage, alighted.

Clay was the first to come down from the bus. The flood was about ankle deep. Before he alighted, Clay had already folded up his black trousers and pulled out his shoes. He and some other passengers began wading along the muddy road to their various destinations. The flood was so heavy that they could hardly pull their feet out of it. Clay still had roughly three-kilometer distance to walk. The weather was cold, so Clay clenched his jaw to control his mouth quaking with cold. With the spirit of courage and peace, Clay trudged down his way home through the puddle of muddy road. The cloudy sky caused more darkness than it used to at that hour of the evenfall. It was difficult for the pedestrians to see safe spots to tread along the road. Some of the pedestrians slipped and tumbled a thousand times into the muddy water. Clay too got his own share of the fall. He was trying to cross over to the other side of the road when suddenly he slid into a gutter. The current of the flood rushing downhill through the gutter was very strong. It was a stroke of luck that Clay quickly grabbed at a metal beam that supported a storefront. The forceful rushing flood did not sweep him away. God really saved him from certain death that evening. He did not sustain a serious injury, just a scraped knee. His clothes were soiled with mud stains, but he was not concerned about the stains. He was rather grateful to God that his life was spared. Clay made it safely home. He got back very late, exhausted, drenched, and shivering in cold.

## A Comfort Zone

By the time he arrived home that evening, Clay's sister-in-law had already prepared supper. On the table at the kitchen were sitting his plates of food. Clay grabbed the food. Within a short time, he devoured it as though he was starving for days. He lurched into his sleeping room to get some sleep. His Bible was sitting on his bed.

Each day, at the end of his morning offering, Clay usually left his Bible open on his bed. This was to remind him to meditate on the word of God every evening before retiring. On that particular day, he felt very tired. And so he prayed a short prayer. Clay had already lain on his bed when it occurred to him that he had not read his Bible. He felt drained of energy. He could not get up to pray. He placed the Bible on his chest and prayed, "Lord, speak to me as I read your word." After a short silence, Clay opened the Bible in a random manner. He hoped to receive some words of promises or blessings. The passage that rather jumped out was a familiar passage from the Book of Revelation. It read as follow, "Moreover, you have endurance and have suffered for my name, and you have not grown weary. Yet I hold this against you: you have lost the love you had at first. Realize how far you have fallen. Repent, and do the works you did at first. Otherwise, I will come to you and remove your lampstand from its place, unless you repent" (Rev 2:2–5).

"Surely, this is not referring to me. I got the wrong passage," Clay reasoned. "God would not say this to me. He knows how much I desire to serve him in truth and in spirit. He must have something else than this to say to me." Clay opened the Bible a second time. This time, the passage that emerged was this: "Am I now currying favor with human beings or God? Or am I seeking to please people? If I were still trying to please people, I would not be a slave of Christ" (Gal 1:10). These words too were not what Clay anticipated. "God, you know that I'm not seeking to please people. I'm seeking rather to please you, my Lord. How could this passage apply to me?" Clay closed the Bible and prayed silently. He tried to fall asleep but he could not. His heart was accusing him that God might be speaking to him through the passages.

A voice whispered in Clay's heart: "Do not resist the word of the Lord. Do not justify yourself. Reflect on the passages. Ponder the truth of the word of the Lord. If you have searched yourself and your conscience justifies you then pray for the grace to remain steadfast in faith in your time of trial. Who knows, God may be instructing you to be spiritually alert against certain temptations that may come your way. Maybe God wants you to recognize the weakness of the flesh and rely more on grace. The flesh is fickle, unreliable, but grace is unfailing. Remember Peter who thought that he could remain faithful no matter what. The impulsive disciple said to Jesus, 'Though all may have their faith in you shaken, mine will never be' (Mt 26:33). Without divine aid, the warmth of our zeal for the Lord can never endure. If your conscience gives testimony of your love for the Love, then possibly God is calling your attention to the future. Stay close to the Lord and you will remain faithful when things may not go your way. When his word will challenge you to come out of your 'comfort zone,' do not resist the word, but rather embrace it to make progress in your spiritual life. When people will begin to blame you or flatter you, be spiritually awake so that you may not be buffeted by a feeling of failure or puffed up with pride. When the ancient serpent will try to persuade you that your efforts and good works are not appreciated enough, be ready so that you may not grow weary in doing good. When the enemy of truth will try to seduce you into seeking people's respect and approval, be on your guard against the tendency to succumb to the evil idea; when the serpent will try to lure you into adhering to certain superstitious and different doctrines than those of the faith, be awake in spirit so that you may remain faithful to the Church. When the Serpent of Eden will suggest that you listen not to the authority of the Church, you may rebuke him and take authority of the Gospel that the Church is established by the Living God who made it 'the pillar and foundation of truth' (1Tim 3:15). So remain in the Lord so that you may not fall into the trap of the enemy. We live in the world where many voices compete to attract our attention. Staying focused on the Lord will help you not to drift away from the path of life." After reflection on the reading, Clay fell asleep. He woke up in the morning refreshed and joyful.

## The Noble Novena

Clay and his friend had planned to spend a few days at his (Clay's) home at the end of the semester. On the last day of the semester, they set forth for the little village. They arrived there at night. After taking their supper and praying Compline (Night Prayer), they went to bed. Clay slept for a few hours and then woke up. It was as though sleep fled his eyes. He was unable to return to sleep. The night seemed endless for him. At 3:00 a.m., Clay prayed the Divine Mercy prayer. Then after some time, several cocks (roosters) began crowing repeatedly. Clay knew it was dawn. He reached for the oil lantern kept under the table. He turned up the flame of the lantern to give brighter light to the room. He raised the lantern to see the clock on the wall; it was 5:00 a.m. He got up and woke his friend for Lauds (Morning Prayer).

Clay and his friend had begun a novena to the Holy Spirit. It was the last day of the novena. They had planned to conclude it at their local parish chapel called Chapel of Perpetual Adoration. At noon, Clay and his friend prayed the Angelus and headed to the chapel. Fortunately no one was in the chapel when they arrived. It was unusual. The chapel was more often than not crowded with devotees, who rarely passed each day without taking time out to make a visit to the Blessed Sacrament. It was surprising to Clay that they did not find any single soul in the chapel that afternoon. They wondered what was going on in the parish. At the same time, Clay and his friend were happy that the quiet of the chapel was providential, for it afforded them the solitude they needed for prayer.

The parish priest had earlier warned the members of his parish against what he referred to as the culture of "pietism," an exaggerated religious passion. He was referring to the attitude of those who came to the chapel to sleep rather than to pray. Some of the individuals often lay prostrate sleeping and snoring in the chapel, thereby creating a noise and distraction in the chapel. "We should avoid creating unwanted sounds and movements in the chapel," the priest warned. He added, "The chapel is a place of silence, where we come to stay awake in order to commune with Jesus Christ. Take care not to turn that holy place to a comfortable sleeping room." Clay and his friend were not aware that the priest had warned the parishioners not to intentionally sleep in the chapel. He had reiterated this time and again.

Clay was not used to sleeping in the afternoon, but he was seriously tempted to sleep that afternoon. He almost dozed off in the middle of the prayer. He decided to stand up to ward off sleep. Clay and his friend completed their novena in good spirit. They wanted to spend some time in the chapel to do mental prayer. Clay sat in the back pew of the chapel while his friend knelt beside the altar. The weather outside was very hot. The coolness and silence of the chapel were so tempting that it could lull one into sleep. Soon, Clay began to fall asleep again. He stood up, stretched himself, and returned to his meditation. Clay's friend, on the other hand, fell into the waiting net of sleep. His posture gave him away. He knelt down continuously for about one hour. When he became tired, Clay's friend lay on the clean, cool, sparkling colorful marble floor. In a flash, Clay's friend was caught up in the intoxication of sleep. Shortly after falling asleep, Clay's friend began to snore very loudly.

Unfortunately for him, the priest was coming into the chapel. As he came in, the priest heard the snoring sound behind the altar. Reaching the back of the altar, he found Clay's friend lying deeply asleep. The priest gave him a mild spank, but that didn't seem to do it. He tapped him on his back, but it was like a soothing puff on a sore spot. The priest then gave him a hard knock on the head. The pain penetrated deep into his *medulla oblongata*. He jolted and sprang up quickly. He stared at the priest and ran his eyes over the chapel, as one regaining consciousness after a deep coma. "Young man, I see you are hard of hearing. You know that I have asked that everyone stay away from sleeping and snoring in the chapel." The priest was still talking when Clay drew close to them. "I'm sorry, Father, we were not aware of your warning." "Shh! I did not ask you, Clay. Allow him to answer for himself; he's not a kid." Clay's friend pleaded with the priest that they had returned from school only a day before. "Please, Father, I didn't intend to fall sleep." The priest mustered up a slight smile and said, "Yes, but you wanted sleep to fall on you, right? Did you intend to lie on the floor? Or were you just pushed down to the floor?"

The priest was tenderhearted. When he learned that Clay and his friend returned from school a day before, he apologized for the hard knock he gave Clay's friend. "You may have been tired from exams. I understand how stressful it is to pass through the rigors of exams. Are you getting enough rest? Come to the rectory for some snacks." They went to the presbytery and had some snacks together. They had good conversation. The priest also gave them some pocket money.

As they walked home, Clay and his friend talked about their encounter with the priest. Clay's friend said that when the priest woke him up he was in a dream. He was washing his hands to eat a very tantalizing pounded yam and vegetable soup, which were served before him. "Maybe it was bad food. I am glad that the priest interrupted it. I would have eaten it. Who knows what it would have caused me." "Say you were hungry," Clay said jokingly. "Now you have taken real snacks and wine."

Clay's friend recalled that he had recently fallen asleep a number of times while meditating. He expressed his concern about this. "I hate sleeping while praying. I hate it but it occurs to me. How will I combat this ugly attack?" Clay had a knack for humor. "All works for our good, right? Where it not for your sleep, we wouldn't have gotten the opportunity to have a good time with the priest." Looking at his friend teasingly, Clay ran his tongue over his lips and added, "You had not taken some wine for a long time, but today you had a whole bottle to drink. You had not eaten short bread for over ten years, but today you had a whole pack to enjoy. You were talking about money to buy some stuff, now you have more than enough in your pocket, all because you slept in the chapel. Your sleep worked well for us, didn't it? Maybe you have to consider sleeping in the chapel often so that we will be getting free food, wine, and money."

Clay's friend gave Clay a friendly side look and laughed softly. "What about the hard knock on my head? You listed the pleasures without mentioning the pain. Okay, it is your turn to sleep so that we may get some more free stuff." Clay continued, "You know, my friend, your sleep in the chapel reminds me of the day I woke Chibu (their classmate) from sleep in the school chapel. He was obviously snoring loudly, just as you did today. Some of us who were there felt disturbed. I tried to wake him up. Do you know what he said to me? 'Leave me alone, Clay, I'm not sleeping, I'm resting in the Lord.' Those who were there burst into laughter. May God have mercy on the poor soul and you too!" Clay's friend interrupted, "Clay, you don't know when someone is serious. I really felt awful for sleeping in the chapel. I wouldn't like to sleep next time no matter what. Clay, you may take your turn in sleeping in chapel."

With a grin, Clay's friend tapped him on the shoulder, saying, "Clay, do you know what? When the priest was talking to me, I recalled Peter and the two other apostles who were overpowered by the clutches of sleep at Gethsemane. You know they were supposed to keep vigil with the Lord in that garden, but they fell asleep. As the priest talked to me, I could hear the same words of Jesus to the apostles resonate in my heart: 'So you could not keep watch with me for one hour? Watch and pray that you may not undergo the test. The spirit is willing, but the flesh is weak' (Mt 26:40–41). I know what caused this. Maybe I had too much trust in myself instead of relying on grace. Though my spirit was ready to subdue the temptation of falling asleep, my flesh was still so frail, so weak that it would again and again succumb to sleep. Unless strengthened by grace, the flesh will certainly draw away the spirit. I think I need to acknowledge my weakness and rely more on the grace of the blessed Lord. I need to think more about mortification by way of more fasting and self-denial. God permitted this weakness in me in order that I might learn to put all my trust in his grace, rather than on my fallible self. By acknowledging our shortcomings, we admit, in truth, that we are not in control. We are in need of his help. Total surrender requires that we give to Jesus our whole hearts, mind, body, and soul, into his safekeeping. And so, he will use us to accomplish the impossible." "Good idea," Clay answered, "maybe standing or taking an unrelaxed posture will be helpful to you while meditating."

## Set for the Story

Clay returned from Mass around one o'clock in the afternoon. He sat on a couch in their parlor, trying to rest awhile after the long walk from church. Casting his eyes over the parlor, Clay caught sight of a pen lying under an armchair at the west side of the parlor. He had misplaced the pen a few days before. He reached down and picked it up. Holding the pen up, Clay fixed his piercing gaze on it and said, "Now it is time to put you to work." He got to his room, pulled out some sheets of paper from his shelf. Clay was now set to write his story in compliance with his mentor's request.

Clay thought that writing his story would give him the opportunity to share the testimony of God's graciousness and goodness in his life. He had hoped that his life story would encourage some persons, especially those struggling with difficulties, challenges, and faith in their lives. On a personal level, Clay seemed to understand the healing effect of telling one's story. He thinks that telling his story will somehow help him to purge some tinge of emotional strains of life. Clay spent some time praying for divine inspiration to write his story.

## A Personal Note

In reading Clay's story, one may notice that there is something definitely particular about it. One of Clay's friends jestingly remarked that Clay always rambled on with stories after stories, with endless scriptural quotations and prayers. In any case, I think Clay's story is quite inspirational and fascinating. I once told a friend that many people have their own life stories, but only few actually tell their stories. Some people enjoy reading or hearing others' stories, not necessarily because they are just stories but because they are stunning stories.

Clay is one of the few who have told their stunning stories. His story is unique and enthralling, not because it is a great work of literary skill, but because it is one of great struggle and amazing triumph of faith. It is one of the few stories that bear witness to God's goodness. Those who are going through trials and struggles in life, especially in their callings in life, need not miss reading and rereading Clay's story. Having been inspired by Clay's story, I feel compelled to share it with others. To avoid detracting from this fascinating story, to avoid failing to do justice to it, I am presenting Clay's life story in the first person's point of view, in Clay's own words.

As you read, take time to ponder, to reflect on some points that strike you. When you have finished reading, consider sharing the good news by giving a copy to your friend or relative.

# Part Two

## My Philosophy of Life

## Considerable Clarification

Dear Father Serene, at your request, I have the joy to write my life story. You asked me to share in the story the significant events and lessons of life that come from my life experiences. I shall endeavor to cover all of them as much as I can. I understand that you intend to share my story to others who may be interested to read it. I want to share testimony of God's goodness and faithfulness to me.

It is my hope that my readers will find my story interesting and inspiring. Before I proceed, I have one request to make. Some individuals who have made remarkable impact in my life have indicated to me that they do not want their names mentioned in this piece. I have decided not to use their real names so as to preserve their privacy. I will also make up some names of places for the same reason. Still, I don't intend to put down accurate dates of events that took place in my life. I figured that doing so will not matter; it will not take away from the heart of my story. As you know, charity obliges us to protect certain personal matters in life. I hope you will understand me.

My life journey has been very tough. I have gone through innumerable failed expectations, setbacks, hardships, pains, and disappointments. I have tried not to brood over them. I do not even want to hold my age in

19

thoughts, I mean, appraising it based on what I have achieved or failed to accomplish in life. Experience has taught me that success and adversity in life do not come to us according to our age. I understand that God apportions his gifts and blessings on earth to whoever he wills and at the time he wills it. None of us knows why the Divine Potter does his things in this fashion. No one has right to question him for sharing his graces as he pleases.

I reject living in the spirit of the world which makes one measure life by material possessions. It is the spirit of the world that moves one to believe that one's life is determined by how successful one is: "His life has meaning because he has many things." "She is nothing because she has nothing." "He has dignity because he is a dignitary." "He is somebody because he has bodyguards, because he has power and prestige." Some who don't have much become envious of those who have made it materially in life. I believe that to be envious of someone's success is to grumble against God: "Why should God give this person this or that gift? It should have been given to me." Early in my life, my father taught me not to be envious of the success or gifts that my neighbor received from the Lord. Envy breeds such evil as gossip, contempt, deceit, rebellion, oppression, hatred, and destruction. Envy is a spiritual cancer that destroys the vitality of spiritual life. I have found the key to joyful life: to love the Lord above all things, to be happy and grateful for my own gifts, no matter how humble they are, and to rejoice in the gifts of others.

## The Good Gifts

Should I compare myself with others? No! Wisdom has taught me not to do so. "But when they measure themselves by one another and compare themselves with one another, they are without understanding" (2 Cor 10:12). Those who may think that they are better than others are still ignorant of the uniqueness of each person's calling in life. The Lord creates each person unique, unrepeatable, and irreplaceable, endowing him or her with certain gifts to serve God and humanity, "For building up the body of Christ" (Eph 4:12).

All good gifts are from the Lord. I have my own God-given gifts. No matter how lowly they may be, I am contented with them. I must put my humble gifts to work, lest the Divine Giver take them away (cf. Mt 25:28–29). Of course, I have prayed for certain gifts that I admire. I believe that if they are in accord with his will, God will grant them to me for his own glory. There is hope to receive tomorrow what I do not have today, provided that it concurs with the divine will. Why should I lose heart?

What is it that can shake off my faith in God? Nothing! By his grace, I'll not turn away from the unchangeable Lord who creates a way for his people through the sea (Ex 14:21), who makes waters break forth in the wilderness and fountains in the dry land (Isa 35:6), who rains down bread from heaven to satisfy the hungry (Ex 16:14–15; Ps 78:24–25; Neh 9:15), who makes rivers of living water flow out of the hearts of those who believe in him (Jn 7:38), who breathes life into the dead and makes dry bones wear flesh and come to life again (Jn 11:43–44; Eze 37), who writes "straight with crooked lines"? What more should I say, nothing is impossible for my Divine Master Potter.

## Pride and Despair

The spirit of pride makes one think oneself as better or more important than anyone else. Pride consumes the root of virtues; that is, humility. I do not esteem myself as better than anyone. I have prayed against the temptation of being inflated with this negative spirit. I have prayed that the Lord may save me from this spiritual leprosy. "LORD, my heart is not proud; nor are my eyes haughty . . . I have stilled my soul; like a weaned child to its mother, weaned is my soul" (Psalm 131:12).

On the other hand, I do not think that others are more blessed than I am. I am confident and grateful that I have many graces and blessings of the Lord to live for. I have prayed that the Lord may deliver me from the spirit of despair (loss of hope). The spirit of despair blinds one's inner eyes from seeing hope in the world of seeming hopelessness, gleam in the midst of gloom, streak of dawning light in the darkest hour of the night. Despair blocks one from envisioning sunrise after sunset, from enjoying peace in the midst of persecution, from expecting appointment in time of disappointment, from discovering life amidst certain death. Despair blocks faith's eyes from recognizing God's presence and blessings in one's life. It blocks the heart's door against the flow of God's healing grace. From these two evils, despair and pride, Lord, deliver me!

I have also prayed that I might never seek to please the world, to fulfill the expectations of temporal matters which people have of me. I have rather come to embrace the mission of love which the Lord has called me to do. Jesus is the Lord of the mission. It is he who calls; it is he who justifies. It is he who glorifies those he calls. My part in the mission is to say "yes," to be open and to follow the Holy Spirit, who leads in love and in truth. The Spirit directs me to the way to life; he keeps me in the truth, in Christ. The Spirit of the Lord breathes life in me and directs my steps from the pit of pride and the dungeon of despair.

## Glorying in God

My calling in life is in Christ. It is this: to love in Christ, to serve in Christ, and to be a channel of Christ's grace. How truly blessed is he who has discovered his call in the mystical body of Christ! God has given me certain spiritual and material gifts for this mission. Everything I have is given to me by the Lord, for the service of him and neighbor. Yet, I am not to be defined by any material gifts that I have or by that which I do not have. Gifts are given in time and can be taken away in time. If one is incapable of doing a particular thing which people expect one to do, does the individual cease to be a person? No, I am a person despite what I can do or what I cannot do. I do not cease to be a person because of what someone thinks or says of me. I am a person because the Lord has said so, because the Lord has created me so.

My Divine Potter tells me that he knew me before he formed me in my mother's womb (Jer 1:5). It is he who calls and prepares me for the mission of his love. If I exercise a particular enviable gift, should I glory in it? No, I should neither glory in any gift I have nor be disturbed by any gifts which I don't possess. The Divine Master Potter commands that I rejoice and glory in my personal relationship with the Lord. "[L]et those who boast, boast of this, that in their prudence they know me, know that I, the LORD, act with fidelity, justice, and integrity on earth . . ." (Jer 9:23).

Divine Wisdom teaches me that my life is not measured by abundance of material possessions but by virtuous and faithful life in the Lord (Luke 12:15, 31). I have learned to rest my faith on God alone. He is my precious treasure and in him my heart finds true rest. In him I find meaning of life. What a grace the Lord has lavished on me that I should be called a beloved Son of God! (1 John 3:1).

## New Numbering

I have prayed that God may teach me to count my days aright in order that I "may gain wisdom of heart" (Ps 90:12). How then do I number my days well? I have found this new way of numbering my days: the way of wisdom, the way that makes my heart ever youthful, ever thankful, and ever joyful. I have learned to appraise my age in the way of the Lord, working submissively with God's time and accepting with joy the turn of events in my life. I realize that in this world all human beings, rich and poor, faithful or faithless, share certain things in common. Trials, sickness, weakness, failures, and death are no respecter of persons. Misfortunes in life have no regard for age or social status. Any person can experience some form of trial at any time, at any age; but while people of faith benefit spiritually from it, those without faith despair and lose all.

The world numbers time according to the ticking of a material clock. I do not bother about human calculation of time; I do not even hang on to the times that I set for myself, time I expect to attain this goal or that goal, to become "somebody" in the standard of the world. What I called "my time" had not worked out well for me. I had gone through several failed times, and thoughts of them left me with interior disquiet. I had been whacked with worries when things did not go my own way. I had felt dejected when I did not fulfill the expectations that people had of me. Is there any need for depending on my timing? It surely does not profit me to do so.

What greater power and prestige, what better privilege would I seek than accepting my dignity as a precious child of God? God alone is enough for me. Whoever has the Lord has all good things. I have learned to be concerned with only God's appointed time. God's time goes with his divine plan. His divine plan goes with his divine love. No one can comprehend the motion of God's time. The expected and the unexpected events, trials and trophies, are all in some way connected to his great plan. Those circumstances, everything that happens to one in life, good or bad, are directed toward one's eternal good. Each condition appears in its time. I affirm with the Teacher that everything on earth has its own time (cf. Ecc 3:1). As the cliché reminds me daily, "God's time is the best." God's time is not the same as my time. I give my time value by the ticking of the clock. I schedule when to work, to pray, to play, to sleep, to eat, to go to school.

Obviously, as long as I am in this world of time, I must work with physical time. The Lord ordains it so. He wills that I work diligently and generously within my time. Yet I keep in mind that I can't fathom God's time. Using my time to the glory of God, identifying with the Lord of time, is a way of sanctifying time.

How do I use my time to the glory of God? I have learned to see each time as a fresh moment of grace to grow in my relationship with the Lord, to improve in doing the work of the Lord. I have learned to abandon myself to his divine will, to generously use every opportunity to share the Gospel in thoughts, in words, and in deeds. I find that in doing so, I gain time rather than lose time. In exercising the virtues of patience in times of pain, hope in times of trouble, faith in times of uncertainty, perseverance in times of difficulties, time gradually heals wounds that time has inflicted on me. I trust that my struggle today will become a thing of the past tomorrow. The great dawn is fast approaching when the night's darkness will be dispelled forever. My lips will eternally shout the joyful song of praise, the song of victory of those who, through the Blood of the Lamb, have triumphed over tribulation (Rev 7:14).

## The Step Process

It is true that the greatest story ever told is not one of easy life but one of great suffering and struggle. When I am in pain, I remember the Divine Master Potter, Jesus, who himself walked the world and carried the cross to Calvary. Through his wounds, he brought me healing; through his pain, he gave me peace; through his passion, he brought me happiness; through his crucifixion, he set me free. What a paradox! The Creator took on human flesh that I might share in his divinity. He chose to be poor that I might become rich in grace. He won life for me by laying down his life. I have to carry my own cross and walk with the Lord. He says that whoever wants to be his disciple must carry his cross and follow him (cf. Mt 16:24). The dawn is fast breaking when I will share my story of the great triumph. Oh, what a cause for joy that the Divine Master Potter has granted me the privilege of sharing in his suffering! At each moment, I hear the Lord calling me to follow him through the narrow way. Where is he leading me? He does not give me the road map. He has the big picture of the way. He just bids me to follow him, to bear with patient endurance the pain of the hard journey. He spoke in the silence of my heart saying, "Whenever you feel tired walking the rough road, prostrate yourself before my cross, connect your pain to my redemptive passion, and I will renew your strength as the eagle's" (Isaiah 40:31). The Divine Master shapes me up for this mission.

My life passes through stages, like the process of molding a vessel of clay. Each stage is essential. The Lord blends, trims, and fires his clay. He does not want to form me in a hurry, but slowly and steadily, he moves the process so that I might not tear apart. The Divine Potter's work of molding me will be completed within his time. Any adverse situation that I may face is part of the process. All my toilsome life experiences make me pliable in the palms of the Divine Potter. They make me humble, knowing that I am not in control. I trust that all things work for my good for I'm called according to his purpose (cf. Rom 8:28). Oh yeah, the tomb of tribulation cannot hold me long; the dawn of Easter is breaking forth. Soon I shall shout my own "Exultet," my own "resurrection" proclamation. Then I shall invite all my family, relatives, friends, and people of goodwill to come join me in gathering the abundant harvest of God's blessings.

## Marking Time

A friend once asked me how old I was. I told him jokingly that I had stopped counting my age. He jested that I was the product of my people's culture. He was right. I was nurtured in the cradle of our culture. Before western education came to my country in the nineteenth century, there was no device to tell time, no timepiece, no clock. Yet, my people read time pretty well through natural signs. Cock (rooster) crow alerted them to time. The peeping of the seasonal birds signaled time for planting. The weather, rainy season or dry season, also helped them to determine time to plant, time to harvest, and time for annual festivals. The setting of the sun pointed to the closing of the day. The new moon marked a new month. Stars helped them to identify directions. Harmattan, dry, dusty wind rang a bell for the end of the year.

It was not customary among my folk to ask someone about his or her age. Supposedly, the reason was because, until recently, my folks were not formally educated to keep birth records. They estimated their ages by recounting certain remarkable events that they witnessed in their lives. Sometimes, they could tell someone's age by looking at one's physical appearance: wrinkled face, shriveled skin, gray/white hair. However, they understood that certain circumstances—hardship, sickness, troubles, and struggles of life—could push forward the hand of the clock in one's life, making one look older than his or her real age.

Another way my folks told one's age was by one's spoken words. They believed that you can tell one's age when one speaks. The admonition of Sirach may come to mind, "Do not refrain from speaking at the proper time, and do not hide your wisdom; For wisdom becomes known through speech, and knowledge through the tongue's response" (Sir 4:23–24).

For my people, a child speaks like a child, without much experience, without deep wisdom. They thought that as a person grew, so did his wisdom and understanding grow. Probably, Job was speaking in this perspective when he said, "So with old age is wisdom, and with length of days understanding, (Job 12:12). The spirit of wisdom has taught me not to be so much concerned in numbering my age based on the ticking of a material clock as to counting it based on my growth in relationship with the Lord. A child who walks in the fear of the Lord is by far wiser and more mature than the aged who have no place for God. I reexamine myself daily to deepen in wisdom "to the extent of the full stature of Christ, so that" I "may no longer be" an infant, "tossed by waves and swept along by every wind of teaching arising from human trickery, from their cunning in the interests of deceitful scheming. Rather, living the truth in love," I "should grow in every way into him who is the head, Christ" (Eph 4:13–15).

## Spiritual Wisdom

It is no doubt that wisdom and understanding can grow with age. Yet, there is a wisdom that does not come from age and experience but from the Holy Spirit. The wisdom infused by the Spirit of God is different from the wisdom one acquires through experience and practice. The wisdom from the Spirit of God can be found in the old and the young.

The friends of Job who visited him during the moment of his trial did not demonstrate this Spirit-given wisdom. It is most probable that they had grown gray hair. They had got extensive experience. And so they evaluated Job's plight according to human wisdom, based on what experience and belief system had informed them about suffering. Oh, how ignorant they were about redemptive suffering! They were unaware of the suffering that God allows, not because one has sinned but because it is permitted for the greater good of the individual and the greater good of others. Still, one may suffer because the Lord allows that to manifest his glory. Job's friends did not get it. They would not get it until Job prevailed through his patient endurance and firm faith in the Lord. Elihu, one of Job's friends, has the conviction that human wisdom and understanding cannot compare with God, for God is wisdom himself and from him is the source of our wisdom: "I thought, days should speak, and many years teach wisdom! But there is a spirit in human beings, the breath of the Almighty, that gives them understanding" (Job 32:7–8).

Yes, the wisdom which comes from the Holy Spirit can be given to the little ones. I'm talking about the wisdom which makes the mute speak, the wisdom which inspires children to express themselves in an eloquent and wise manner (cf. Wis 10:21). The wisdom from the Holy Spirit was infused and stirred up in the young boy named Daniel. He boldly stood for truth. He spoke without fear against unjust judgment meted out to the innocent woman, Sussana (cf. Daniel 13). Jeremiah thought he was not of age. He reasoned that he was devoid of the wisdom that comes from age and vast experience. For this reason, he pleaded with God not to send him to the mission since he was still young and inexperienced. "Ah, Lord GOD!" I said, "I know not how to speak. I am too young!" (Jer 1:6). In other words, Jeremiah was saying to God, "I have not grown gray hair, please send someone else. Choose someone who has seen more years and got great experience." Jeremiah tried to back away from the prophetic mission. But God's strength is revealed more clearly in our time of weakness. God endowed Jeremiah with the wisdom and power from above to carry out the divine mandate.

Like the inexperienced prophet, I have not developed gray hair. I have not had much experience which widens human wisdom. Even so, I'm not discouraged by my inadequacy and limitedness. In the spirit of St. Paul,

I trust that my sufficiency is of the Lord. I have prayed that my faith may supplant the fear of my frailty. I have prayed more often than not for the wisdom that comes from the Holy Spirit. I remember the well-known words of the Bible, "The beginning of wisdom is fear of the LORD, and knowledge of the Holy One is understanding" (Pro 9:10). The infused wisdom is meant for those who are docile, for those who humbly open themselves to encounter the transforming power of our blessed Lord, Jesus Christ.

Those that possess this heavenly wisdom are quick to love, to forgive, to serve, and to share the joy of the Gospel in words and in deeds. I find the way of this true wisdom through the teaching and guidance of the Church. I receive it through obedience, through humility, and through self-emptying of my own way and my own will in order that the Lord's will may be done in my life. Constant prayer, faith, and works of mercy dispose my heart to receive this divine gift. Age is never a barrier to this wisdom, for even infants have burst out in praise of the Lord (cf. Mt 21:16).

Oh Lord, set your people (young and old) ablaze with the fire of the Holy Spirit, the Spirit of wisdom. May our youths catch this divine fire. The time has come, Lord, the time of the fulfillment of your promise to pour out your Spirit upon us (Joel 2: 28). I thirst for this wisdom. I hunger for this wisdom. May your Spirit of wisdom ever find a dwelling place in my heart. With all my heart, with all my soul, with all my will, and with all my strength, I praise my Lord, the source of all good gifts. I pray: Oh, come, wisdom! *Amamihe, bia! Veni, Sapientia! Venid, Sabiduria! Ba, Hakmah! Ela, Sophia!* Come, wisdom from above, and dwell eternally in my heart.

## My Perpetual Peace

My peace begins here on earth and will come to its perfection in heaven. To encounter Christ is to encounter peace. Christ is true peace, the "tranquility" of my soul. One who is in an intimate relationship with the "Prince of Peace" (Isaiah 6:9) has found true peace. It was St. Augustine who teaches me that my soul remains restless until it rests in Christ. Didn't the Lord say to those who are weary, those who are weighed down by their crushing loads to come to him for solace and rest? (Mt 11:28). Granted that sufferings, persecutions, sicknesses, and death are part of the journey of life, the peace which Christ gives is incomparable with the peace that the world gives. The peace that the world gives lasts for a short time, but Christ's peace lasts forever.

The peace from above dwells within the hearts of those who seek and resign to God's holy will. This peace cannot be taken away from my heart. It is the peace that is abiding; it is never ceasing. Christ is the anchor of my hope. No storms can sweep my peace away. No tribulation, no persecution, no disappointment, no rejection, no humiliation, no principalities, no powers can rob me of my peace in Christ (cf. Rom 8:35, 38).

My peace is not one attained in slumber, but in keeping vigil, in prayer, and good works. It is a peace received not by avoiding war, but by getting into a spiritual warfare, using the sword of the Spirit (the word of God). Mine is a peace enjoyed not by seeking to save my life, but by risking it for the course of the Gospel. By pouring out my life for the sake of Christ, I save it (cf. Mark 8:35). The eyes of faith enable me to see this peace. I savor it by carrying my cross to follow Christ. I share it by love, by generosity, and service. Without the peace of Christ in my life, my heart would have remained in internal turmoil in this world.

# Part Three

## My Life Story

### The Lament of Life

Now let me set about the task of writing the subject matter, the story of my life. I know quite well that I was born nearly a decade after the great plague which ravaged our land. My mother told me that during the period of nine months that she was pregnant with me, she did not feel much stress that usually goes with pregnancy. She worked on the farm, danced with the traditional women, walked long distances and traded in the market. She remained strong until she went into labor. The period of her labor did not last long. Before the pain of labor could come upon her, she gave birth to a bouncing baby boy. Immediately, Mama delivered of me, the nurse turned me upside down and gave me a spank on my tender butt. To Mama's dismay, I did not cry. "Is he stillborn?" she wondered. Mama watched anxiously as the nurse tried to spark off breath in me. The forceful nurse gave me a second stronger spank. At this point, the pain penetrated deep into my brain and broke my numbness. I cried, "*Uwa-a–a! Uwa-a–ah! Uwa-a-a-a-!*" Note that in my language the word "*uwa*" means "the world." My folks play on the sound of a baby's cry. They say that a newly born baby cries "*uwa-a-a!*" that is, "this world!" Yes, I cried "*uwa-a-a!*" for I sensed that I had come into a different place. My cry announced to those around, including Papa and my older siblings who were sitting anxiously at the waiting room, that I had come alive into the world.

I wondered why I did not cry at the nurse's first spank. Well, I reasoned that it might be because I did not sense at once that I was no longer in that comfy womb, a place of tenderness and warmth. I was not aware that I had left the place of tranquility, free from stress, noise, and hurt. I felt as though I was still in that serene nest where I received love and care, without any idea of what it meant to give love. When I kicked from inside her, Mama affectionately caressed her paunch, soothing me, "I love you." At that cool lodge, I did not feel the pang of hunger or the torture of thirst. I was constantly nourished by my mother's body without any effort of mine. I felt secure, tranquil, and joyful.

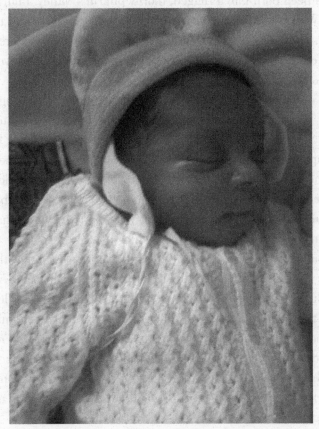

The baby Clay is born into the world, and the Divine Master Potter continues to mold and shape him as His vessel of the healing balm of grace.

On that memorable day when I arrived into the world, the nurse bade me welcome with a painful shake and bitter pinch. She received me by inducing pain into my tender body. What a wakeup gift to a slumbering visitor! The sharp pain signaled me that I had transitioned to the world of tears, toil, and pain. I needed not to be told that I had embarked on a battle of life, on a painful pilgrimage. At that point, I sensed that I had started a journey riddled with struggle and suffering, hunger and thirst, hard work and trials. The coldness of the world rang in my budding interior ears a bell, summoning crosses and sacrifices. It called me to prepare for the sting of illness, for the irk of aging, for possible persecution, suppression, humiliation, and rejection. Ultimately, it was a bell reminding me of the inevitable debt of physical death. Yeah, the cry *"uwa-a-a!"* was a sign that I had been born into a rugged, thorny pilgrims' valley. I hurt. I cried for help. Who could lift me out of the pit of pain? Mama could not grant me relief. Papa was physically absent and left me in the mercy of the nurses. Yet, in their tenderness, my loving parents kept their eyes on me compassionately.

They did not stop me from receiving the pain, for they thought that I needed it in order to be alive. Mama shed tears as she listened to my cry for relief. She laid me on her chest and rested my head between her neck and her upper left arm. Gently, she stroked my delicate skin. She jiggled, kissed, and sang an exciting lullaby. Mama did not hold me for a long time. The nurse grabbed me to get me ready to be taken out of the labor room. Oh, how quickly that consoling moment was aborted! Wasn't that a first sign that no exterior consolation and delight lasts forever?

My budding mind might have committed to memory that the world is not our lasting city. It is not a place where the human race will attain the fulfillment of our deepest, ultimate desire of our hearts. Little wonder then that the world is dubbed a "valley of tears," a place of admixture of sorrow and joy, good and bad, success and failure, poverty and richness, light and darkness, vice and virtue, clean and dirty, friendship and enmity, love and hatred, success and failure, health and sickness, life and death. It is a world where evil works against good, lie against truth, and darkness against light.

As my tender ears began to hear sound, the Lord of life whispered to me: "Don't seek the comfort which the world offers. Your solace is in carrying your cross to follow me. By carrying the cross, you find rest. Through my yoke, you find freedom. By fighting for truth, you find peace.

By dying with me, you drink life in abundance from me, who is the "Life-Giving Fountain." My heart finds rest by flying into the abyss of Christ's love. I find eternal consolation and life by allowing myself to be found by Christ.

## Mama's Mediation

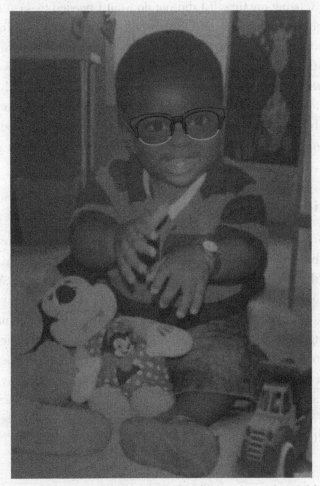

The baby Clay is easy to please, gifted with a tender and joyful heart.

I learn that as the hand of the clock ticks, time gradually diminishes my days in the world. Time brings changes to my body and mind. I grow in wisdom and in body. Yet, internally I feel the Spirit telling me that I should allow myself to grow in my spiritual life. Body and mind grow in time, diminish in time, and disappear in time. The soul, however, cannot die in time. It is meant to live on, primarily in Christ. In this light, the deepest desire of my heart is to nourish my soul with the food of Life, Jesus Christ. I seek to grow in the grace and knowledge of my Lord (2Pet 3:18).

I thought that each stage of life called for diligence and responsibility. God will hold me accountable for the way I use the time he gives to me. I would be wasting my time if I did not do what I needed to do at the right time and in the right place and in the right way. How did I begin early to think about my spiritual interest? Well, at my tender age, my mother prayed a beautiful prayer for me: "Lord, ignite the light of your love in your little baby. Give him the grace to work diligently, to desire to do only what is pleasing to you." The Divine Master Designer heard Mama's prayer that evening. In time, the dusk was to give birth to the dawn of God's grace. The Divine Potter continues to mold and shape his clay into a vessel of his grace.

## Clay Circumcised

When I was just eight days of age, a nurse in the hospital circumcised me. She did not anesthetize me before cutting that portion of my anatomy. As a result, I screamed with pain as she cut off the foreskin. My elder brothers and two other persons were present. Each of them held my delicate tiny limbs. Mama fanned some soothing air on me, while the nurse did the cutting. Mama said that I was in great pain during the first week. During breastfeeding, I would sob with tears. It hurt Mama to behold her tiny child wriggle in pain. She would fix her tearful eyes on my flushed face. It was a keen look of love, a gaze of tenderness from a heart deeply wounded with compassion. When someone mistakenly hit the sore spot, I would yell in pain.

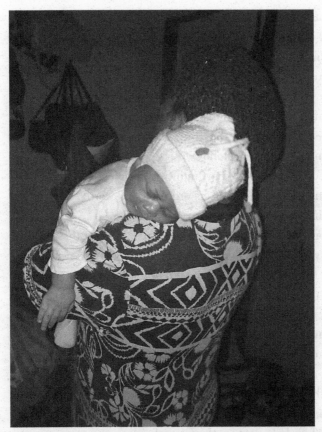

Clay is resting in the arms of his mom, whose motherly embrace and
bountiful affection lent a certain peace that lulled him to sleep.

Sometimes, when it became hard to soothe me, my mother wrapped her
arms around me and tucked my head in the crook of her neck. Then she
softly drummed her fingers on my back as she sang her beautiful lullaby:

Who beat up my son? Who hurt my heart?
Oh, my beloved son, a gift so precious!
Don't cry anymore. I am here for you.
Don't cry, my precious child.
God gave me my womb.
He asked me to lend it to him to prepare his vessel of clay.
I heartily gave it to him for it belongs to him.
Gradually, the Divine Potter began to mold his vessel.

Lo, he made a baby in his image and likeness.
The Lord entrusted the baby boy to my care.
I feed him, but God nourishes him.
I take care of him but God keeps him safe.
I educate him, but the Holy Spirit fills him with wisdom.
I clothe him, but the Almighty Father girds him with virtue.
I bandage his wound but the "Balm of Gilead" is his healer.
I give him an example to follow
But the Lord directs his heart into God's way
The Divine guides his steps according to his word.
Oh, my son, you are a gift so new
A gift more precious than all the gold and silver of the world!
My gem, you are more delightful than the world's treasure.
My heart throbs at the sound of your sob. Be at peace, my son.
Comfort, my son, comfort!
O mother of the Savior, come and soothe your baby.
O my heavenly Father, come and console your son.
O Prince of Peace, come and grant him your peace.
O the Breath of God, come with your driving wind upon my son.
Come with your healing breath and blow away his pain.
Set him on fire with your love.
Stir up in him holy zeal for the Gospel.
Come from the south, come from the east
Oh breath so divine
Come from the four corners of the world.
Come and spread your warm arms around him.
Come and encompass him with your tranquil presence!

The soft melody of the lullaby penetrated deep into my innermost being. My inner ear could hear it. My undeveloped mind could discern it. My delicate flesh could feel it. As Mama sang, her voice whizzed like a gentle breeze that soothes the sweltering summer heat. The tapping of her finger on my back was like blowing a gentle air into a wound. Her arm that wrapped around me was like an impenetrable fortress that gave me a sense of security. The warmness of her cheeks that brushed against mine swept away my pain. Her motherly embrace steadied my shaking knees.

Her bountiful affection soothed the sore spot. The gentle pace of her song lent a certain peace that lulled me to sleep.

## The Symbol of the Circumcision

I have said that I was circumcised on the eighth day of my birth. In my culture, circumcision is not a ritual practice. It does not have any religious significance. We know that the Hebrews circumcise their male children on the eighth day after birth. This is symbolic of their covenant with the Lord. Circumcision is a sign that marks them as belonging to the Lord. I thought it was beautiful that they dedicate to the Creator of life that part of the body from where the seed of life comes out. There are other religious or social reasons why some peoples circumcise their babies. It may be an initiatory rite before marriage. None of these reasons is applicable to me. Yet it is customary among my people to remove that portion of the anatomy after birth. Some of my folks hold a sort of superstitious belief that those who are not circumcised become promiscuous when they come of age. I find that this belief is unfounded, since most of those with unrestrained sexual behaviors today were actually circumcised in their infancy.

In any case, I believe that what is essential in our Christian life is the spiritual circumcision that God makes available for those who trust in him. God circumcises the hearts of those who accept him as their Lord and Savior so that they may love the Lord with all their hearts. A circumcised heart receives and lives out the Gospel. Such heart is aflame with love for God and neighbor. My parents prayed that God might circumcise my heart. They prayed that God might circumcise my ear in order that I might hear and receive the word of God. They prayed for me to receive a circumcised body and mind so that I might serve him with chaste body and pure mind. They prayed that God might grant me circumcised eyes so that I might avert my eyes from the filth of this world (cf. Ps 119:37), so that my eyes might be opened to the vision of his revelation. Circumcised eyes see the beauty and wonder of God's creation. My parents prayed that God might circumcise my lips so as to proclaim the Gospel to all nations. I received circumcised feet that I might hasten to bring the good news to the poor. When the whole body is circumcised, the whole being harmoniously becomes an eternal dance, a joyful symphony of praise to God.

Mama related that nursing me was not an easy feat. I often cried to be breastfed. I was not bed-friendly. When I fell asleep and Mama laid me on the bed, I would soon lie awake, fidgeting, wringing and chewing on my fists, and whimpering. My mother was so loving and self-giving that all this did not bother her. Instead, she was joyful to attend to my endless need for her presence. Wait a minute! Those infantile games for love were not without significance. Recall that through the prophet Isaiah God uses the imagery of mother and baby to announce his promise of comfort: "So that you may nurse and be satisfied from her consoling breast; That you may drink with delight at her abundant breasts . . .You shall nurse, carried in her arms, cradled upon her knees; As a mother comforts her child, so I will comfort you; in Jerusalem you shall find your comfort" (Isa 66:11–13).

Isaiah is not alone in the prophetic words. St. Peter adds his injunction, saying, "Like newborn infants, long for pure spiritual milk so that through it you may grow into salvation" (1 Pet 2:2). Early in life, God put in me a keen appetite for divine milk, for the milk of his saving word. As physical milk nourishes a child and promotes his physical growth, so the spiritual milk of the Gospel fosters growth in my spiritual life. Lord, feed my spirit with your spiritual milk so that my soul may grow up and stay alive in you.

## Born Again

When I was a baby, I had a craving for my parents' loving touch. It was a delight to feel Mama cradle me in her arms. I enjoyed Papa's warm embrace whenever he cuddled my tender body. I cherished Papa and Mama's loving gaze into my eyes, to which I always responded with a smile and cooing sounds of joy. The prayer that remained in my parents' heart was, "God be with my child all the days of his life." Mama had an intuition that my soul had a longing for something higher than human comfort. She felt that it was time for me to receive the life of Christ. My heart pounded to receive the breath of Christ's life.

At four months of age, Mama could not wait any longer. "I think it's time for my son to be baptized," Mama suggested to Papa. Papa thought it was a good idea to have me baptized without further delay. They were planning to meet with the parish catechist for registration when they ran into a Protestant friend of theirs. Learning that my parents were going to baptize me, she suggested, "Why not wait until your son gets old enough to decide on his own?" "No, no, that is not what we believe," Mama interrupted. "I do not wait until my baby is old enough to eat on his own, to bathe himself, to dress by himself, to go to bathroom by himself, to educate himself. We know that all of these material things are necessary for our children. Even if a child cries while a mother is bathing her child, the mother does not stop doing that simply because the child does not want it. Love compels her to continue cleaning up the child because the child needs it. If parents are so keen to give their children their bodily needs without waiting until their children are old enough to decide, why would one defer their spiritual needs?

"As Catholics, we believe that the grace of baptism cleanses Christians from the sins they committed and from the original sin; that is, the sin that all human beings inherited from Adam and Eve. In baptism, Christ washes us of these sins and gives us a new nature, his life. We know that babies are not old enough to commit a sin, yet they bear the stain of original sin. We don't want to deny our children this grace of purification." Mama was right. Through baptism, Christians are buried with Christ, and through the power of his resurrection they share in Christ's eternal life.

## A Ride Through the Rough Road

The following day, Papa and Mama met with the catechist to arrange for my baptism. "What name will we call him?" Papa asked Mama. "We don't need to give him another name than his native name Chinonye," a name in Ibo language which can be translated: "God is with us"; that is, "Emmanuel." "The church usually requires another name for baptism." "Okay, we can give him the name Clay." An inspired choice of name indeed!

On the morning of the baptism day, my mother bathed me. I usually screamed at the touch of water. The case was different on that blissful morning. I was calm and peaceful as Mama gently dabbed my body with warm water. She gently stroked over my supple body with a soft sponge. Then she dressed me in oversized white pajamas, white stockings, and a white hood. She wrapped me in a beautiful piece of *abada* cloth to keep me warm. The day was bright. I must have felt peaceful. With warmth and affection, my sister held me in her arms. "Is he asleep?" Papa inquired. "I think he is about to fall asleep. He closes and opens his eyes," my sister replied cheerfully. As though I heard what she said, I opened my eyes and began to blink them rapidly. Then I started kicking my legs. "Ah, he is awake!" my sister said with excitement. She pushed her tongue outward, wagging it close to my face. She wanted to see if I could see it. I turned my eyes from side to side, following the direction of her tongue. "My goodness! Clay can see! He follows the movement of my tongue." "Yes, he is of age to see. I discovered yesterday that he has actually begun to see," Mama affirmed.

Soon, my parents were ready to go to the parish. Firmly and gently, Papa lowered his bicycle for Mama to go aboard. Mama carried and held me with tenderness. They set off for the parish. My father's bicycle was old and the frame was bent. The screws that held the pedals were loose and worn out. It had been so for a long time since he had not got enough money to fix it. Papa tied them with rope. Some of the spokes were disjointed. Even so, Papa was confident that the bicycle would make it safely to the parish. The pedals generated an impressive noise as my father pedaled along the road. The loose spokes also jingled along the way. The two sounds produced a steady melody that sounded somewhat like this: *"Tan-gan-chi-i-i, tan-gan-chi . . ."* The noise continued all the way, sounding like a locomotive. For Papa, it was not a noise but a melody of praise. He sang praise songs along with the jingling of the spokes.

Though poor, Papa and Mama were content with what they had. The poverty of the family did not take away from them the inner peace and joy of those who trust in the Lord. Papa and Mama were ever grateful to God for all his countless blessings upon the family. Papa liked to hum and whistle either Christian or traditional songs while working or riding his bicycle. Hence, the noise from his bicycle became for him a background music as he hummed worship songs along the road. Papa might have added, "My bicycle, praise the Lord. Make a joyful noise onto the Lord."

The road to the church bustled with people and activities because it was Ore market day. Some of the villagers were so poor that they could not afford to buy even a bicycle. As a result, there were many pedestrians on the road carrying heavy stuff on their heads. It was not hard for them to carry bulky things on their heads. Poverty had forced them to be accustomed to doing hard labor with relative ease. Some who had bicycles or motorcycles were also on the road, transporting their goods or people or their stuff. A couple of cars that ply the rough, dusty route were owned by rich people.

Even though they were poor, my parents were well-known in the town. Mama nearly lost her voice in responding to greetings and exchanging pleasantries as they rode along the way to the parish. I was busy licking my fingers, my eyes fixated and blinking in the bright sky. My senses were opening. What a joy to behold the beauty of the blue sky!

Papa was riding slowly. We were not far from the parish when suddenly the sun rose. Mama noticed that I felt the sunrays on my face. She covered my face with the hood. We arrived at the parish church safely. Two other families who also came to baptize their babies were already seated. The baptism was about to begin when four other families entered the chapel. All together there were seven families present for baptism.

## The Sign of the Servant

It was significant to know that seven families were present at the day of my baptism. The number seven, as you know, symbolizes completeness and perfection. The Bible uses the number seven a lot. To give instances, God took six days in creating and rested on the seventh day. In accordance with Elisha's order, Naaman plunged himself seven times into the Jordan River and was cleansed of his leprosy (2 Kings 5:10). One of the offerings of the first day of each month in the Mosaic Law is seven unblemished yearling lambs (Num 28:11). In the Book of Revelation, we learn about the seven stars and seven gold lampstands, which symbolize the angels and the churches respectively (Rev. 1:20). The seven angels were given seven trumpets (Rev 8:2). I believe that the seven babies were anointed as special messengers of God. Those tiny messengers in the arms of their mothers were chosen vessels of God's love and grace. God never despises those who truly yearn for his Spirit, those who sincerely desire the fire of the Holy Spirit. I pray that God may make me his fiery messenger of love, a sounding trumpet to shout the Gospel to all the corners of the world.

## The Rite of Rising

Father Onye welcomed the families to the celebration. The parishioners were used to his croaky voice. Obviously, age was no longer on his side. But his mind was still very sound. Looking directly at the faces of the parents of the babies, Father Onye cheerfully called each of them by name and said: "We rejoice with you for the blessings of these babies."

He drew close to my parents who were sitting on the first pew. Father Onye questioned them in his strong Enu-Onicha accent: *"Kedu afa ichoo ka' baa nwayi* (what name do you want to give to your baby)?" Papa wanted to respond but blanked out. He did not remember the baptismal name. My mother cut in and almost yelled the name: "Clay." It is worth noting that my folk do not simply give a name to their child without meaning. Names are significant for them. A person's name may mark certain lived experience of the parent(s). A name may be given to one as an expression of devotion or gratitude to God. Still one may bear a name which points to the person's role. By giving me the name Clay, my parents seemed to have had a prophetic intuition that God was at work in the life of their tiny baby.

Anyway, during the beginning of the baptism, I was asleep and snoring in my mother's arm. My mouth was hung open. However, I think at that time I was sure of one thing: I was at peace, confident that my parents were there for me. As soon as Father Onye made a sign of the cross on my forehead, I woke up. I blinked my eyes a thousand times. Then I stared at the priest as he signed the forehead of the other babies. Who knows what was going on in my budding mind? Of course, a baby is not of age to think, but he or she is not devoid of intuition. Mama and some others were captivated by the way I held my gaze steadily on the priest. Then I turned and began to suck my fingers. Mama knew I was hungry. She used to make a joke of me that I suckled heavily at infancy.

The rite of baptism was in progress. Hunger didn't let me stay still. I screamed loudly. It was not a good time for breastfeeding, so Mama tried to hush me.

After the scriptural reading, Father Onye gave a brief sermon. Mama still remembers some of his message: "Today, we are celebrating the birth of these babies into our Christian life. Thank you, parents, for cooperating with the Creator in bringing these children into the world. I exhort you to take seriously your responsibilities as parents in raising them in the way of the Lord . . ." Then Father Onye turned to the godparents and continued, "Godparents, I trust that the parents of these babies have reliably chosen you to cooperate with them in the responsibility of assisting these children grow in the discipline and morals that come from the fear of God." He went on to address all present. "All of you have to be actively involved in raising these children in the faith. Christ has entrusted these children to your care. Bring them always to church. Pray with them.

"Teach them, by words and deeds, how to pray and how to live well. Guide them with care. Take time to direct them with love. Do not hinder them from coming to Christ. There are many wolves out there in the world. If you allow them to stray from the path of life, they will be under the mercy of the ravenous wolves lurking in all corners of the world." Father Onye addressed the fathers: "Sometimes, it is easier for me to speak to mothers than to you, fathers. You know that women listen with their hearts but we men tend to listen with our heads. I pray that the Holy Spirit may bring this message to our hearts. Some of the crises we have in today's families could have been avoided had the fathers played their part in parenting their children. Christ invites all of us to help our children encounter him through our examples. Be men of prayer. Pray with your family. Be men who work hard to provide for the family. We know that life is hard in our country. It is not Christian to leave women to suffer alone in the struggle to raise the beautiful children whom the Lord has given to us. Beg the Lord to touch your hearts so that your love for your family may not grow cold. It is love that will bind your family together. If we neglect our duties as fathers, as mothers, and as godparents, we are hindering our children from coming to Christ." Father Onye cleared his voice and then said, "Amen." The sermon was over.

After the sermon, the catechist asked the families to move to the waterfront. My parents held me, positioning my head on the font. The priest poured water on me, saying, "Clay, I baptize you in the name of the Father." He poured water on my head for the second time, and continued, "and of the Son," still he poured water on my head the third time and continued, "and of the Holy Spirit." I did not cry but I wriggled to catch a breath. Father Onye anointed my forehead with charism. I was sealed forever with the mark of Christ's life. He placed a piece of white cloth on my chest, symbolizing the new life of Christ that I had received. Papa held a lighted candle. The burning candle signified that Christ is "the light of the world" (John 8:12). At the end of the baptism, the families joyfully exchanged greetings. It is my delight to think about that beautiful day. In my infancy, my parents presented me to God to be cleansed of the original sin which all the human race inherited from Adam and Eve. Now that I am of age to make my own decisions, I present myself to God in prayer and through the sacrament of reconciliation so as to be purified of my own personal sins. "If we acknowledge our sins, he is faithful and just and will forgive our sins and cleanse us from every wrongdoing" (1Jon 1:9).

The Divine Potter continues to mold and shape his clay into a vessel of his grace.

## Sting of Sickness

Soon after my baptism, I took ill. I lost appetite for food. My parents felt that it was malaria. They feared that my frail frame would not withstand severe sickness. Mama was upset. She thought about how to get some food into my stomach. She prepared pap and mixed it with some medicine, which she bought at a local pharmacy. My sister scooped the pap into my mouth while Mama held me firmly, blowing air on my face to enable me swallow it. Mama feared that I might throw up. Luckily enough, I did not vomit it. But after taking the pap, I felt drained of energy. My heart was beating rapidly. My eyes were heavy and closing in sleep. Mama signaled my siblings to quiet down to enable me to sleep. I slept for several hours. By the time I woke up, it was already noon. The pap and the pills seemed to have worked. Mama could tell that my vitality was gradually coming back. I stroked Mama's face with my tender palm and reached the "food bank" to suckle. You could imagine the joy of a loving mother seeing her beloved baby bouncing back to health. She kissed me and sang for me some exciting cradlesongs. Little did she know that another sharp sword of sickness was on the way to pierce her compassionate heart.

About one month later, there was an outbreak of measles in the village. My mom tried to keep me from contracting that dreaded virus. One night, I was up all night crying. Mama sensed that something was wrong but she was not sure what was causing me discomfort and pain. She wondered whether I was teething. In the morning she discovered that rashes and red spots had covered all over my body. I had contracted the dreaded measles! In my town, we had no pediatricians, doctors who specialize in treating children. And so she took me to a nurse for treatment. When cooking or doing her house chores, Mama back-carried me. She would sing and pray for my healing. My folks believed in divine healing more than in a cure from medical treatment. They had faith that the power of healing comes from God. In the Bible, Ben Sirach's advice to his son comes to mind, "My son, when you are ill, do not delay, but pray to God, for it is he who heals" (Sirach 38:9). It was in this light that some of our local physicians adopt the mottos: "We give medicine, but God heals," "We are servants of the Healing God," "Healing comes from the Most High."

## Walk to Wellness

Two days into my sickness, no medicine seemed to be working. Mama got ready to take me to the maternity hospital in our town. My dad's bicycle had a flat tire. Mama's bicycle was not in good condition too. So Mama had no other option than to walk the four kilometers to the maternity. She firmly wrapped me on her back. When we reached the maternity, about ten women were already seated, patiently waiting to see the nurse. (The nurse had been attending to a woman who had been in labor for several hours.) My mom joined the queue. She sat on a wooden stool and tried to breastfeed me. But pains would not let me enjoy my favorite "food." One of our family friends was sitting beside us. Stretching her hands, she beckoned to carry me in her arms, but I turned her down, pulling my face and clinging to my mother's wrapper. Mama said that I never allowed strangers to carry me. When I refused her to carry me, the woman smiled at me. I returned her smile. She thought I would let her carry me this time. She stretched her arms pleading that I allow her to carry me. I quickly ducked and clung to Mama like metal sticking to a magnet. After nearly two hours of waiting, the nurse attended to us. She checked my vital signs and gave Mama some medication. She asked Mama to return for a check-up after two days. Like a miracle, after two days my health improved greatly. The red spots and rashes gradually healed. Within a week, I bounced back to good health.

## Soothing Stroke

At six months of age, I could crawl and move pretty fast. I could recognize faces and voices. Apart from the members of my immediate family, I could identify those relatives and neighbors who were close to our family. I could vocalize some names like Papa, Mama. I was easy to please. However, once hunger struck me, I pushed my way to my mom. One day, one of my sisters went to fetch firewood. My other sister was out in the woods to collect fodder, grasses to feed our goats. My older brothers went to play soccer. My mother was preparing to go shopping but there was no one home to look after me. She breastfed me and sat me down in our parlor. She went into the garden to pick some pepper and pumpkin leaves that she would use to prepare soup. I began to play with toys. At some point, I felt lonely. I didn't see anyone or hear any voice. "Where could they have gone?" I might have wondered. I reached for my empty feeding bottle and began gnawing on it. A couple of minutes later, I cooed to signal for attention. There was no response. Mama heard my voice and moved stealthily into the parlor. Turning my neck around, my eyes caught hers. She smiled at me and waved. I smile back at her and cried softly. I bade her to carry me, but she tossed me a piece of biscuit. She waved goodbye. While she waited for my sisters, Mama started washing some of the napkins she soaked in the hot water a night before. Hardly had Mama started washing the napkins when her sister-in-law Ada came in. "You take care of Clay while I go to market," Mom requested. "Where is Clay?" Ada inquired. "He is in the parlor. You can hear him gurgling." I recognized the woman's voice. And so as soon as she came in, I smiled at her. I stretched out my hands and threw myself toward her. She sprang instantly to catch me, but she wasn't close enough. I banged my head against a side table. I bruised my forehead slightly. I rubbed the sore spot with my palm.

Surprisingly to her, I did not cry. Perhaps I did not cry because I felt the touch of love. Love can relieve pains and heal all ills. Yeah, at that age, I could understand the language of love. I was filled with high spirits for being cared for. Ada seemed to have known her child's psychology very well. She knew what she could do to please me. She wrapped her arms around me, kissed me on my forehead, and gave me some cookies. I began to nibble on it without minding the pain. She took me to her home while Mama left for market.

# The Missing Moment

I was happy hanging out at Ada's home. Mama did not return from market in time. She thought that I would be very hungry before her arrival. When she came back, Mama stopped by Ada's house to take me home. Ada was busy pounding fufu for dinner. "Is Clay hungry?" Mama asked. "No, Opanwa, my daughter, carried him visiting the neighborhood. I'm not sure where they are right now." "I guess Clay is not crying. Otherwise, she would have brought him back. When they come back, please ask Opanwa to bring him to me."

For over two hours, Opanwa and I were nowhere to be found. Night was closing in. Ada was apprehensive about our whereabouts. She called out to Opanwa: "Opanwa! Opanwa! Opanwa-e-e-e-!" Mama went back to Ada's house to check for me. She did not see any soul outside except that the goats were bleating. Ada had gone to the neighborhood in search of us. Opening the door, Mama peeped inside the room. Lo and behold, there we were lying on the bed, deeply asleep. Mama heaved a sigh of relief. She gently walked in and woke Opanwa. She took me home, thanking the Lord for keeping us safe. How Mama needed to learn to overcome her fear with faith! "My soul, be at rest in God alone, from whom comes my hope. God alone is my rock and my salvation, my fortress; I shall not fall. Trust God at all times, my people! Pour out your hearts to God our refuge" (Psalm 62:6, 8).

The Divine Potter continues to mold and shape his clay into a vessel of his grace.

# The First Step

As the months slid by, I was coming of age. When I was seven months old, I was able to stand holding on to any furniture or some other object that could support me. At nine months, I took my first steps learning to walk. I could stand up without clutching Mama's arm or holding on to anything. But I often wobbled to my feet because they were not yet strong enough to carry me. One evening, I tried walking but I staggered and fell. I hit my head against a little chair. Luckily enough, I did not sustain any wound, but my head hurt for hours. I cried softly and stopped. Papa carried me in his arms and comforted me. He lifted up my chin, looked straight into my eyes, and smiled. Then he said, "I love you, my precious son." The joy of being loved swallowed up the sharp ache. The next day, my dad tried to help me learn to walk. He held me up and left me standing without support. Staying two feet away from me, he watched my trembling feet. He held up my feeding bottle to attract me to his direction. "Come, Clay," he said. I stretched my right arm to reach the bottle, but it seemed too far from me. Pulling my right leg and raising the second one, I lurched myself toward Papa. I missed the third step. Before I could land on the floor, Papa grabbed me on my right hand. Papa stood me up to try the second time. I made an effort to walk, but this time I fell before the second step. I fell headlong to the ground. I sustained a small bump on my head and a scrape on my right elbow. My father picked me up, wrapped his arms around me, comforting me. Oh, it was not the first time I had fallen down! By this time, it was beginning to click in my developing mind that the journey of life is a continuous struggle. Pain is inevitably part of the journey.

Later, I would learn that Christ did not overcome the world without the cross; that success does not come to one without suffering; that no one becomes a hero without some experience of sorrow; that a winner is not one who does not experience weariness, but one who perseveres to the end. At that tender age, I had not grasped that perseverance brings progress. In my infantile trepidation, I relented from persevering until two weeks elapsed. As I think back, I see the fact that the beginning of learning is the hardest part of it. Failure is part of the learning process. One is not a failure simply because one fails while learning, but only when one gives up persevering and fails to learn from one's failure.

At the time that I was learning to walk, I was also learning to speak. The first words that I learned to vocalize were "mama," "papa," and "taata." My siblings and my parents help me to say words and names correctly. Before I reached the age of one, I had already started walking around, slowly and carefully. I was also able to make a few intelligible sounds. I could say the names of some of my siblings. I thought that at that tender age I started well in the broad world of wisdom and knowledge.

# Smeared with Scum

I loved to play with the children in our neighborhood. We played at cooking food, building houses with mud, and celebrating Mass. One day I soiled my new dress with mud. Mama was coming back from market. I was very excited to see her. Mama never missed buying for me *moi-moi* or groundnuts or eggs. I ran to greet her. She knew that I was dirty but that did not bother her. As she carried me in her arms, I smeared her white dress with mud. With a sense of innocence, I showed the stain to Mama. "You did it," Mama replied to me. "What do you want me to do now? Look at yourself—very dirty!" I hung my head in guilt. Mama looked at me, smiled, and said, "Don't worry, my child. I'll clean you up and wash my dress, okay?" I felt forgiven. I pointed my finger to her bag. "I know what you are looking for," Mama said with a grin. When we got home, Mama opened her bag and brought out an egg, my favorite food. I took hold of it with excitement. Without waiting to remove the shell, I began gnawing on it. Mama peeled the egg for me. I went to our front door, sat at my little chair, and began to munch it. I did not care to share it with my siblings. My younger sister begged me to give some portion to her, but I refused. Mama met me there and said, "My son Clay, share with your sister, okay?" I bit off a small piece of the egg and gave it to her. Now I know that at that time Mama was instilling in me the culture of care and generosity. She was forming my heart to cherish the joy of sharing. She was teaching me the language of love. She was helping me to learn to give without counting the cost, to be always mindful of my brothers and sisters.

I think of the main drama of that day. Mama embraced me despite my dirtiness! It meant the world to me; there is a deeper meaning to that expression of love. I reflect on my relationship with the Lord. Oh, how I frequently soil my soul with sin! How my merciful Lord embraces and cleanses me again and again! Each time I damage with sin my relationship with the Lord, I hear God say to me: "Come now, let us set things right . . . Though your sins be like scarlet, they may become white as snow; Though they be red like crimson, they may become white as wool" (Isa 1:18).

# Informal Formation

We had no nursery school (kindergarten) in my village. The state government built an elementary school for us. It was located at about three kilometers away from our home. The eligible age for entrance into the elementary school was six. I had to wait for three more years to begin my formal education. My parents, older siblings, and relatives educated me informally before I started school. We prayed together as a family every morning. The first prayer I learned was the sign of the cross. When I was learning it, I was able to sign only my right shoulder and my abdomen. My sister held my hand to help me sign the prayer in the right order.

I was taught certain basic cultural behaviors. I learned to eat with a spoon, to greet people properly, and to respect others. I also learned some other cultural rules of etiquette. To give examples: it was considered disrespectful behavior to use the left hand to give something to someone, especially elders. Eating with the left hand was not a socially acceptable table manner. Mama said that I had a hard time learning to eat with my right hand. She kept reprimanding me to change my spoon from left hand to right hand while eating. At some point, my mom had to tie a heavy metal bangle around my left wrist to make it heavy for me to lift it when eating. That helped a great deal.

As a family, we ate from the same plate and drank from the same cup. After meals we shared some pieces of meat or fish. While eating with my siblings one day, I sneaked a piece of meat into my mouth. I was chewing it slowly to avoid being noticed. My elder brother stared at my mouth, which was evidently popped out. He knew I had something else inside my mouth. "Heh, I see you! Come on, open your mouth wide!" he ordered. "You have taken your own share of the meat!" I regretted such bad attitude. It was evident that I sniped a piece of meat in my mouth. My brother had made it known. I could not hide it. I kept silent and took some time to chew the meat. I knew I had eaten my own share of the meat. That was my punishment. My sister generously gave me a bite of her own share. Papa reproved me for such bad behavior. He encouraged me to be honest and just in all things, even in small matters.

Papa's admonition sank deep into my mind; right from that time, I strove daily to be honest and sincere in all I do. Recalling Papa's words brings to mind the words of St. Paul, "[P]ut away the old self of your former way of life, corrupted through deceitful desires, and be renewed in the spirit of your minds, and put on the new self, created in God's way in righteousness and holiness of truth" (Eph 4:22–24). After a meal, it was our custom to say "thank you" to parents and to older ones. Up till today, greetings are still an important part of our culture. I learned from my parents the basic courtesy and respect to all persons.

## Christ in Disguise

My parents were fervent in their Catholic faith and lived out what they believed. They modeled moral values for me. They knew their responsibilities as Christian parents, especially in training their children to fear the Lord and see Christ in others. Mama would often remind me about the biblical command for children to obey their parents. She remarked that obedience is an attitude that is very pleasing to the Lord. It attracts God's blessings, as we read from the Bible, "Children, obey your parents (in the Lord), for this is right. 'Honor your father and mother.' This is the first commandment with a promise, 'that it may go well with you and that you may have a long life on earth'" (Eph 6:1–3). I learned early in life to obey not only my parents but also those in authority. All temporal and spiritual leaders deserve my obedience, provided that they are not leading us into sin.

My parents taught us to respect every human being, leader or follower, poor or rich, beautiful or ugly, handicapped or whole. All persons deserve my respect because of who we are as sons and daughters created by God. I learned to treat each individual with dignity as a child of God, no matter one's state in life. I confess that when I was about five years old I was guilty of disrespectful behavior toward a man who was mentally challenged. He used to visit our home. Whenever he came, my parents would give him something to eat or other stuff he might need. One particular day, he called in. My parents were not home. I was playing with my friends in front of our house. The man showed up in ragged T-shirt and dirty trousers. The trousers were torn at the back, exposing his butt. My friends and I laughed and shouted at him, *"Onwa n'eti"* (the moon is shining), a sarcastic way of saying that his buttocks were exposed. The man simply smiled at us and said, "Don't laugh at me, my little children." Some of us began to throw stones at him. He was holding a loaf of bread. Holding out his hand, he said, "Take some bread and eat." None of us were interested to accept such a gift from a palm that seemed to have never touched water for decades. Even mere looking at his hand was disgusting to us. So we spat and turned away. Oh, what childish behavior!

When word reached them, my parents scolded me very seriously. I felt bad for treating the man that way. He was such a kind man. As a child, I did not realize the great love he showed us. He was willing to share with us the little he had. We made sport of him, but he never clung to hurt; he never held it against us. I remember him with great affection as I pray that his soul may find rest eternally in heaven. When my parents learned of our disrespectful behavior toward him, they scolded me: holding his right ear, he ordered me to hold mine: "Get it into your ear now! Let this be the last time I'll receive any report of such rude conduct." Mama added, "I have told you, always treat the poor and the sick with dignity. God created every human person. The Lord can come to us any day in the disguise of a beggar." I nodded in agreement, ruminating about the image of Jesus coming to me in a poor state. I never wanted to offend my beloved Jesus. Since then, whenever I see the poor, I think of Jesus who bids me to help him in them.

# A Tale of Eternity

Papa had a small radio. He usually turned it on in morning and evening to listen to news. I liked the radio. Whenever Papa brought it out, I would lean in his arms, watching as he tuned it to a station of his choice. I would flip randomly at the other switches. I remember one day I sneaked into Papa's room. I took hold of the radio. Not sure of the right knob to turn, I flipped one knob after another. All of a sudden, a deafening hissing sound blasted from the radio. I had turned it on. But I neither knew how to reduce the volume nor how to turn it off. Papa had earlier warned me not operate the radio. My stubbornness has found me out! I failed to obey Papa. I was afraid that he would punish me for not giving heed to his warning. I wondered how I would get out of the trouble.

The noise of the radio caught my brother's attention. I knew for certain that word would get to Papa. "So you have spoiled Papa's radio, eh? Okay, you'll see, I must let Papa know about this," my brother threatened. I stood still, casting my head downward. I was filled with fear that Papa would surely whip me. My brother turned off the radio. When he came back, Papa sent for me. He gave me a penetrating look and then said in low voice, "Why do you choose to be stubborn? I have warned you time without number not to touch this radio, but you went ahead to do what you wanted." He pulled me with his left arm and gave me a little spank on my butt. It didn't hurt. That was a mild discipline from a loving father! Every good parent disciplines his child with love (cf. Heb 12:7b). I yelled, not because I was hurting, but because I wanted him to think that the spank was painful. I didn't want him to give me the second one. I cried loudly, calling out to Mama, but she was not home. My brother liked to see me scolded because he thought I was very obstinate.

Mama came back in the evening. She gave me *"akara,"* a kind of bean cake. Mama sat close to me while I was munching my *akara*. She began to tell me a story about heaven and hell. She so described hell that it instilled fear in me. "My son, remember always that those who are disobedient and the wicked will be condemned in hellfire," she said. That was the first time I heard of hellfire, and so I inquired, "What is hellfire?' She began to explain to me how those who die in sin would live forever in the agony of hell, a fire that never goes out. It was a pretty smart way to get children to behave. It is true, children learn to behave well when they know that they will be punished by acting contrarily. "I don't want to go to hell," I resolved. "I'll no more be disobedient, and I'll never laugh at those who are poor or handicapped."

Over time, I came to learn that God wants my faith and not my servile fear. Such enslaving fear toward God arises from dread of being punished in hell. God does not want this to be the reason for me to obey his commands. God does not want me to have a picture of him as a stern judge who is ever ready to cast into hell anyone who misbehaves. God rather wants me to have that filial fear that should move me to avoid offending him who is such a loving Father, who deserves all my love. He wants me to see him as a Father who is full of mercy and compassion, a God who loves me with an everlasting love (Jer 31:3). St. John teaches me that perfect love casts out all fear (1Jn 4:18). God wants me to live a good life out of the love I have for him and my neighbors. I love the Lord, because he is worthy to be loved, for, as the Psalmist says, His "love is better than life" (Ps 63:3).

## Elementary Education

Clay begins his formal education with a curious gaze to see and connect with reality, with an open heart and mind to learn the Truth, with docility to be transformed by the truth, with passionate zeal to share the truth, and with self-sacrificing love to pour out his life as a tool for the transformation of his generation.

On August 23 of that blessed year, I turned six years old. My parents had waited for this time to get me started with my formal education. They wanted me to begin school so that I could stop playing all the time. They desired to see me cease from endless wandering in the woods in search of fresh fruits, palm nuts, mushrooms, and wild animals. Early in life, I had a keen desire to learn to read and write. I enjoyed listening to my siblings recite their lessons at home. At the same time, I took delight in playing with other kids in the village. I feared that school would interrupt my cherished plays. And so when Mama told me that she would take me to school, I objected. Papa threatened to whip me should I refuse to go to school.

Unwillingly, I went onboard Mama's bicycle. As she rode away from home, I started weeping. Mama hated seeing me weep. She tried to hush me. But I didn't stop crying. Some people in the neighborhood who heard my cry came out to see what was going on. Some thought that I was stung by a scorpion. Mama ironically responded to them, "Don't mind him! He is just overjoyed and wanted to let you know that he is beginning school today."

It was the first day of the school year. The bell had just rung when we arrived. The school assembled for new student orientation. There were some other families who came to register their children for school. Some of the children were my friends. When I saw them, I felt happy and encouraged, thinking that school wouldn't be hard and boring. The headmaster asked us to wait at his office until they finished with the orientation. He was flexing his newly shaped stick, which he used to whip students who were recalcitrant. I had heard about the headmaster. He had the reputation of being very strict and cold. He whipped any student who misbehaved until the student peed on his or her dress. Yeah, in my society, teachers enjoyed unlimited power to give their students corporal punishments. In the school, once a student violated the rules and regulations, no one would be able to deliver the student out of the clutches of the headmaster. I tried to behave myself to avoid the "baptism of fire," as some dubbed the headmaster's lashing.

While waiting for the headmaster to attend to us, I stood by the window watching the students who lined up in the green field according to their class. I caught sight of my sister who stood at the end of their queue. I saw five pupils who were already admitted to begin primary one.

Before one was admitted to primary one, there was a sort of "arm test" that was carried out. Without passing this test, the candidate would not be eligible for admission. How was this arm test done? Well, the principal would hold the child's right arm, move it over the child's head to touch the lobe of the child's left ear. If the child's arm was not able to touch the lobe, the child would be disqualified. I passed the test. I was registered to begin my primary school.

# A Slingshot to School

On Tuesday that week, I was ready for school. I was passionate to go to school because my friends were also attending. I dressed up, carried my little bag containing my slate (wooden writing tablet), two pieces of chalk, a water bottle, two African cherries, and some palm nuts. I hung my slingshot (catapult) around my neck. "No! Take it out. You are not going to the woods but to school," Mama ordered. "Are you going to school or to hunt squirrel?" my sister queried. I stood dumbfounded, my head cast down. I grumbled against my sister. I tried to pull the catapult out of my neck. Before I could take it out, Mama and my sister snatched it from me. I was annoyed with my sister. Were it not for Mama, I would have used the sling to throw a stone at her. I felt that she took advantage of Mama's presence to attack me. Wait a minute, was my sister really attacking me? No! She did not intend to attack me. Rather, she was directing me to detach myself from the object of distraction. I let them have the catapult. I knew I would still get it back from them.

Two of my friends were waiting for me at our porch. Without any further delay, I hung my school bag over my left shoulder. We gallantly set off for school. Mathematics was the first subject we had that morning. At 8.30 a.m., our teacher began her introduction to mathematics. She taught us in our mother tongue, Ibo, since we had not yet learned to speak English. Holding some pieces of stones on her hands, the teacher began to count them loudly and had us repeat after her. "Say after me, 'One *bu otu*, two *bu ibua*, three *bu ato*, four *bu ano* . . .'" She was teaching us how to say the Arabic numerals in Ibo.

The drilling progressed with endless repetitions. We were fascinated by the class because we thought we were learning a new chant. At one point, some of us began to lose concentration. Some of us yawned. Some stretched themselves. Some turned their seats backing the teacher. Some were drowsing. Still some put their hands on their heads. I was bored and wanted to play. I excused myself to use the rest room. I stayed there for some time and ate a cherry that was in my pocket. Then I returned to the class. The teacher kept teaching. I dipped my hand into my bag, took out some palm nuts, and began sneaking them into my mouth. I noticed that the boy who was sitting close to me was falling asleep. In a stealthy manner,

I pinched him at the back. He jolted from sleep and turn around to see who did it. I pretended to be listening to the class. He did not think it was me. I also did the same thing to those dozy pupils who were sitting within my reach. Noticing that some of us were distracted, the teacher approached our pew and stroked her long cane on our heads. "If you don't pay attention now," she warned, "I'm going to flog the hell out of you. Do you hear me?" We nodded and said, "Yes, madam!" Shortly after she resumed her teaching, the school bell rung for break. There was a deafening howling joyful sound resonating from all the classes. "Rec-re-a-tion!" shouted our teacher. "It is recreation time. Go out and play. Now listen! Make sure you play with care. Don't be rough, okay? Make sure you don't hurt yourself or others." We responded simultaneously, "Yes, madam." Without much delay, we all dashed out of the class and moved different directions.

As my folks say, an African domestic fowl stands with one leg when she is brought newly into a homestead. I was new in the school. I did not know exactly where to go. I sat at the window of our class and watched students bustle about with great excitement. I saw a group of boys bouncing a ball toward the football field. A group of girls rushed down the hall. Still some students hastened toward the sales booth. I walked to the sales booth. They were selling *akara*, *moi-moi*, groundnuts, biscuit, *agidi*, and some other stuff. I did not have any money. "Clay, have you eaten your *udala*?" my sister inquired. I answered her that I had eaten them even before the class ended. She bought some *akara* for me. I was eating it when one of my friends drew close. He stretched out his hand, begging me to share it with him. I gave him some to eat. We sat on a stump at the edge of the field and watched the senior boys play football.

## Firewood in the Fireplace

The school dismissed at one o'clock. Before we arrived home, Mama had prepared fufu and *egwusi* soup. "Clay, I want to celebrate you for beginning school," Mama said. "I have prepared your favorite meal. I slaughtered a rooster, and I have kept aside the head and the entrails for you." I laughed quietly and thanked Mama. My sister sent me to fetch fire from our neighbor's house so that we could make a fire to warm the soup. With the oil lamp dangling from my hand, I hurried to bring fire from our neighbor's glowing ember. Before I returned, my sister had already arranged the firewood in the fireplace, ready to start the fire. I handed over to her the lighted oil lamp. She sprinkled some kerosene on the hard wood to help them catch fire quickly. She lit a broom stick and set it on the firewood. At once the wood caught fire and a large flame burst forth. Our thatch kitchen was almost engulfed in flame when I quickly pulled out some of the blazing wood. When the fire settled down, my sister placed the soup pot on the tripod which was sitting over the wood fire. It did not take long, our soup heated up. My siblings and I had our lunch together. It was delicious. My sisters were slow eaters. I made fufu balls pretty fast. Before they could swallow one, I had already taken in three or more. My sisters did not mind. They were used to my fast-eating habit.

After eating, I said, "Mama, I like going to school." "I'm glad to hear that from you," Mama replied. "Make sure you do what you say." On Saturday that week, I got up early and took my bath. Mama saw me rubbing palm kernel oil on my body. She understood why I bathed so unusually early. I thought it was school day. "Where are you going, Clay?" she asked. "School!" "No, today is Saturday." Ah, my passionate zeal for school had made me lose count of days.

After our breakfast, my sisters and I set out for the woods to collect firewood and fodder for our goats. My brothers had gone to fetch water from the public water pump at the village square. I held our small machete while my two sisters carried two big ones. Together we headed for the bush. My sisters had big bundles of firewood and fodder. They added some to my little firewood that I collected. They made ropes out of palm fronds and tied the fodder and the firewood. I undid my shirt and looped it to form a pad. I sat the looped shirt on my head, and my sister helped to lift the bundle of firewood and laid it on my head. I carried it and started to walk back home. I had barely walked two hundred feet when I tripped over a stone. I fell with my face to the ground. The firewood scattered all over the place. I scraped my right elbow. My sister lay down her bundle of fodder and came to hold me up. She threw her arms around my neck and wiped my tearful eyes. Then she helped me to set the firewood on my head. "Go gently and look carefully. Don't fall again, okay?" she encouraged.

# An Encounter with Hunger

As we trudged down the narrow path, we came across two of our country boys, Opara, who was six years old, and his younger brother, Obere, who was four. They were sitting on the ground on the narrow path. Both of them were deeply sobbing, and wrapped their arms around each other. Flood of tears and running nose wet their shabby shirts. My sister stopped and asked them, "Who beat you?" Obere sobbed and stammered as he told his story. My sisters had difficulty understanding what he was saying. I heard all he said. But my elbow was hurting and the heavy bundle of firewood was causing me pain on my neck. I felt uncomfortable to wait any longer. So I walked ahead, carrying the heavy firewood home. My sister held her firewood with one hand and held Obere's hand with another hand. All of them walked along the road to our home.

As we drew close to our kitchen, which was located near our stable (goats' house), our goats saw the fodder and began to bleat repeatedly. But they had to wait until the next morning to be served with the fresh fodder. Mama was very pleased that we were able to gather such huge bundles of firewood and fodder. She was particularly appreciative of me for giving her a hand with the chores.

Mama came into the porch and saw Obere and his brother leaning on the wall at the facade of our house. They had not eaten since morning. Their mother had no money to buy food for them. She left early in the morning for paid farmwork. The children had to endure hunger until she received some wage to buy food. They barely had one full meal a day. Hunger was written all over Opara and Obere. Their eyes were sunken like those who were confined in a "concentration camp." Malnutrition had left them with an emergent bloated belly.

Their unkempt hair was brittle and almost gray. Their oversized polo shirts were dirty and ragged. Their feet were cracked. They needed help. They needed food! They seemed to understand their mother's struggle and toil for their survival. Their mother would reassure them of her love for them despite their suffering. The joy of knowing that their mother loved them gave the children strength to endure the pangs of hunger. When Mama asked what was going on with them, I related to her their story.

What happened on this particular day was that Opara's little brother was very hungry. They thought they could pick some *udala* (African cherry) to hold their hunger until their mother returned from work. They went into the infamous Obiokute's farm. Unfortunately, Obiokute apprehended them and began to flog them. Obere had started crying at the top of his voice before Obiokute could turn to him. Still wringing his hands and sobbing, Opara knelt and pleaded with Obiokute to give him double punishment instead of touching his frail brother. "Please, please," he pleaded, "my brother is sick and hungry. If you wouldn't mind, give me his share of the lashes. Please, please, sir!" Obiokute did not listen to him. "Shut up!" Obiokute raged. "Oh, you want to prove you are a strong boy." Having said this, Obiokute gave Opara an extra whip before turning to Obere. Obiokute's attitude was not surprising to the people. Obiokute was well-known in the village as a very cruel man. He was just as his name, Obiokute, which means "heart of stone." His name influenced his life. Compassion, mercy, sympathy, and kindness had no place in his heart.

Mama was greatly moved by the pathetic story of the children. She hastened and served them with heavy plates of fufu and *egwusi* soup. Within a few minutes, Opara and his brother gulped down the whole food. They thanked Mama. Feeling satiated and refreshed, they went back to their home. "Amen, I say to you, whatever you did for one of these least brothers of mine, you did for me" (Mt 25:40).

## A Treasure in an Earthen Vessel

It was another school day. Some of our schoolmates were already at our front door waiting for us. Almost all the students had their gifts for our "madam" (that was how we addressed our teacher). Some had got some cobs of corn and pears. Some had some oranges. Madam did not request them, but we loved bringing some gifts to her. She was very kind and motherly, and all the pupils loved her very well. When we got to school that morning, the pupils presented to her all sorts of fruit. Her table was filled with many fruits available in that season of the year. She was very grateful for our generosity to her.

Madam thought that I was a smart boy. She tried to encourage me to form the habit of reading instead of playing away my time. I appeared very quiet but she discovered that I could be at times stubborn. Yet, she was patient with me. "Clay," she advised, "make sure you are always attentive in the class. Class time is never a time for play. Once you are in the class, be attentive, listen well, ask questions, and you will learn. You told me that you want to be a doctor, right?" "No!" I replied loudly, shaking my head. "What is that again that you told me that you want to be when you grow up?" "I want to become a priest," I responded with a sense of firmness. "Great!" Madam affirmed. "You know that Father Onyuka, our pastor, is a priest because he did not play away his time in the school. He worked hard and prayed well. People see priests as those who are smart, intelligent, and prayerful. It will be hard for one to become a priest if one does not pay attention in class." Madam stooped and patted me on my shoulder. Then she looked straight into my eyes and said: "Clay, promise me that from this time forth you will no more play in class?" I stood still as though I was struck dumb. I hung my head, looking down on the earthen floor, because I felt shy and abashed. She repeated the question. I gave her a sidelong glance and said softly: "I promise."

When we returned to class in the afternoon, Madam taught us the Ibo alphabet. I remembered her counsel and so tried to be attentive. It was hard. Before the end of the class, I began to feel feverish. Before long, I started shivering. My head was pounding as though two persons were beating drums on it. It had been long since I was sick. It was like a heavy storm after a lull. I lay down on the floor. "Clay is not used to sleeping in the class. He would rather play and distract others. Is he ill?" Madam wondered. She drew close and saw that I was shivering, my lips drooped, my face looked pale, and my eyes were weak and partially open. I felt drained of energy. She felt my body and found that I was running a temperature. "Clay!" she called, "Are you all right?" I had no strength to respond to her. I struggled to shake my head. My breathing was heavy. I dribbled, and before our madam would clean my saliva, I had started throwing up. She hurried and called the headmaster, who gave me a ride to our house.

When we arrived at our home, Mama was working in our garden. As soon as she heard the honking of our headmaster's motorcycle horn, Mama came to see who was visiting. Mama saw the headmaster trying to help me lie on Papa's workbench. She became upset. "What's happening to him? Did he fall from a tree? Hit by a car . . . ?" She flung a thousand questions to the headmaster. Emotions surged from her vulnerable heart. The headmaster interrupted, "Take it easy! He is not dying. He has a fever. He needs only some aspirin to relieve his pain. It's not a serious matter." Mama carried me up and laid me in Papa's bed. She covered my body with a blanket and daubed my head and face with a wet towel. She called, "Clay, Clay, what is happening to you?" She prayed over me and then brought a bottle of holy water and sprinkled it on me. Afterward Mama brought out one tablet of aspirin. She knew that I dreaded taking medicines. So Mama formed a ball with some piece of fufu and inserted the tablets into it. She dipped the ball of fufu in soup and put it into my mouth. I swallowed it, but after a few seconds I vomited up both the fufu and the medicine. She brought a bottle containing palm kernel oil, which she rubbed on my head and body. Mama also rubbed on my body an ointment that had a burning sensation. She covered me with a blanket. Within a few minutes, sweat poured forth from my body. Cold symptoms fled away from my body, but I still felt weak. Papa thought it was malaria; hence, he prepared some malaria herbs. Each morning and evening, he would give me one cup of the liquid herbs.

After three days, I did not experience much improvement. I lost a great deal of weight, and Mama was much concerned for my health. One evening, I was so weak that I passed out. Mama was greatly troubled, for she thought that I was dying. Papa sent for a nurse. After running some tests, it was found that I had typhoid fever. The nurse began treating me with many injections, drips, and pills. Before I got over the illness, the school session was nearing its end. Our madam suggested that I wait until the next academic year. I had to repeat first year. That year passed fast, and before we knew it, we were already in another academic year. My former classmates were in primary two while I was starting afresh in the first year. Even so, it didn't bother me because I trusted that my God had a great plan for my life. I did well in school. I was made the head boy at the senior level and I carried out my task with zeal and devotion. In spite of occasional illness that struck me, God continued to refresh me with strength and fervor to press on.

# A Tinge of Naughtiness

The Divine Potter's Clay was gradually coming of age! I was slender, dark complexioned, notably nimble in movement, committed, reserved, and self-possessed. I know that I was bashful when I was growing up. One thing that most triggered this feeling in me was one of my sister's friends. She was about four years older than I was. She was very beautiful and always cheerful. She visited our home from time to time. She was very fond of me and called me "sweetheart." Even though I loved her so much, I didn't want her to call me by that name. It made me blush. My siblings and some of my friends used to jest with me, saying that my "sweetheart" had come to see me. I felt abashed and uncomfortable being around her. Whenever I heard her voice around our house, I would quickly dodge and hide in our room. I remember one day I hid under Mama's bed until she left our home. When she discovered that I was hiding from her, she started to come to our house in a stealthy, sneaky manner. Later she got married and left home for the city to be with her husband. I felt relieved.

As you know, I grew up in a village where there was no constant electricity, but I used our charcoal iron to straighten my clothes. I dressed with care to make sure I looked nice. However, I did not dress with the intention of impressing someone but rather to express my belief in the common saying that "cleanliness is next to godliness." My effort to keep myself exteriorly clean was to remind myself of my call to be interiorly pure. Purity is essential for entering into heaven.

As I have remarked earlier, the review of the strands of my childhood is not one of complete record of excellent behavior. I have to confess that there was some negative side of me, which I want to share with you. Apparently, some of my childhood unruly behaviors were due to ignorance. It was not that my parents didn't teach me to behave. It was rather because I forgot it, thinking that such negative behaviors could make me stronger and self-actualized. Those bad attitudes were really an indication of my humanness, immaturity, and imperfection. It was Jesus Christ alone who took on human flesh without any stain of vice. This is not to justify my naughtiness, but to call your attention to fair estimation. Again, my parents played their part well; they did not relent in forming me in the way of the Lord. However, the fallen nature reared its ugly head occasionally in my life. In my childhood days, my older brother and I lived like cat and dog. We quarreled often, even over trivial matters. It was not my brother's fault. I guess it was because I was disrespectful and stubbornly rude to him. He was four years older than I was, but sometimes I looked down on him. As a result, he beat me up very often, but I would always offer him a tough resistance. His fear was not how to beat me, but how to get away from my strong grip. No matter how hard he thrashed me, I would not yield to him until he exhausted his strength. I longed for the day when I would grow enough strength to overcome him in a fight.

I remember one day Papa bought us a loaf of bread. Mama gave each of us two slices of bread. My brother came to me and asked, "Do you want to be stronger than I am?" "Yes," I replied. "It is easy," he continued. "If you press a piece of hot bread on your chest, then you will have a heart of a lion. You will be very strong, fight without growing tired, and no one would be able to overcome you." "Is that so easy?" I inquired with curiosity. "I want to have a heart of a lion." My brother took me to our fireplace. He used tongs to heat up some piece of bread. He withdrew it when it was hot and said to me, "Open your chest fast." Without hesitation, I undid my shirt with eagerness. He pressed the hot piece of bread on my chest. At an instant, the hot piece of bread seared my chest and I screamed with pain. When he saw my singed chest, my brother ran away through the back door. All the family—Mama, Papa, my sisters, and some of my cousins—who heard my cry had their hearts in their mouths as they rushed down to the kitchen. They thought I was bitten by a scorpion. With Mama's eyes wide open and her heart heavily throbbing, she inquired, "What is the matter?" I sobbed my story out while they listened passionately. Papa sighed and said sarcastically, "Why then are you crying? You will have a heart of a lion only if you can bear the pain. If you continue to cry, you will surely lose the power that you have received. Strong men do not cry, no matter how they hurt!" I knew Papa did not mean what he was saying. We are used to his ironic comments. This was a serious matter. It was not a time to laugh. I was hurting seriously. Mama brought her first aid box to treat my wound. She applied some ointment on it and bandaged it.

I got some pebbles and stones, with my slingshot hanging on my neck. I sat at the front of our house waiting for my brother to come back. "He must certainly get his own share of the pain," I muttered. I sat patiently keeping watch and grumbling, ready for a battle against my brother. Mama approached me and started to stroke my head, asking me to forgive my brother. "Forgive him, my son, okay? Remember Jesus wants us to forgive the offenses of our brothers and sisters. It does not please God if we refuse to let go of everything our brother or sister has done wrong against you. Think about this: if you kill your brother or your sister, who will stay with you?" "If he dares offend me next time, I'll certainly strike back," I warned. Having said this, I dashed into Papa's room. Papa's radio was turned on. It was playing some relaxing countryside music. I lay down on Papa's couch and listened to the music to lift up my spirit.

The music coming from the radio pierced my heart like a sharp sword, deflating it from the swell of resentment and anger. The second music penetrated my soul, and like a blazing fire, consumed the dross of negative emotions. I remember some of the words of the music: *"Onye egbule nwanne ya. Onye egbule nwenna ya. Onye gburu nwanne ya mgbe obuna anya mmiri ga eju ya anya . . ."* (May no one kill his/her brother/sister. Whoever kills his brother/sister will remain in tears [agony] day in and day out). As I listened to this music, I began to ponder Mama's words to me. She said that Jesus wants me to forgive and love my brother. I thought over how much I had felt to forgive and love my siblings. I regretted the day that I gave my sister a black eye. In fact, many thoughts raced in my mind: "What if my anger had cost me my brother's or sister's life? What if I had maimed any of them? How would I stay alone if I had killed them?" I dissolved in tears. It was a turning point. I felt sorry for being naughty. I regretted having offended God by not loving my siblings enough. I felt the hand of God drawing me into his heart. I made up my mind to forgive my brother. I felt very peaceful and calm because the weight of those negative emotions had been purged from my heart.

Over the years, I came to understand love. I could hear love inviting me to love without measure, without condition. I learned from the Bible that love "does not seek its own interests, it is not quick-tempered, it does not brood over injury, it does not rejoice over wrongdoing but rejoices with the truth. It bears all things . . . endures all things" (1Cor 13:5–7). With a contrite heart, I prayed, "Lord, forgive me for not loving my brothers and sisters and my neighbors as you wanted me to love them. Transform me and make my heart glow with love so that I may love everyone without putting any condition for loving." God answered my prayer and began his gradual healing process in my life. I handed over to the Lord all my vices, my obstinacy and rebellion, my stubbornness and vindictive spirit. God continued to work in me, transforming my heart to learn to endure and to bear all things for the sake of Christ.

## False Face

In my teenage days, some of our youths took pride in being acclaimed as a "strong man." Some thought that to be a man was to be a bully or a troublemaker. "Are you not a man?" "Act like a man!" "Be brave!" They would urge. They chose nicknames that they loved to be called. I remember vividly such names as: "Area-Scatter," "Oke-Nkume (Great Stone)," "Isi-Udele (Head of a Vulture)," "Ogbu-dimkpa (Man Killer)," and numerous others.

Power tussle was not uncommon in those days. Little matters could cause them to fight against each other. They would verbally abuse or curse the other. They would wag fingers, flex and shake fists, and slap chest to demonstrate their power. One of the opposing parties would yell at the other: "Do you know who I am?" "Don't you fear face?" "Are you not afraid of playing with fire?" "I'll show you who I am." If one of the parties did not give it back to the opposing party, some spectators, who were mischief makers, would make some flattering comments to instigate fight: "Don't let him go free;" "Deal with him," "Show him who you are." If the other chose to stay calm, they would boo and jeer at the person, labeling him a coward. In other words, not to take a stance against the intense confrontation was seen as a sign of disgraceful weakness and cowardice. If one offered resistance or struck back, then fight ensued, and whoever got the better of the fight became the "local champion," the "strong man."

Personally, in those days, I never intentionally cause trouble or harm. However, in a few occasions, I engaged in physical fight with some persons. I fought because I felt offended. I felt offended because of what I thought about what was done to me. I remember a number of times that I used the common phrase of those who had forgotten who they really were, "Do you know who I am?"

One instance was during the time we were practicing our cultural dance. A lad who belonged to a different dance group came to spy for their group. He came secretly to observe our dancing styles. Such an act was customarily offensive. When we saw him, he tried to escape, but I caught up with him and dragged him by his shirt. Holding him firmly, I questioned him furiously: "Do you know who I am?" The boy thought that my small body frame would make it easy for him to lift me up and throw me away. It was not as he thought. As he attempted to resist me, I swooped down upon him, lifted him up, and threw him to the ground. I left him and walked majestically back to our house, puffing heavily like a wrestler who had conquered a giant. How ignorant I was! In retrospect, I wish I knew then who I was made to be. After asking people, "Do you know who I am?" I now ask myself, "Who really am I?" I pondered this question for a while. Its answer would unfold as I grew in my personal relationship with my Divine Potter.

I was caught up in the common crisis of self-identity. How I needed to recognize that "who I am" was not defined by physical power but by the power of love! Some of us do not realize who the human persons are created to be. As a result of this lack of understanding, some are crushed in the illusion of who they think they are. In their indiscreet drive to uphold their false identity they lose the light of faith, hope, and love. Oh, the shepherd of my soul found me in time and illuminated my mind. I allowed myself to be found by the Divine Shepherd. He pulled me out from that deadly pit of illusive world.

Now I know who I am. I am a son of light and love. I am called to be light to the world darkened by ignorance. I'm called to be visible love in the world diffused with hatred. I am a child of God called to peace. I am one called to love.

What do I mean by love? St. John reminds me that God is love. I was created by love. God has poured the ocean of his love into my heart. The fountain of love is brimming over, and I cannot hold it to myself. I let myself become a channel for God to turn the dry land of hatred into a spring of love. I am called to love others for God's sake. In my relationship with God, *love* took flesh to save me. His name is Jesus Christ, Emmanuel (God with us). In my relationship with my fellow human beings, LOVE is an acronym which guides me in relating with others: "[L]isten, [O]pen, [V]isualize, and [E]ncourage." L stands for listening to others. O stands for opening my eyes to see the good in others, opening my heart to care for others, and opening my hand to help others. V stands for visualizing Christ in others. E stands for encouraging others to spiritual growth through my words and actions. I have recognized who and whose I am. I couldn't know who I am until I know truly who created me. I couldn't know who created me until I appreciate that I am wonderfully created. I couldn't appreciate the wonder of his creation in my life until I began to see the Creator in my neighbor.

Oh, how blind I was not to see the Lord of love in my brothers and sisters in those days that I fought against them! How I did not know myself because I walked away from myself in those days that I failed to love others around me! By the power of God's grace, I'll no more forget who I am. My true self is never in bullying or fighting others. My true identity is not in hating or crushing others, but in helping and caring for them. Now I strive daily to love without measure. I become truly alive when I live to love. I know I am not yet perfect. I grow in love every day. Alleluia! the Lord's strength is continuously made manifest even in my weaknesses (2Cor 12:10).

## My Veritable Village

Growing up in the small village in southern Nigeria, I experienced a peaceful life there. I call my village a tranquil place for the lowly. It was a place where material poverty did not erode from the hearts of the people contentment and joy. It was a community where the language was love. The people were mindful of others and sought together the common good. Their smiles truly came from their hearts. My village was a place where the presence of one another delighted the lowly souls, and communion was seen as an estimable value. The chieftains had symbols of unity inscribed on their seats. The maxim which they uttered and strived to live out was *"Igwe-bu-Ike"* (Unity is power). Now and then, families, relatives, and friends gathered around a table of kegs of nature-made wine tapped from palm trees and raffia palms. The wine cheered the people's hearts and fostered in them a spirituality of communion. The people valued the culture of life and morality. Their unique sense of hospitality, especially the tradition of presenting kola nuts to visitors, was a testimony of their value and love for the human person.

Their cultural life was bound up with their deep sense of the sacred. For them, Chukwu (the Supreme God), Chineke (God the Creator) was very involved in their lives. They revered the Creator in all they did. They offered prayer regularly when they went to bed for a night's rest, when they woke up at dawn, when they planted or harvested their crops, when they married or gave in marriage, when they celebrated life or the arrival of a new baby.

Of course, there is no perfect society on earth. In my village, there were a few scoundrels, but they shamefully confined themselves to their closet.

Before this time, my folks read time with nature. Weather rather than a watch spoke to them the time of day. A cock rather than a clock informed them about the time. The crow of cocks (roosters) sounded the bell of the time to retire and the time to wake.

The Creator furnished my village with beautiful natural scenery. I loved the evergreen vegetation that enveloped the village like a fortress, shielding her from the sweltering sunrays of dry season. The leaves on the trees often swirled in the wind, transporting cool breeze to the threshold of our homes. The lush palm trees extended their fronds to all corners (north, east, west, and south) as though in adoration to the divine. It was a delight to behold the cluster of green bamboo trees swaying in the gentle wind as if they were in a worship dance. I loved the luxuriant blooming shrubs, the heavy blush of various ripe fruit trees, the blossoming of naturally grown lilies, and enchanting flowery meadow with various shades of color. Whenever we went into the bush, I would not stop sniffing the scented aroma of the flowers. Each day, different species of birds hovered and peeped with varying melodious sounds. I enjoyed observing the multiple colored butterflies which often flew over and perched on the meadows, satiating their thirst with the sweet nectar of the bloom. Hawks, kites, vultures, and eagles elegantly soared the heights into the clouds, skating southward of the serene sky. Every evening, especially during rainy season, I could not wait to listen to the sweet symphony of the cries of crickets, frogs, toads, and grasshoppers. At night, I would gaze at the sky, attempting to count and name the uncountable stars. Once in a while, the sky revealed a colorful rainbow, which signaled to me the sacred color bank from where the Divine finger drew the colors that decorated nature. The green grasses of the bush supplied our sheep and goats with nourishing fresh fodder. The large tall trees once in a while shed their dry branches to supply our need for cooking fuel.

I remember one day when I stood in wonder as I gazed at the trees laden with fruits. Then I raised my hands to heaven to praise the Creator for the profundity of the power of fecundity bestowed on his creation. I burst out whistling my favorite traditional lyric in celebration of the gift of nature. What more can I say? My village was a place where the natural scenic splendor stirred my warm heart to yearn for the eternal beauty of the Creator. The natural beauty, the culture of communion, life, and morality, and the deep spiritual life of my people are very appealing to me. Oh yeah, I prefer the simple, peaceful, organic lifestyle in the village to the luxurious and sophisticated city life.

## Moonlight Match

Some individuals who came from the cities to visit my village thought that life in the village was monotonous and boring. For me, village life was very rich in exciting variety of social, cultural, and religious activities. As children, we played and had fun together. Every day, we longed for the evenfall. We would make haste to complete our chores in time in order to play. None of us loved to miss our recreational moonlight plays. We spiced up our eventide with variety of plays.

I recall one occasion, after evening meal, all the village children gathered as usual under a large African cherry (*udara*) tree. The first person who arrived at the playground gave a signal, howling a song to summon other children. We hurriedly washed our plates and ran fast to the arena. We got there almost at the same time with some other children from the neighboring houses. When we all gathered, we started to chant different traditional songs. I do not remember all the songs we chanted that very day, but two of them are still vividly fresh in my memory. One was titled "One blood, One Love." The words are translated literally thus:

"Who has gone to fetch firewood with her brother and left him there? Who has gone to gather grasses with his sister and left her there? One can forget his bundles of firewood; one can forget her piles of fodder. But none forgets her brother and none forgets his sister. When you eat, when you drink, do not forget your brother; do not forget your sister. Love your siblings and be their keeper. Be supportive of them, for you and they are one. You are in your siblings and your siblings are in you. Do not forget your brother. Do not forget your sister. For your siblings are a precious gift to you."

Another song that we sang that night was titled, "The Message of the Little Angels." It goes this way:

> Listen, all the ends of the world. Listen all the dwellers of the east. Give ear all the inhabitants of the west, all the settlers of the north, and all the citizens of the south. We come to you with a message from the Messiah. It is an oracle uttered from the mouths of little ones. We received the message because we are little children of God. It is only those who are "little" who can enter the little gate of heaven; it is the little who are light enough to fly to the sky. Listen now! Our mouths will utter the oracle. Come! Beckon to the deaf to draw near; lead the blind to come. Bring the aged; whisper in your friend's ear to come; call out from the mountaintop. Carry your baby and come. Bring your children to hear the words of the Lord. Teach them by example to live out what we reveal to you today, and make it known to generations to come. Do not say that we did not tell you. Now hear the message: The Lord is love. Love is life. Life without love is lackluster; it is a body without breath. Love is the spring of life. The Lord of love invites you to come and drink from the life-giving spring without pay. This spring is welling up into the threshold of your heart. Open the door of your heart to be inundated with the current of love. Love your brother and your sister. Love those around you. Love the Lord's creation, and then you will have life. Whoever has an ear to hear should hear the message of the little angels.

After the songs, we played hide-and-seek and tug of war. We were still playing when one of us noticed that it was getting late. So we dismissed for night rest. When we got home that night, our room was very hot because of sun. Our bodies were wet with sweat, and we needed to take our bath to cool off. Unfortunately, we did not have enough water. We had only a handful of water in our large earthen pot, and we would use it to prepare our breakfast in the morning. The community tap water supply was faulty. For over two weeks, we had been walking a long distance to buy water from water dealers. Bathing twice a day would make it impossible for us to afford the high cost of water.

We had to bear the sting of the heat. We had no electricity, not to talk of air conditioner to cool the room. We did not need to bother ourselves about electric fans or air conditioners, for nature supplanted what poverty deprived us of. So we brought out our straw mat and spread it outside to get fresh air. My siblings and I scrambled to secure a better spot to lie down. We snuggled on the mat and nestled against each other, and before long, sweet, refreshing, peaceful sleep took its course. Mama checked on us regularly to see that we were in good state. We were not afraid of "human wolves," armed robbers or evil people. We were rather at peace for in those days, the menacing anti-life spirit was uncommon in the village.

## The Warmhearted Woman

In my village, we had one elderly woman whom we fondly called "Ezinne" (good mother). Sometimes, on bright moonlight days, we gathered at her home. Ezinne was a very kind, joyful, and jovial woman. She was a delight to be around. Her caring and generous heart revealed her love for the Lord. She treated us as her children. She never ate without reserving some portions of food for us. She never drank without thinking about us. She had a special knack for telling stories, and she was exceedingly experienced in matters of culture and well versed with folklore.

On the days we visited her, she would sit down on a large log of wood at her veranda. We always scrambled to sit closer to her to listen to her beautiful, inspiring stories. She would always begin her story this way, "Children, I would like to tell you a story." And we would respond, "Tell us so that our hearts may rejoice!" We never grow tired of hearing those exciting stories.

Age had pulled out all Ezinne's teeth. She could not chew food, and she had difficulty saying some words clearly. However, we were used to her unique way of pronouncing certain words. My little cousin, who was about three years old at that time, amused us one day. As Ezinne was telling us some story, the boy inserted his finger into her mouth, saying, "Bite me."

Ezinne mumbled his finger. She had no teeth to bite. Feeling tickled, the little boy laughed loudly. I pulled his fingers out because he was disrupting the story. Before Ezinne could resume with the story, another child asked her, "Ezinne, did you ever grow any teeth in your life?" Ezinne chuckled and said, "My teeth were very beautiful to behold; they were sparkling white and proportionate, evenly spaced, with a fine gap between the upper incisors." Holding my beautiful niece Ochakomaka, Ezinne teased her, "See, I was far more beautiful than you are." "Ooh! It is not true," we bellowed almost at the same time.

We cast our eyes over Ezinne. We saw that age had eaten deep into her, leaving her with no tinge of physical beauty to be reckoned with. Her skin was shriveled, her face was terribly wrinkled, her eyes and cheeks were sunken. There was not a single tooth left in her mouth, and all her hairs had turned gray. There was no evidence to show that she was beautiful when she was younger. We tried to hold back our laughter as we gazed at her. One of us said to her, "Ezinne, you were never as beautiful as Ochamaka."

With her characteristic sense of humor, she remarked: "Believe it or not, because of my beauty, some people used to call me 'Ugomma' (Beautiful Eagle). The saying is true that 'when a woman grows old, she looks as though no bride price was paid for her.' Wait until you get to my age. In the next seventy years, you will see for yourself how your youthful luster and energy will gradually fade, as age chisels on you each day." "No, I will not lose my teeth when I grow old. I will not like to miss eating meat," Ochamaka retorted. "My daughter, when you face the touch of the reality of aging, it is not a matter of what you want but what fate gives to you," Ezinne remonstrated. "You won't understand all this now," Ezinne continued. "You are still too young to experience the challenges of old age. Now let us move on with our stories." "Yes! yes! tell us more stories," we echoed excitedly.

Ezinne told us many folktales, riddles and fables, such as the slyness of the devil, and the crafty tortoise who deceived all the members of the animal kingdom. We also learned about what caused the sky to go up to unreachable elevation. Still she told us the story about how a group of children went missing because they did not follow their parents' instructions.

The warmhearted woman also taught us a number of songs. Two of them were titled "One Blood, One Heart," and "The Message of the Little Angels." Ezinne told us many stories that contained moral lessons. Sometimes I think back on how we had fun together around Ezinne in those days. I reminisce how we clung to her as she taught us those exciting songs and stories. I heartily remember her with great affection.

## The Busy Blacksmith

I wouldn't forget my frequent visit to our village market. In the market was a blacksmith's workshop. Sometimes when we visited the market we stopped by the workshop to watch the blacksmith forge his metals. Two levers of manually operated compressors were mounted on both sides of the kiln (the furnace where he fired metals). With his hands holding the levers firmly, the old blacksmith blasted air into the kiln at a rhythmic speed to heat the piece of metal. It was fascinating to me to hear the chiming sound that resonated far away as he used the levers to blow air into the kiln. The sound echoed: *"Pum tum putum, pum tum putum . . ."*

After I arrived home one evening, the sound of the kiln kept coming to my mind. I reflected on the blacksmith's amazing work. After heating up the metal to flame red, he used tongs to pull the metal out of the kiln. He set the metal on the anvil, a heavy metal, and repeatedly hit hard on the hot metal to forge a tool of his choice. Impressively, I found that after passing through such intense heating and hard hammering, the metal wore a new shape, giving birth to a new tool. Through this process, the blacksmith forged axes, pickaxes, hoes, shovels, and many other tools.

I thought that the simple work of the blacksmith could be analogous to God's work in my life. All the process of fashioning a piece of metal spoke to me about the work of the Divine Potter in my life. The sound of the firing of the kiln was echoing to me, "God is working, God is working . . . God is working in me . . ." True, God is at work in my life. He places me in the kiln (crucible) of trials. My pains, disappointments, difficulties, failures, weakness, humiliations, and struggles are a part of the process of forging me into a tool of his choice. After the firing and hammering, I'll turn out to be a brand-new tool in the hand of the Divine Potter.

# My Brandmark

As a person of faith, in all circumstances I'm consoled that I am walking the way to Jerusalem with Christ. How could I be a true disciple of Christ if I did not carry my cross to follow him as he demanded? My heart is at peace that I am privileged to bear the brandmark of the Risen Lord (Gal 6:17). My hardship in the discipleship indicates that I am a slave, not of the world, but of Christ. What a way of freedom and peace! After his resurrection, Jesus took time to show to his disciples his wounds on his hands, sides, and feet. Those who doubted his resurrection came to the light of conviction that he was truly the wounded Messiah.

Some of his disciples also bore marks of suffering. St. Paul suffered the pains of persecution, the hurt of hardship, and the sting of sickness (cf. 2Cor 12:7). He was beaten, stoned, and shipwrecked. He experienced hunger and thirst. He had sleepless nights, and was exposed to harsh weather (2Cor 11:23–28). Despite his trials, St. Paul rejoiced because he thought that he was privileged to share in the suffering of his Savior. St. Peter exhorts me to rejoice as I partake in the Cross of Christ (1Pet 4:13). Still, St. James encourages me to count it as a blessing when I experience certain adversity, for it is part of the process of purifying me for himself (cf. James 1:2–4).

In our time, we have numerous people of faith who experienced terrible tribulations in their lives. Not long ago, I read the story of St. Vincent de Paul. He was held captive by the Turkish pirates. Before he was captured, St. Vincent received the thrust of the pirate's arrow. He recounted that the wound of the arrow served "as a reminder" throughout his life. Time will come, and it shall be on that glorious morning when I shall show my own scars. It will happen on that day when the Divine Porter will have completed the work he began in my life. On that day, the heavens, the host of angels, and the earth will rejoice as they chant the celestial hymn of triumph. Yes, I shall enter through the glorious gate.

Before receiving the garment of glorified body, I'll show the scars of my faith journey, my resigning to God's will, my patient waiting, and my service of charity. At that beautiful gate I shall lay out my heart that is pierced by the sword of sorrow. The saints shall see my heart flaming with the fire of love and steaming with zeal for the Gospel. They shall see my skin chapped by frequent exposure to the harsh weather in the course of the sacred mission. I shall show my palms calloused by toils for the sake of Christ. They shall see my cracked feet that walked the roads to preach the Good News to the poor. I shall show my knees hardened by long hours of kneeling in prayer. They shall see the scar where the deadly "arrow" pierced me while I was on the line of the holy mission. They shall see my sunken eyes that kept vigil in prayerful watch. They shall listen to the litany of trials of my life.

Then I will join the saints to praise the Lord for his abundant grace that he poured upon me. Yes, God's grace has been abounding in my life— grace so transforming that I do not hold back my smile to those who needed it; grace so inspiring that I do not hesitate to give words of consolation to those who needed my support; grace so powerful that I do not hold back from "ministry of presence" to those who needed my accompaniment; grace so sufficient that my heart does not run dry with compassion for those who are hurting; grace so redeeming that I do not give up persevering in faith. Praise the Lord, for he has poured in me grace upon grace.

## Dance of the Dreamer

Growing up in my little village, I was involved in our cultural dances. I participated in three dance groups: the Abanko, the Ogba-nkpada, and the Agaba.

Abanko dance is for the male youths, and it is made up of one or two dancers and five or more others who beat the percussion instruments. The instruments include wooden and metal gongs, drums, whistles, rattles, and cymbals. The dancers costume in bunches of seed rattles worn around the ankles and waist. They also wrap around their waists straws made from raphia palm trees. They cover their faces with masks, and wear pajama pants, stockings, and gloves to cover their bodies. They hold straw hand fans which they use to receive gifts, to create air when they feel hot, and also to control their body movements in dancing.

Like Abanko, Ogba-ngbada is also for male youths. It is made up of two or three dancers and about six persons who beat the percussion instruments. Ogba-ngbada has more additional percussion instruments and dancing styles than Abanko. Sound of flutes adds an exciting melody for Ogba-ngbada dance. Agaba dance is made up of persons of different ages. Males and females of all ages can be members of Agaba dance. Agaba dance has more complex dancing style and more elaborate pattern of beating of its percussion instruments. It involves folksongs, and the dancers and the instrument beaters sing the refrain after the soloist. Agaba dance may be composed of roughly thirty members, which include about eight beaters of percussion instruments, one or more flutists, two or three distinct masquerades, a guard for the chief masquerade, which is always on leash. A long strong rope is tied around the chief masquerade's waist to restrain him from hurting spectators. The rest of the members are uniformed dancers finely costumed in colorful traditional garbs.

Odogwu dance is another dance that my folks perform. It is a dance for the nobilities, men and women of substance. Odogwu is danced during coronations, new yam festivals, marriage celebrations, ordinations, and other outstanding celebrations. We learned odogwu dance, but we never debuted it. When we were preparing to perform it for the first time, some of our members migrated to the cities in search of greener pastures, so to speak. We could not continue with odogwu dance.

We performed our cultural dances for the most part during the festive periods of Christmas and Easter. However, we also danced at any period of the year for those who hire us for special occasions, like celebrations of weddings, anniversaries, coronations, conferment of chieftaincy titles, ordinations, thanksgivings, and the like.

Cultural dance was for us an important means of raising funds to support the financial needs of our families. At the end of the year, we shared the money that we raised and other material donations we received in the course of the dance. I used some part of my own share to support my parents for our school fees and other pressing needs of our family.

Some have asked me about the part I played in our cultural dance. I danced and also played drums for the dance groups. I thought I was a pretty good dancer. My siblings would not agree with me on this. They used to tease me that I was the most untalented dancer among the group. They might be right, but I didn't feel discouraged anyway. I thought I did better in beating drums than in dancing. My parents were proud of me and their affirmation helped to urge me on.

I loved being with the dance groups. I joyfully gave my best to them. I didn't consider our participation as a matter of competition but of cooperation; it was about collaboration. We shared together in building up one another by loving, by serving, and by entertaining. I remember that the eve of each new year was always a special day for us. We masked with banana straws and carried tin cans or wooden or metal gongs. Then we went house to house, beating the stuff and chanting, "May the year go empty handed. May the year go without taking any life. May all the evils go with the year and may the New Year bring good fortune, health, peace, and prosperity." Most of the people we visited showed their appreciation by offering us some gifts. We usually returned home with a lot of gifts, and this perhaps was because all the people wanted to receive good wishes and blessings of the New Year.

## Hunting and Hurting

Hunting was one of my hobbies. I did not learn hunting from Papa because he was not a professional hunter. However, Papa had a local gun that he used to shoot wild animals that came around our homestead. When I was about six years old, Papa bought for me a new slingshot (catapult). Oftentimes, I hung my catapult around my neck. I used it to fire at birds, bats, and squirrels around our compound. I did not kill any animal with my sling for a long period of time. I guess the reason was that I didn't know how to aim well in shooting. After trying for a long time, I succeeded in killing one bird. The first bird that I killed happened in our garden. I was weeding the garden when I noticed that a songbird perched on our pumpkin vine above my head. I watched the bird peck on the fluted pumpkin. I gently pulled out my catapult from my neck. But I did not have any stone to use. So I tiptoed a few feet away and found some dried palm nuts. I picked one and placed it in my slingshot. I hurled it hard on the left wing of the bird. The bird wobbled and fell down. I took hold of it with great excitement. I celebrated my first catch. This made me more passionate to hunt.

The following day after school, I selected a number of smooth stones from a heap of gravel from our neighbor's house. With my slingshot ready at hand, I set off for the bush for hunting. I was with two of my friends. I returned in the evening very tired and without killing any animal. Mama scolded me for leaving out the house chores because of hunting. "He came back without killing even a lizard," my sister taunted. Yet I did not say a word to her. I knew that what I did was wrong. When they saw that I felt sorry for doing it, they did not talk anymore about that.

In the village was a famous hunter named Ezeanu. He had two hunting dogs, which he used for hunting. He had a group of friends who often accompanied him to hunts. On one occasion, I decided to join them for hunting. I was thrilled seeing how the two dogs smelled out animals and signaled Ezeanu to where the animals were hibernating. As we walked into the bush, the smaller dog came to Ezeanu, wagging its tail excitedly. I had no idea what that signal meant, but Ezeanu understood it quite well. And so he whistled to summon us. "The dog has smelled out an animal. Be alert!" he instructed. We all followed the directive, while the dog took the lead to show us where the wild animals were. Soon we arrived at heavy foliage of bamboo trees. The dog began to scratch a huge hole at the bamboo base. That was a sign that an animal was in the hole. "A big bunker for rabbits! They are in the hole," Ezeanu affirmed.

He instructed us to take vantage positions to block the animals from escaping. Some men started to dig out the rabbits. No sooner had they begun digging when two big rabbits swiftly pushed themselves out from the base of the tree. One of the rabbits ran between my legs at high speed. None of us could hit or catch them. The dogs chased after the rabbits.

As I ran after the rabbit, I held out a club ready to hit it. All of a sudden the rabbit ran toward me as the dog chased after it. I tried to hit the rabbit. Before the club could strike the rabbit, the dog had already captured it. Unfortunately, the club banged the head of the dog. The dog flung the rabbit out of her mouth and howled frantically in great pain. She was seriously hurting.

When Ezeanu heard the dog's cry, he became deeply upset. He feared that the dog had sustained a fatal wound. The dog was still wiggling and shrieking when the master anxiously rushed to us. He picked up the dog in his arms, rubbing its head, trying to alleviate the pain. Staring at us with his wide opened eyes red in rage, he stammered his reproof. I apologized to him. He stood transfixed liked a defeated giant. He bit his lips and shook his head as a disarmed soldier in a battleground. He sighed and reproached me with a fierce glance. Then he warned strongly, "I see that you guys are hard of hearing. Now I'll say it again! you must be careful. Many have maimed their colleagues and hunting dogs in their bid to kill game. My dogs are more important than thousands of rabbits. It would have been far better that the rabbit escaped than harming my dog."

When we got home that day, we talked about the incident. We knew that Ezeanu reacted with an unusual tenderness. He had never put up with anyone who hurt any of his dogs. One of my friends thought that Ezeanu mellowed down because he had great respect for my father. Personally, I considered it as divine grace. Sometimes, in his mercy, God changes the hearts of our enemies so that they may be at peace with us (Prov 167).

As time went on, I learned the skills for hunting. I used traps to catch wild fowl and bush rats. I also had a special trap for hawks and kites. I used chicks as bait to catch them. The cheeping of the chicks attracted the predators. It was always exciting coming home with one or two bush animals. Papa warned me to be careful with digging out animals in holes. "Snakes sometimes hide in holes," Papa cautioned, adding, "It has been reported that a number of people were bitten by snakes while they were trying to dig up animals in holes."

One day, we ultimately had such a chilling experience. A friend saw a fresh hole and thought that a rabbit lived there. We started digging it. One of my friends tried to dip his hand into the hole. I recalled what Papa told me—to beware of snakes in holes. So I restrained my friend from inserting his hand into the hole. My friend shoveled out some sand, and all of a sudden a huge black cobra popped up out of the hole. My friend bolted from the ground and shouted, "Snake! Snake!" I sprang over a log of a fallen tree and ran very fast like a deer escaping from a wolf. I stopped at some distance away, looked back, and saw the snake crawling fast into the bush. Right from that day, I dreaded digging holes.

Reflecting on this experience, I think of how poverty pushed us to risk our lives. We looked for food to eat while some in other parts of the world threw away their excess food. What a world! My heart goes out for many people in the world today who are suffering poverty and hunger. Some are starving because they lacked food, while some are overeating because they have overabundance of food. I pray that the Lord may move my heart to cherish charity.

In my plenty, Lord, prompt my heart to remember and reach out to the impoverished. In the midst of surplus, Lord, stir up in me the passion to provide help to those suffering certain scarcity of needs. Oh how I yearn for that Promised Land where we all shall no longer lack any good thing, a kingdom where there will be no more poverty or hunger, no more fear, no more sorrow or suffering. How I long for the kingdom of love, of peace, and of happiness! How I hunger for the kingdom where I will no more wander in the woods in search of food, a kingdom where wants and starvation will lose their grip forever. How I await in hope for the kingdom where I will never again experience the rebellion of creation; snakes will never scare me anymore, for "they shall not harm or destroy on all my holy mountain; for the earth shall be filled with knowledge of the LORD . . ." (Isaiah 11:9)

My hope rests firmly upon my Lord Jesus Christ who grants me that kingdom where there will be no more evils, no more moral decay, no more natural disaster, no more corruption, no more crimes, no more sickness, no more diseases, no more war, and death will be slain forever!

## Initial Inspiration

Clay learned early to pray in the Catholic tradition.

A group of the village children in a "Block Rosary" prayer meeting.

Right from my childhood, I have had a strong passion to grow in morals and in spiritual life. Certain experiences helped to shape my spiritual life. I have the blessing of coming from an active Catholic family. Hence, I learned early to pray in the Catholic tradition. When we were children, we founded a block rosary prayer center in our house. It was named "Seat of Wisdom Block Rosary Center."

Within a short time, the group grew from five to about forty children from around the village. Occasionally, a few adults joined us in the daily rosary prayer. At times, we made house-to-house visits in our village, praying with the families. Most of the villagers received us well, partly because the people were predominantly Catholic and partly because they were faithful people who loved the Lord and put their trust in the children's intercession.

I remember how we prayed together with great devotion. As I cast back, I can still picture us kneeling before the small altar in a prayerful mood, with palms joined together and eyes closed. I can still hear our gentle voices as we faithfully recited the endless decades of the rosary with moderate pace that inspired devotion. Most exciting was our house-to-house visit.

Once in a while, after evening rosary we filed out, visiting the families in the neighborhood. It was really inspiring to behold our beautiful procession along the narrow paths of the village. We were like little angels. Our little girls wore long scarves which extended from head to waist.

As we marched along the road, we sang praise songs while some of us beat musical instruments. One could hear from a distance the echo of our voices, chiming of metal gong, clashing of cymbals, and sound of drums. Each of us held a lighted candle, and the light from the candles diverged far into the dark bushes dispelling the spine-chilling gloom of the village. When we arrived at each house, we knelt to offer prayer for that family. The warmness of the villagers' reception of our visitation uplifted our spirits. Most of the families testified that our prayer brought blessings to them. Most of them joyfully offered some gifts to us.

Sometimes, we attended certain religious functions in the parish. Even though our parish was distant from my village, we never grew weary walking several kilometers to attend Mass and meetings. During their internship around July, some seminarians visited with us. I remember one of the seminarians told us a story about how St. Dominic used the rosary as a spiritual weapon to overcome the "Albigensian heresy," which held, among other doctrines, that all the physical things were evil and were not created by God.

Our parish priest also visited us once in a while. We admired him greatly. He had a good sense of humor, and he was a very humble, devoted, and loving priest. He always began his greetings with "Ave!" to which we would roar our response, "Maria!"

One evening, the priest unexpectedly showed up when we were concluding our rosary. His presence made us feel uneasy and distracted, but we pretended to be recollected as we chorused the "Litany of the Blessed Virgin Mary." He gently knelt beside us. We acted like we had our whole attention on the prayer. But now and again, with half-closed eyes, we sneaked a peek at him. Ah, he understood such kids' stuff. After the prayer, he mimicked our behavior.

His encouraging words that day were memorable. He read a passage from the Gospel of Matthew, which speaks about being like little children in order to enter the kingdom of God (cf. Matt 18:3–4). Then he offered a long reflection that was difficult for our budding minds to put together:

"My little children, I'm very impressed that you are steadfast in your prayer. God has blessed all of you abundantly. Continue to pray for your future, for your families and for the entire world. Remember that 'block rosary' children are known for their good behavior and prayerful life. Our Lord Jesus Christ loves little children. And he wants us, who are adults, to learn from you. In a sense, you are my 'teacher.' I have some things to learn from you. Yes, Christ tells me that unless I become like you, it will be difficult for me to enter heaven. In what sense do I become like you? The Lord wants me to have a childlike heart, a heart filled with such virtues as obedience, humility, simplicity, and total confidence in the Lord. Does it sound like Christ was talking about children like you? Are you humble, obedient children? If yes, then know that you are my teacher. Christ is talking about you if you respect and obey your parents, if you do your house chores well, if you are docile, opening yourselves to learn from your parents and others who teach you. You teach me simplicity through your happiness, joy, care, readiness to forgive, purity of heart, and your single-mindedness in what you do. You teach me to have total confidence in the Lord, through your trust that your parents will supply all your needs. Remember that as you are growing in your physical life you are also growing in virtue and in spiritual life. If you do not drift from the part of faith, you will surely increase in true wisdom, the fear of God. When you remain in the Lord, his blessings will remain with you. I pray that God may continue to guide you and daily draw you ever more closer to his Sacred Heart." The priest blessed us, signing us with the sign of the cross in the air.

## Holy Communion

At fourteen, I enrolled and started taking First Communion classes. I had a burning desire to taste the Eucharist. I once asked my siblings how the Eucharist tasted when they received the Lord, but none of them were willing to tell me. It was a secret that they never shared with any person. I hoped that one day I would have a taste of my Lord in the forms of bread and wine.

After attending classes for three months, I finally received my First Communion in July that year. On that memorable day, I dressed in white pants (trousers), white shirt, and white sandals. During communion, all of us who were first communicants filed out and knelt in front of the altar. I joined my palms together, with my head slightly bowed in reverence to the Lord. I was ready to receive the Lord who condescended to make himself food for my soul.

As the holy bread entered my mouth, I found that the taste was nothing extraordinary, yet I could feel that something marvelous happened within me. True, the Eucharist was not so delicious that my tongue would desire for more. Rather, the sacred species was full of ineffable sweetness which unceasingly drove my soul to yearn for more. It was a sweetness that was not felt in the tongue but in the heart and in the soul. It was a taste that brought into my soul strength, peace, joy, and consolation. I remembered that in my infancy I yearned for my mother's breast milk; after receiving the Lord, my soul yearned increasingly for the milk of Christ's love, the Holy Communion. "Like newborn infants," my soul longed for the "pure spiritual milk" of Christ's Body and Blood, in order that I might "grow into salvation" (1Peter 2:2).

Like the disciples of Emmaus, my inner eyes were opened as soon I received the Eucharist; I could see the Lord going into me in a tangible way. I could see the Divine joining himself with the human. How wonderful a privilege for a mere creature to become one piece with his Creator! You could imagine the current of life that flowed into a fish which was washed ashore for a moment and then thrown back into the ocean. I felt like someone who could breathe again after being deprived of oxygen for some time. I became more and more passionate to live in God's presence. In that mood of spiritual sweetness, I resolved not to offend my Lord in thoughts, words, and actions. I strove daily to be an obedient, docile, respectful, and honest child. I became more intentional in prayer and in charity. It was like my smoldering fire of holy fervor was fanned into flame. I felt new inner promptings to offer myself in the ministry of saving souls.

Right from my tender age, the good Lord set me on fire with the desire to serve him as a priest. Every Sunday, I listened to the priest give homily. I had heard him preach on how Jesus called the disciples and each left everything and followed him. I yearned to leave everything behind to follow the Divine Master in the mission, to devote myself without reservation in service of the Gospel. As I grew in body, in mind, and in faith, that desire for the sacred ministry steadily grew stronger.

It is interesting to note that the mystery of God's way is beyond our comprehension. I proposed to enter into seminary at the time that I considered early in my life, but the Lord of vocation had his plans. I had a dream of the Lord's calling, but the Lord had the blueprint of the dream. He began the process of bringing it into reality in accord with his own will.

As time went on, I came to the realization that the blessed Lord designed to take my vocation journey, not through a shortcut but through a detour. Throughout the stormy voyage, He guarded the flame in my heart; the windstorm could not put out the flame. Through the ruts, the Lord continued to push the wheel forward; I did not get stuck on the way. Through the long, rough road, the Lord continued to renew my strength and refresh me with hope; I did not despair.

I remember the first high hurdle that I encountered along the way. My family had practically no financial resource to cater for my seminary studies. The seminary education was very expensive. Despite the reality of our material poverty, Papa continued to encourage me, giving hope that God's plan would prevail in my life, though it might take time. So it was that the calling seemed like a gem in the sky too high to reach. Yet I did not relent in trusting that with God nothing is impossible.

## The Father's Farmyard

Our lands were not very fertile for farming. We did not have large farmlands in the village. However, the villagers did small-scale farming to support their families. My parents were very industrious and persevering. In addition to other works they did, they cultivated the land, growing some crops in order to augment their meager income. They grew yam, cassava, maize, and a few other vegetable crops. Because we did not have large farmland, we rented lands for farming. I remember asking Papa why our grandparents did not acquire enough lands for our family. He told me that his parents were poor.

In those days, wealth was measured by the size of one's yam barn, and land ownership was based on how much farmland one was capable of cultivating. Those who acquired and developed large farmlands were those who married many wives to increase hands in the fields. I know of a family whose great-grandfather married sixty wives and had many children and grandchildren. There was such a sea of heads in his compound. As a result, he had a hard time putting a name to the face; he could not recognize some of his children.

Anyway, my parents were poor but they were contented with the little they had. God blessed them with sustained strength and vitality. They inculcated early in our life the spirit of hard work. They set us to work on the farm, and every person in the family worked according to his or her capacity. During planting season, we cleared and tilled the field with machetes, hoes, and shovels to prepare it for planting yams, corns, cassava, and some vegetables. All the works on the farm were done manually. My parents did not bother about how much work we did on the farm. They were interested to instill in us the spirit of diligence and hard work.

In the village, the child Clay is set to work; he does household
chores well and learns early to carry bulky stuff (like
bundle of firewood or fodder) on the head with ease.

When we went to the farm, we would work until evening. Then we returned home to prepare for dinner. It was from my parents that I learned tremendous lessons about hard work, patience, and perseverance. As I worked on the farm, my heart longed to serve in the Lord's vineyard! I contemplated the earth and everything in it. By God's words, all things came into being. He rules over them with love.

The Lord of the vineyard created multitudes of human beings and entrusted us with the care of his wonderful creation. Unfortunately, some deserted the duty of looking after the earth. Some, instead of caring for it, worked to destroy the earth. The Lord says that "the harvest is abundant but the laborers are few." The Lord asked that prayers be made for increasing true laborers (Mt 9:37–38). I pray, Lord, send your true laborers to cultivate the earth with the Gospel, to clear the forest of fear in our hearts, to boldly plant the seed of your word into fallow and desolate hearts, to water and weed the souls through personal witness and care for Your people. Sanctify me, purify me, fill me with your Spirit so that I may be counted among your chosen "laborers." You are the "master of the harvest," and to whoever you choose you provide the necessary tools for the task.

Oh, how the world needs your true laborers! Your vineyard is ravaged by swarms of locust. How we need your true laborers to drive them away! Your farmland is pillaged by the enemies. How we need more laborers to keep watch! Master of the harvest, I beg you grant to those you have chosen the grace to bring your healing presence to those who are wounded: restore the grace of faith to those who have lost their faith in you; provide the needs of the poor; heal those who are sick in mind and in body. Grant your strength and hope to those who have lost hope. Grant your Spirit to your chosen ones so that they may grow daily in strength and in wisdom. Choose and send me forth, O Lord, to continue the work you did when you walked the earth, "to bring glad tidings to the poor . . . to proclaim liberty to captives and recovery of sight to the blind, to let the oppressed go free, and to proclaim a year acceptable to the Lord" (Luke 4:18–19). Yes, Lord, I pray that you heal the sick, feed the hungry, clothe the naked, and shelter the homeless. You alone know what every individual needs at this moment. Grant, O Lord, the needs of each individual who trust in you. You alone are the Lord of the harvest. Amen!

# Livelihood and Light

Handicraft was one of the sources of income in my village. My siblings and I crafted baskets and brooms to support our parents. We got all the materials for making baskets and brooms from palm trees. My sisters used the leaves to make brooms while my brothers and I used the stems for making baskets. At my initial stage of learning basket weaving, I made all kinds of awkward, flimsy baskets, unevenly and coarsely knitted. But as I practiced each day, I gradually became proficient. I made different forms of baskets: grilling baskets for smoking fish or meat, baskets for sieving cassava, and baskets for carrying farm tools or produce.

Some of my friends were skilled in trimming palm trees and cutting palm fruits. I did not learn to climb palm trees. My parents did not let me climb trees for the reason that my older brother once fell from a palm tree and sustained a severe injury. He was almost pierced through by some pointed bamboo woods which were used for staking yam stems at the base of the palm tree. The palm tree was very tall, and it was a miracle that my brother survived the accidental fall. He did not fracture any bones, but he had deep bruises and the scar is still there today. I hired palm tree climbers to cut the palm fronds for me.

On market days, we went to market to sell our baskets and brooms. We usually left home before daybreak. We had a big rooster (cock) who crowed regularly. He let out its first crow around three o'clock in the morning. We usually set off for the market at the second crow of the cock, which was around 5:00 a.m. I recall one particular day I was getting ready to leave for the market. My companions were already waiting at a narrow path close to our house. I heard one of the guys call out loudly, "Clay!" I yelled out my answer, letting them know that I would be there in a short time. I hurriedly loaded my baskets, a dozen in all, on Papa's bicycle. I pushed the bicycle, rushing along to catch up with my friends who were waiting for me. The sky was still dark that morning. And so I groped my way down the path, my eyes squinting through the dusk of the dawn. One of my friends was carrying a lighted kerosene lamp to light the way. There were five of us. Three of us were carrying our baskets on bicycles, while two carried theirs on their heads because they had no bicycles. The bundles of baskets were heavy and the way to the market was distant, about seven kilometers from our village. They had no choice but to bear the pain, carrying the load on their heads. We tried to see if we could fit their baskets on our bicycles, but it did not work. We agreed to take turns in carrying the loads on our heads.

As we trudged along the narrow, hilly, and eroded road to the market, a car with high-beam headlights on was coming toward us. The brilliant light blinded our eyes. We could not see our way. We stopped at the edge of the road to allow the car to pass. For a few seconds after the car passed, our eyes remained dazzled by the light. I tried to push my bicycle along but I suddenly fell into a gully. Immediately, my bicycle tumbled and my baskets scattered in all directions. I felt helpless. The two fellows leaned their bicycles against some trees at the edge of the road and came to help me out. I got up and rubbed out mud from my body. I felt a burning pain around my left knee and my left elbow. It was certain to me that I had scraped off my skin.

One of my friends cut some leaves of "ojigachi," a common plant used for healing wounds in my village. The plant grew rampantly in all places in the village, and it could easily be recognized by its strong smell. My friend squeezed out the fluid and dropped it on my knees and my elbows. It was very painful. Then the two guys gathered my baskets. The other two who were carrying their baskets on their heads waited for us pityingly. Even though they were still under the weight of the load on their heads, they kept empathizing: "Clay, *ndo* (Clay, sorry)!" I always remember the concern and care we showed to one another as friends. We were passionate to be there for one another, to help in carrying one another's burdens (cf. Gal 6:2).

As I reflect on that incident, my stumbling along the rough dark road, I can't help but think about our spiritual journey. Without light, we cannot see the way. And without seeing the way, we stumble and fall. Christ tells us that he is the light of the world. Those who follow him walk in light and those who do not follow him stumble and fall in their darkness (John 8:12). I thought about how the bright headlights of the car blinded our eyes. Light is not meant to shine directly on the eyes. When light shines directly into our eyes, the light blinds our eyes. Who gazes at the brilliant sun without his or her eyes being dazzled? Eyes are meant to see things illuminated by the light. Light drives away darkness and helps us to see things that would have otherwise been hidden in the shadow of darkness. If I try to see the mystery of Christ with my natural eyes, without the eyes of the heart, without faith, I would be in the darkness of unbelief. In our spiritual life, we walk by faith and not by sight. Christ who is light comes to enlighten my heart and mind. He comes to shine his light not directly into my physical eyes, but into my heart and into my mind, so that I may love and be enlightened by his revelation. Those who are physically blind can also see the way of life through the eyes of the heart. St. Paul prays that the eyes of our hearts may be illuminated that we "may know what is the hope that belongs to his call, what are the riches of glory in his inheritance among the holy ones" (Eph 1:18). When the Lord shines his light on our hearts, we begin to love and serve him with our whole hearts; when he opens the eyes of our minds, we begin to see and understand the vision of his revelation. We begin to appreciate his mighty power, his presence and love in our lives. I pray that Christ's light may dispel my darkness, that the Holy Spirit may open the eyes of my heart and mind so that I may grow in love and understanding of the truth of the Gospel.

## Fair Sale

After we rearranged my baskets and tied them again on my bicycle, we proceeded to the market. Reaching the market, we were very happy to find that the turnout of basket sellers was few. Basket buyers were waiting anxiously for business. This meant that it would be a good market for us. The sale went quickly. The highest bidder paid cash and carried the baskets. The fair sale was a consolation to the travail that we passed through in the whole process of making and conveying the baskets to the market. We bought all the stuff we needed from the market and headed back for home.

When I got home that day, I still felt the pain of the fall. The wounds on my elbows and knees took some days to heal. As I stumbled that morning, I remember asking God, "Why me? Why did you allow me to fall?" I prayed before I left home. As I looked at my rosary dangling from my neck, I remembered the rosary which we prayed on the evening before. We prayed the Sorrowful Mysteries. A thought came to me: in the fourth Sorrowful Mystery, the Lord carried the heavy cross, and under the weight of my sins, fell to the stony ground several times. The heartless executioners forcefully flogged and struck him repeatedly. They made sport of my Lord. No one was there to console him. My fall and pains were nothing to compare with the Lord's passion. I was comforted and cared for by my friends. The friends of Christ, on the other hand, turned away from him. "Why not me?" was a question that came within me as I pondered the mysteries of the cross. Then I prayed, "Lord, I realize the many graces that you poured upon me on that day when I fell to the ground. O my loving Divine Master Potter, You have been at work in me. Let the pain of my fall and every pain that I may suffer in life meet with the flood of blessings that flowed from your cross. You said that if I wish to come after you that I must take up my cross and follow you. May I always keep in mind that your love for me is unconditional, boundless, and everlasting. May I constantly appreciate your presence and power in my life, even in moments of adversity. Amen.

## My Leisure Time

I was not a talented sportsperson. Yet, I loved juggling. I also loved biking and playing ping-pong. My parents usually restrained me from playing football. One of my brothers sustained an injury while playing football. As a result, my parents became apprehensive whenever they heard that we were out playing the sport. The villagers never encouraged sports in those days. Spending much time on sports was seen as a lack of sense of responsibility. They thought that sports was another name for playing away precious time that should have been spent working on the farm or giving a hand with the chores or making some handicrafts for sale. One poor villager once scolded his son, saying, "Once you come back from school, you disappear from the house to play. You don't think of how to help in the family. You don't think of any important thing to do. Do you think that food will fall from heaven?" It was because of this negative view of sports that made some of us, the village youths, lose interest and commitments to sports activities. However, I spent some great time with my friends, visiting relatives, taking a walk, and fraternizing with colleagues. When I learned to read and write, I began spending much of my leisure time in reading and writing. I loved reading spiritual books. My heart and mind is not set on "what is seen but to what is unseen; for what is seen is transitory, but what is unseen is eternal" (2Cor 4:18).

## Changes and Challenges

So far I have shared with you what it was like for me growing up in my little village. I have given you a picture of my life story from infancy through childhood. In the following topics I shall share with you my life story from high school to college days.

After a successful completion of primary education, I entered a government-run secondary school in my town. The school was located roughly six kilometers away from my home. It was very affordable to the poor villagers. It had poor facilities and was understaffed. Evidently, our students were not on par with the average student who studied in the cities. City schools had better educational resources. I had a poor primary education and I was studying in a high school that could not meet my educational needs. To make matters worse, it was a school where truancy, recalcitrance, and bullying were a prevailing way of life. I shall later describe the school life and how I made headway.

Two years after entering secondary school, I felt bashful about some of the activities in the village. Some of those who grew up in the cities used to jokingly call me a "village boy" or "bushman," or "a local champion." They used the names to refer to us who grew up in the village. But the name-calling was not the reason for me to pull back from some of my cherished village social activities. I was coming of age, and that meant more noble responsibilities. I had increasingly significant commitments that needed more time and attention: I needed more time to study, to learn more about other cultures, to fraternize with friends and colleagues. Still, I needed more time to be with the Lord in solitude, to think about what the Lord really wanted me to do with my life. It was in this light that I withdrew from cultural dance, hunting, and moonlight games. I did not stop making baskets. Rather, I continued to make baskets for sale and I also made some free of charge for some of the poor villagers who needed the baskets but had no money to pay.

## The Four Friends

"Which of you wishing to construct a tower does not first sit down and calculate the cost to see if there is enough for its completion? Otherwise, after laying the foundation and finding himself unable to finish the work the onlookers should laugh at him and say, 'This one began to build but did not have the resources to finish'" (Luke 14:28–30).

The school had just reopened for a new session, and registration for new students was in progress. My four friends (Omike, Alika, Ego, and Egwu) and I had slated our registration for Wednesday of the resumption week, having got all our paperwork ready. They visited me on the eve of our registration day. We gathered in our courtyard to have a conversation about the school. We talked about the infamous disciple problem in the school. We had been warned about the group of hooligans who instead of studying busied themselves with bullying other students.

We were very concerned about this, wondering how we could put up with the challenges of such an unfriendly study environment. Omike remarked, "I will make sure I do what I am expected to do, but believe me, I'll not hesitate to use my catapult (slingshot) on anyone who harasses me. I'll make sure that I break his head. Then I will bolt into the bush and never set foot in the school anymore." We all cast a look at one another and laughed. We knew he was not interested in school in the first place. His family was forcing him to go to school. Ego said to him, "I have seen that you are not ready to complete your education. Now tell me, when you withdraw from school what will you do next? You go to learn bicycle repair or you become a palm wine tapper?" Omike replied, "Are you saying that without education I would not be 'somebody'? Did the richest man in this village go to school?" Standing with hands on hips and with eyes wide open, Omike continued with firmness in his voice, "Look, I'm destined to be rich whether I go to school or not. Of course, there are many things I can do to make it in life." Alika said, "I shall not resist any of those bad guys who bully me. If they step on my toes, I shall be on the watch for them in my village. Once I see any of them, I must pounce on him and deal with him in a way that he will never forget in his life." "Haw-haw," I laughed. "Alika Nnaa (as I fondly called him), what will you do to him? Tell us. You don't have the stamina to catch a cat, not to talk of attacking those lions in the school." Egwu cut in, "Well, my mom told me not to fight in the school. I have to obey her, otherwise . . ." He was still speaking when all of us burst out laughing. We know him as a timid and fearful person. Omike spoke up, "Simply tell us that you have no strength or temerity to fight."

Alika looked at me and remarked, "Wait a minute! Clay has not said anything. Clay, tell us what you think." I hesitated a little bit, for I did not know what to say at that point. They fixed their gaze on me, waiting to hear what I would say. I cleared my voice and adjusted my posture against the wall. Then I folded my arms and began a long sermon: "We need to ask ourselves, first and foremost, what our aim for going to school is. I guess we do not go to school in order to be acclaimed as supermen. School is supposed to help us grow in virtue and not in vice. As we plan to begin our secondary education, each of us needs to open up himself to be educated in mind and in morals. We are not going to school to fight those bullies, nor are we going to take revenge against them. We want to be good Christian gentlemen and live exemplary lives as Christians. In this light, we should be focused more on how to get the most out of our time in the school. As for me, any other matter that will not work for my good and the good of others is not my business. I hope to be useful to myself and to my community. I want to study well, learn as much as I can, and avoid any distractions against my dream in life.

"Yesterday, I reflected on the horrible bullying in the school. I likened the school to a bus park where there are several buses that are going to different destinations. Before he or she goes aboard a bus, the passenger wants to find out where the bus is going. You don't want to just hop on the bus without knowing about the itinerary; otherwise, you will get on the wrong bus. When you find that the bus is going to your destination, then you get aboard. In school, some groups or individuals have different goals or destinations in life. Some have good goals and some have bad goals; some are going in the right direction while some are going in the wrong direction. Still there are others who sit on the fence, neither cold nor hot, without any focus, without any definite plan of where they are going with their lives. They are the lukewarm students. They can be lured into the bus of bullies. They can be easily pressured into bullying others, for they fear that if they refuse they will be bullied. The bullies are like *agboros* (unruly freelancers who find passengers for commuter bus owners in Nigeria). *Agboros* are not going anywhere; they have no destination but they can disguise as passengers in order to attract true passengers to the bus. If one is not careful in dealing with the *agboros* they can delay your journey, or stop you from getting to your destination. If you fight with them, they seek to strip you naked; if you are not tactful and prudent, they can rip you off. Some of the students bully others because they have some interior hurt that needed healing. Some bully others because they feel unloved or uncared for. Some bully others because they thought that doing so will make them become 'somebody,' they thought bullying will help them have self-esteem. Bullying is a sign that the bullies are feeling lost in the purpose of life. If you look closely into their lives, you'll find that the bullies feel a void deep within them. They think that bullying will help them to fill their emptiness and hurt. How they needed to know that it is only Christ who can fill those empty places in their lives and give them lasting peace and joy! We have to keep in mind that, like the bullies, it is easy to take up a wrong direction in life. It can be just as easy as keeping company with the wrong person or seeking counsel from the wrong person or keeping company with the wrong group or watching the wrong movies or reading the wrong literature. It is easy to follow the wrong path by giving in to negative emotions and impulses like despair, fear, shame, frustration, jealousy, resentment, envy, and hatred. Since we have our vision, our hope, our dreams, our aims, for going to school, we have to pray for the grace to stay focused and strive to let no one become a roadblock to us. We are not going to join the bus of bullies. We are not going to allow the hooligans to cause us unbearable pain in life. We are going to overcome them with faith, with hope, and with love. When we get to the school, we shall explore the place to get to know the students. We will find out those who have lost true life vision. We'll discover those who know and work for their good purpose in life. It is this last group whom we shall befriend and with whom we will work. It is not going to be easy for us, but if we work hard, if we pray hard, if we stay focused, if we love well, we will, at the end, win the war."

## Scared in the School

The night seemed unusually long. I was awake to the first crow of our rooster, around 3:00 a.m. I waited longingly for the endless night to give way to dawn, the long-awaited day when I would begin my high school.

After a long wait, morning arrived. It was not long before my friends came to our house. I put on my new, sparkling well-ironed school uniform, with my leather sandals neatly fastened on my feet. All were awesomely dressed, except one of us who was wearing his old torn T-shirt. His family was so poor that they could not afford the cost of the school uniform. The little boy worked at a local palm oil mill, laboring strenuously for survival. Poverty and hard struggle had aged and toughened him far beyond his age. As we walked to school, our hearts swayed with mixed feelings: our hearts swelled with joyful excitement for the new beginning of high school, and at the same time our hearts pounded with anxiety about the bullies in the school.

The "big guys," as some called them, had become the subject of talk of the village. Because we were not familiar with the environment, we decided not to ride our bicycles to the school but rather walk the distance, about seven kilometers, to the school. The morning assembly was to begin by 8:00

a.m. We set off for the school at 6:00 a.m. We started a conversation as we walked along the road. Reaching the main road, we ran into a bunch of other students. It was beautiful to behold all of us walking along the road as though we were in a school parade. Some were in blue uniform, some in pink, and some in white T-shirts and black shorts. Step by step, we moved forward.

Before we arrived at the school, the bell for the morning orientation had rung. We were four minutes late. We thought it would not matter since it was our first day in the school. We looked through the school wall and sighted some students racing down to the auditorium. "Please, hurry up!" I beckoned to my friends. We got to the school gate at exactly 8:06 a.m.

We were about to enter through the school gate when a group of students furiously bolted from nowhere, yelling at us almost simultaneously: "Hey, stop there! At-ten-tion! Stand still and raise your two hands! Now, march down here. Left! Right! Left, right . . ." With our hands raised above our heads, we marched toward them. Their spine-chilling, frightening deep voices made our teeth chatter. As we marched toward their direction, our hearts throbbed and our legs quaked with fright. We had heard much about them, but now we had seen and experienced their action. They ordered us to kneel. Alika, one of my friends, was naturally as timid as a rabbit. With his heart in his mouth, he frantically lay down. "No, get up and kneel," I said to him. Flexing fist and a stick at us, one of the guys yapped: "You nincompoops and riffraff! So you think you have the temerity, the audacity, the effrontery to sneak into this school?" As he threatened us, one of his colleagues fiercely queried us at the same time: "Don't you know you are late? You feel you can come to school at any time you like? Do you think your father owns this school? You thought you would be able to escape from a lion. No matter how fast a deer can run, lions know how to capture them."

They overwhelmed us with questions and threats within a second. We kneeled there helplessly like lambs waiting to be slaughtered. Our arms, still held up in the air, were hurting. One of the big guys, who was rather tall and huge, wearing big dark goggles on his eyes, rose from a stool beside the wall and began to quiz us: "Do you know who I am?" "No. I'm a new student," I replied. He conked me and snarled: "Didn't you hear about me at home? You are in trouble." I wondered how he expected me to recognize him without having seen him for the first time. It was only one student among ten of us who knew him by his nickname: "Ogbu-Agu" (Lion-Killer).

Ogbu-Agu ordered us to pull out our sandals and shirts. "You need to be baptized before entering this holy ground," Ogbu-Agu said. There were nine of us whom he said must receive his baptism. What did he mean by baptism? We had no idea what he was talking about. "Excuse me, senior Ogbu-Agu," I said, "we have been baptized." "Hey, shut up your mouth," he hushed. "Did you receive fire when you were baptized? You were baptized with water, but today we are going to baptize you with fire. We are very generous with our baptism. We are going to baptize you *gratis*, free of charge. We are not like pastors in many churches who demand some money before baptism. Our ministry is a free fire ministry. We do a lot of charity to the poor." Each of them was clasping whips: sticks and belts. It was clear to us that by baptism of fire they meant flogging us with those whips. I thought that he did not mean to say "charity," but "tragedy or calamity." Our knees were burning with pain from long kneeling. We knelt there stripped of our shirts and footwear, and sweltering with anxiety and fear.

The teachers were around the school premises but none of them seemed to be concerned about what was going on at the gate. "Did the teachers commission these students to do all this evil? Are they not concerned that these heartless guys are terribly maltreating students here?" we wondered. We were yet to find out the stance of the teachers about this ugly behavior. Raising his whip, one of the big guys who was known as "Akpi-Ocha" (White Scorpion) yelled at us, "Lie down! This is the moment of grace." I thought he meant "graze" (scraping of skin) rather than grace. We went into a spasm of panic as we lay down waiting for the lashing. They were almost set about whipping us when one of them named "Egbe" (Hawk) whispered to us, "Any 'offertory' before the baptism?" Everyone lay still, trying to figure out what he meant by "offertory." It was their figurative term for a ransom or bribe. None of us responded to his demand. "It seems that some of you have some dangerous weapons in your pockets," Akpi-Ocha said. "I have no weapon in my pocket," Alika responded with a sobbing voice. "All right! I want to be sure you are telling me the truth. I can perceive the smell of *igbo* (marijuana). I'm sure someone here has the 'forbidden herb' in his pocket. You don't want to smoke marijuana at this age; it is dangerous to your health. Besides, it defiles this holy ground. I must search your pockets. Now, hands up!" Grasping my shorts, Egbe ordered me, "Get up." He immediately delved his hands into my pockets and found a five naira note, Nigerian money. "Chineke (My god)! So you stole your mother's money?" "No, I didn't steal it. It's mine," I replied. "How do you convince me that it is yours? I have to hold it until we verify from your mother. Go and lie down there." He searched the other boy kneeling beside me and found ten naira in his pocket. Akpi-Ocha said to him, "I can see that you all are bad guys. You have made off with your parents' money. We have to confirm from your parents about this matter. We are not here to train rogues. We are here to discipline you so that you can be useful to yourselves and to the society. Now, keep five naira with you while I hold five naira until we meet with your parents."

Egbe was still searching us one after another when one of their members named "Ajo-Ikuku" (Bad Wind) alighted from a motorcycle. All the big guys hailed him, roaring, "Ajo-I-ku-ku!" Ajo-Ikuku was their president. I raised my head to catch a glimpse of him; behold, he was someone I knew. His father and my father were good friends. He knew me very well. Papa used to send me on errands to their house. I felt he would come to my help. And so I fixed my gaze on him to make sure he saw me. As soon as he caught sight of me, I greeted him. He did not respond to my greeting. I noticed that his face was contorted with rage. Tough guys are always mean. For them, a cheerful face is a sign of cowardice. Perhaps, I had spoiled his business.

Looking at his timepiece, Ajo-Ikuku said, "Okay, it is 8:45 a.m. It is time for class." He turned to us and ordered, "Hey, my boys, get up immediately." All of us sprang like frogs released from a net. We waited for the next command. "Put on your sandals and shirts before I count up to three." Every one of us selected his stuff. Some of us were still lacing our sandals and some others were struggling to button up their shirts when Ajo-Ikuku rushed at us with a long stick. He dashed toward us like an unleashed bulldog, snarling: "You nincompoops! Riffraff! Nonentities! Pudding heads! Dullards . . .!" He called us all the bad names he could remember from his thesaurus. We had no idea of what those words meant but we knew that they were disparaging comments. Out of fear, some us of wore their shirts inside out and their shoes on the wrong feet. Some swapped shoes. Still some grabbed their shirts and sandals without waiting to put them on. Without any further delay, we raced down the classroom blocks like a herd of sheep escaping from wolves.

During midday break, Alika stayed back in the class. The big guy had scared him off. He was trying to take it all in. When the school ended for the day, Alika bade farewell to the school; he would never set his feet on the school ground anymore. He left for the city to apprentice for business with his brother. The other three friends dropped out at different times. When all of them withdrew from the school, I recalled our conversation on the eve of our first day at the school. I had firm trust that by the grace of God nothing would deter me from attaining my dream. So daily I pressed on with renewed zeal and determination, keeping my eyes fixed upon Jesus Christ. I trusted in the Lord's unfailing promise. I knew that the Divine Master Potter had given me the grace not to yield to hardship, failures, and distractions. God provided me with new friends. They were enthusiastic for learning, disciplined and god-fearing. We studied together and shared many things in common.

## The Big and the Bugged

Amid the unrest in the high school, the Lord gave me interior strength to press on. From time to time, the big guys treaded on our toes. They disturbed us within the school property. They disrupted our classes. They harassed us during their frequent unwelcome visits to the classes. Whenever they entered our class, they expected all the students to stand up and greet them: "Good (morning), seniors." We tried to comply with them anyway. They maltreated any student who failed to obey them. Whenever we had no teacher in the class, we would fear that they would pay us their sorrowful visit.

I remember one morning we had just finished our mathematics class. No sooner had the teacher left than the big guys, seven in all, invaded our class as guerillas. As usual, some of them were brandishing all kinds of whips. As they hurled themselves into our class, we stood up to pay them the customary "homage." With a hostile stare and gruff voice, they commanded, "On your knees!" That was their way of ordering us to kneel down. Before we could get down on our knees, they started to hit us indiscriminately. Some thrashed us wildly with sticks and belts. Some struck us with their fists. Still some slapped their palms on our heads, kicking as they forcefully pushed their way around the class. We struggled to dodge the blows that rained down on us as hailstones. I received a heavy blow on my left shoulder, and as I tried to duck the second one, my head hit the window frame. The pain was so deep that I nearly passed out. I crouched under my desk, stroking my head to rub away the pain. When the big guys got tired of beating of us, one of them, named Oke-Udele (Male Vulture), said to us, "Next time, you will not forget to salute your 'venerable seniors.'" Then, they dashed out of the class.

Two days later, all the students gathered at the auditorium for the weekly moral instructions. The big guys came late to the meeting and sat in a group in the back row of the hall. Our moral instructor was teaching on charity and obedience. He read out from the Bible the following passage: "Do not neglect to do good and to share what you have; God is pleased by sacrifices of that kind. Obey your leaders and defer to them, for they keep watch over you and will have to give an account, that they may fulfill their task with joy and not with sorrow, for that would be of no advantage to you" (Heb 13:16–17). The big guys shouted in unison, "Yes, tell them!" One of them stood up and said, "Excuse me, sir! In fact, I was reflecting on this passage this morning. This is a timely message which our students need to hear and take to heart. I hail you, sir! The Spirit is at work in you and me." He gently sat on his stool as if he was speaking from his heart. Then his group lauded him, "Okuru-Ora (meaning 'Spokesman,' as he was nicknamed)." Some of students started muttering. Obviously, Okuru-Ora and the rest of his group members were not submissive to the school authority.

Now they played Pharisees, pointing accusing fingers at others while they themselves were guilty. They thought that it was not them but the rest of the students who needed to hear the good news. They had closed their minds from receiving the transforming word of God. How could the Pharisees have a change of heart when they did not acknowledge their sins and need for grace, when they wallowed in the illusion that they were healthy and thus did not need the Divine Physician, when they believed that they were more righteous than anyone else? How ignorant the big guys were! They wanted to be obeyed but they never want to obey. They "lord it over others" and want to be served, but they say to the school authority "*non serviam* (I will not serve)." Mercy has no place in their hearts, yet they look for help when they are in trouble. They thought that to be somebody is to make a loud noise, but they forget that to be noisy is to be empty. They did not understand the saying, "An empty drum makes the loudest noise." Is it not true that a peddler makes more noise to sell his or her stuff than a tycoon? Think of the noise of street vendors, like ice cream vendors, who push carts shouting and ringing bells to draw buyers' attention. The big guys thought that to be somebody is to be domineering and raise hell. They were ignorant to the fact that one who treats the lowly as inferior beings is attempting to escape from one's inferiority complex. They were yet to learn that true strength is not in crushing the lowly, but in defending them. The big guys thought that to be truly great and powerful one must oppress others. How uninformed they were that true greatness is attained not in being served but by serving. Recall St. Peter's counsel, "Do not lord it over those assigned to you, but be examples to the flock. And when the chief Shepherd is revealed, you will receive the unfading crown of glory" (1Peter 5:3–4). Oh, how could we help our generation to understand the logic of life? To give all to the love of God and our neighbor is to gain all. Vanity is another name for whatever I possess or do without God. To be in a lowly position with God is to be on top of all.

## The Troublers and the Authorities

One may wonder if the school authorities did anything to deal with the bad behaviors of the big guys. Well, recall the old saying, "You can lead a horse to water but you cannot make it drink." The school authorities tried to give all the students the opportunity to improve and grow in virtue, but the big guys chose to grow in vice. The school authorities took measures to restore discipline in the school but to no avail. They introduced moral instructions, but the big guys were not willing to be instructed. They tried counseling to bring them to order, but they were not ready to listen. They called for dialogue. This too did not work. They worked together with the parents and village heads to deal with the defiant students. But all their efforts seemed as though they were adding salt to an injury. Some of the big guys who were expelled from the school continued to come to school to cause confusion. At some point, the big guys directly turned against the teachers who wanted to help them. They rioted and destroyed several valuables in the school. They disrupted classes and physically attacked the teachers. The school authorities called police. The police officers arrived in our school in search of Ajo-Ikuku and his companions. The big guys were nowhere to be found. No one was able to discover their hideout. The next day, they locked up all classrooms, posting on the doors, walls, and windows the inscription, "Today is the day of the lords. Let us rest and rejoice indeed." When asked about the significance of their action, one of them said that the principal must explain to them why he called police on them. On the following day, the big guys blocked the classes to prevent students and teachers from entering the classes. Suddenly a black police truck drove into the school. As soon as they saw the police truck, the big guys scampered and leapt into the bush like gazelles.

When the police officers left the school premises, the big guys resurfaced and started to threaten the teachers. They punctured the tires of the principal's car and damaged school property. For a whole week, the incident disrupted school. The big boys didn't care about study. They were not even interested to learn. The only book which they read frequently was a dictionary. They wanted to show off and sound smart. So they read their dictionaries constantly in search of big words with which to address people. In the daily morning assembly, they would speak to us in high-sounding words, which most of us had difficulty understanding. One could tell that some of their sentences were not agreeable with the rules of grammar. They often jumbled some jargon and quoted out of context.

One who came to our school in those days would notice that virtually all surfaces in the school—walls, floors, doors, ceilings, and even trees—were defaced with graffiti, vulgar, disgusting writings and drawings of all kinds. However, no one dared to correct them. You know that wisdom speaks, but it is only the simple that understand her. The wisdom of Proverbs applies in that context: "Whoever corrects the arrogant earns insults; and whoever reproves the wicked incurs opprobrium. Do not reprove the arrogant, lest they hate you; reprove the wise, and they will love you" (Prov 9:7–8).

The conceited tend to think that they know more than others, and they make sport of the lowly who humble themselves to learn from others. Our students knew what to do to please the big guys: applauding, praising, hailing them. To give an example, the students would yell their flattery, "Your majesty, senior Akpi-Ocha! We hail you!" The big guy would bask in the euphoria of false eulogy. How worldly power puffs some people up with pride! How ignorance leads some away from the path of life! (Hos 4:6).

The principal told us about one of the big guys who came to take his testimonials. The principal did not know what to write about the big guy.

He shrewdly wrote in the testimonial: "He is good in everything but what is good." The big guy did not understand the meaning of the sentence. He thought that it was a good recommendation. He thanked the principal and left. What happened afterward was another story. It is always good to be good.

In all things, I praise the Lord, who has given me the grace of faith to know, to trust, and to glorify him at all times. A soul who encounters the Lord desires and strives to live in right relationship with the Lord and neighbor. This is true wisdom. When one truly loves God, love wells up from one's heart, manifesting in genuine love of oneself and others.

I pray that those who oppress others may have a change of heart and realize that we are one in the Lord. I pray that those who are oppressed, especially those who have no one to defend them, may take consolation in Christ's presence in their lives.

## Senior Student

Time went fast. The seemingly unending six years of rugged conditions of school life were nearing the end. Just within ten months, it would be over. I thanked God that I had become a senior student at long last. To be a senior student was, to some of the students, a period of relief and freedom from the harassment of the seniors, particularly the big guys. To some, it was a license to bully the junior students as a way to avenge the maltreatment that they experienced from their seniors. Some of the students who suffered cruel treatment from their predecessors vowed to vent their anger on their junior ones. Some of my classmates were gearing up to transfer their wrath to the juniors.

Unexpectedly, I was invited by the school senate for an interview. The board had nominated me as the student president, senior prefect (SP). After the interview, the school bell rung, summoning the students for the announcement of the new school functionaries. Providentially, it was announced that I had been chosen as the new SP of the school. There was a thunderous applause from the students. "What is your agenda?" some students asked me afterward. "My agenda is the school agenda," I replied with a grin. For one week, I had series of meetings with the students, primarily to find specific measures to deal with the disciplinary problems in the school. The meetings nearly got me into trouble.

The school authority thought that I was planning to collude with the big guys to war against the school. After explaining to them, the authority understood. The Spirit of the Lord touched the hearts of some of the most hardline students. As a result, within a short time there was an appreciable change in the students' behavior: the seniors desisted from harassing the juniors. Disruption of classes became a thing of the past. Destruction of school property was relatively rare during that period. Yet I knew that we were not yet at the Promised Land. There was still some warfare that required our dedication and commitment. The battle was not ours to fight; it was not mine to direct. It was the Lord who fought and directed us to the way of victory. What we did was to surrender to him in prayer and in faith, to listen and follow our Divine Captain. During our final exam in the school, some guys among us involved themselves in examination malpractice. They fought the examiners and made off with question papers. Consequently, all of us suffered the penalty. Our school result was withheld. But this apparent obstacle did not move me to give up on my aspiration. I kept the hope alive in my heart, with my eyes fixed on the Divine Master Potter who was at work in me. The Almighty Lord was set to replenish the years that the locust had eaten in my life (cf. Joel 2:25).

## Refining Instance

It was a reality that the exam result, which I had hoped to use to enter college, had been withheld. It seemed that I had reached an impasse on the sublime vocation. Naturally, I had some questions about this situation: To where is destiny driving me? How do I make headway in life? I was moved to argue my case before the Divine: "God, you knew me before I came into being. You alone know the plans you have for my life. I don't know the plans but I know that it is of good. I don't know exactly what you have called me to do for your kingdom, but I am certain that you called me for a mission even before you breathed life into me. I want to know what you want me to do for you. Early in life, I heard the whispering of your Spirit within me. With my whole heart I respond in the words of Elijah, 'Here am I, send me.' You are the Lord of the mission. You are the way and the light. Yet I don't understand why you left me in the dark. Is it your will that I should pass through all these distressful years in vain? Where do I go from this moment? If you were not calling me to the sacred ministry, why is there such a blazing desire in my heart? Answer me, O Lord, lest I miss the way." I thought God responded to me as he did to Job, "Who is this who darkens counsel with words of ignorance? Gird up your loins now, like a man; I will question you, and you tell me the answers (Job 38:2–3)!" God might have asked me: "Who owns your life? Where were you before I knit you in your mother's womb? If I take my breath away from you today, where will you be to ask questions about your future? If you have eyes that can penetrate the future, tell me what will happen tomorrow. Who is in control of your future? Who owns the mission? Who calls you to the mission? Who gives you the health and strength for the mission? Tell me what you have that is not from me? You are just worried for many things, but you have neglected the only antidote to all problems: faith in me. The problem is not that you have a problem, but that you *think* you have a problem. Do fish in the ocean worry about water drying up? Do birds in the sky disturb themselves about food to eat or worry about being bereft of space to fly? Are trees at riverbanks anxious about drought? If you remain in me, you'll never lack what you need at each point in time. Be still and know that your Lord is at work in your life."

## The Presence of Peace

I was concerned that my family had no money to pay for me to retake the exam. Besides, I had no idea of any reliable nearby school that would be open to grant me admission. I was worried like one in the midst of storm. I could imagine how the disciples felt when they were pounded by the storm in the sea (Mt 8:24–27). Like the disciples, I too was distressed. How ignorant I was! I focused on the bigness of my problem instead of fixing my faith gaze on the bigness of the Lord. From the human point of view, I saw an insurmountable roadblock. The still voice echoed in my heart, asking me the same question the Lord asked the disciples: "Where is your faith (Luke 8:25)?" It wasn't until I looked at the situation with the eyes of faith that I could see the surpassing power of my Savior.

Over the years, with the grace working in my life, I came to the realization that my Lord is really an unsleeping Savior, always in control of all situations. I perceived the light of Christ leading me through a long rough road. Well, I had wanted to pass through a shortcut. Who wouldn't like a fast route to his/her destination? I knew from experience that any journey with the Lord is not always without a cross, not often easy. There are usually considerable sacrifices to make but the Lord does not fail in granting the grace of each moment. I believed that I would surely arrive safe to where the Lord was leading me. I prayed that the Lord might renew my strength and faith: "Lord, I cannot do without you. The way is rough and full of thorns. I cannot remain steadfast unless you help me. The strength to persevere is yours. May your Spirit stay with me always to renew my strength so that I may go forward with you, to rekindle in me the fire of love so that I may serve you always, to refresh me with faith so that I may rely on you alone in all circumstances, to revive my hope so that I may crave ever more the peace and happiness that you alone can offer. Lord, help me, for you alone are my Savior." After the prayer, I sensed a profound peace within me. I believe that the Lord disciplines those he loves. I believe that when I suffer in faith any pinch of humiliation, the Lord grants me the privilege of divine elevation. When I share in Christ's passion, I receive the grace to share in his resurrection. I trusted that the Divine Master Potter was at work in my life and he would see me through.

## Fanning into Flame

I received the sacrament of Confirmation at the age of nineteen. I often recall that joyful day when the bishop anointed my forehead with chrism, sacred oil. I remember how he extended his hands over me and prayed for the Father to send upon me the Holy Spirit. As he uttered the animating words, "Be sealed with the gift of the Holy Spirit," I felt in a more powerful way the presence of the life-giving breath of God. I knew my life was no longer the same, for I had been transformed by the vivifying fire from above. Truly, this holy fire refined in me the gifts I received in baptism. I strove daily to "fan into flame" the special gift which the Lord gave to me. St. Paul reminds me that I did not receive the Spirit of fear, but the Spirit "of power and love and self-control" (2Tim 1:7).

During my days as a senior student in the secondary school, I became involved in the Catholic Charismatic Renewal. I had Life in the Spirit Seminar, and it was a great moment of encounter with the Spirit of faith, hope, and love. It was in that praying community that the Lord stirred up my gifts and the passion to use them to the glory of God. I joined the group to preach at street corners, and we also did dormitory-to-dormitory visitation, sharing the Good News with our fellow students and workers. I attended retreats, prayer crusades and pilgrimages around the country. The counsel of my spiritual director remains vivid in my memory, "Find time to get away from the noise of the world so that you may learn to hear the still voice that speaks to your heart." I love reading and listening to the word of God. I am sure that the Lord opened my ear through the prayer of Ephphetha, which the priest prayed over my ear on the day of my baptism. On the day of my Confirmation, the Spirit of the Lord turned my "ear to wisdom, inclining" my "heart to understanding."

## Stepping into Mission School

I talked with a priest friend of mine about my withheld result. The priest introduced me to another priest who administered a school owned by a diocese in Nigeria. The senior priest warmly received us. Sitting on his cushion chair in the parlor, the priest crossed his legs, folded his arms, and smiled. Then he gave me a piercing look and said humorously, "Did you say you are from Kparaoma Village? You mean you want to be a priest? Will any priest ever come from Kparaoma?" With a grin I said, "If it is God's will, I'm willing to offer my life to serve the Lord and his Church as a priest." My village was small, poor, and not well-known. No priestly vocations had come from there. It was exciting to him to hear of my desire for the priesthood, and he was willing to help nurture and support the desire in me. In his kindness, the merciful priest thought it would be good to have me spend two years in the school. He reasoned that since my former school had no good academic records, I would not be able to catch up with the final year students in his school. "Because you come from such a poor village school, I would think that you need at least two years to brush up your intellectual ability," the priest suggested. I assured him that if he gave me the opportunity to try, I would be able to do well. "If you feel you can make it, well, I am open to that," the priest okayed. I hold him dear in my heart, and with my deepest gratitude I express my hearty appreciations for all he did for me.

Within two weeks to the school resumption day, I had ready all the necessary stuff for the school, thanks to my elder brother. He was so generous that he did not hesitate to dig deep into his pocket to pay for my education. I knew I was up for a change, beginning a new experience in life, a boarding school where activities were regulated. I would learn certain rules of etiquette: to sleep and wake at regulated times, to eat not as much as I would want but as much as was given to me. I would learn to grow accustomed to intensive study, and most fascinatingly, I would learn to pray in the manner Catholic schools do.

It was really hard for me in the very first month in the school. But because I was determined and hardworking, I pushed on with courage and faith. The warm friendship I had with the students was a great source of motivation to me. I made progress daily. I saw a steady growth in my study habits, spending ample time each day for my private study. By the grace of God, I participated well in classes and I had the consolation of performing well in quizzes and class assignments. I heartily praise God for the many graces he gave me at that period.

## The Dart of Death

The routine life in the school was going well until one bleak afternoon. Eight students and I went to the stream to fetch water. All except me knew how to swim. I had never learned to swim. I guess it was because we had no river or any other body of water in my village. I was intrigued watching the students swim with amazing skill. "Clay, come and swim," beckoned one of the students. "I wish I could swim," I softly replied. "No one is a swimmer by nature. We all learned it by practice. You can become a good swimmer tomorrow if you begin to practice today," the second student suggested. "That is right," affirmed another student. "Come on, Clay! Be a man. Why not try it now? It is not hard. This is how I learned to swim." At this point, I felt defeated to make any excuse. I saw no reason not to try. They had ultimately succeeded in urging me on. So I removed my sandals, folded my trousers, and dipped my feet into the water. Step by step, I moved forward into the stream until the water came to my knee level. I was afraid to go farther into the deeper side of the water. I ducked my head into the water. I could only hold it for a few seconds, because I felt as though I was suffocating to death. "You won't learn to swim well if you stay there. Draw closer to where we are," beckoned one of my friends. I courageously moved toward them. All of a sudden, I dipped my leg into a deep hollow and slid down into a deeper side of the water. The water engulfed me completely and I lost control of myself. The water current forcefully plunged me into the depths of the water and then pushed me up. I gulped down a great quantity of water as I gasped for life, screaming for help. I cried in my heart, "Jesus, my Savior, only you can rescue me! Save me right now for I am drowning!" The water plunged me into the depths of the water for the second time and threw me up again. As the water was about to hurl me into its depths the third time, my friends rushed along, got hold of me, and lifted me out of the stream.

As we got ashore, they gently laid me on the ground. My stomach bulged out because I had swallowed a large amount of water. I could not breathe well. One of my friends pressed hard on my stomach to expel excess water from my system. Some water flowed out of my mouth and nose. I told him to stop. I was drained of energy as though I was hit by a truck. My friends gave me the help I needed at that point, and within a short time, I recovered and we returned to the school. We agreed not to tell anyone about it. The reason was that if word got out our rector would forbid all the students from going to the stream. That would not be to the advantage of the students, because there was not enough water in the school for the students to use for bathing and for washing their clothes. I praise the Lord for the grace of life he granted me. I would have been numbered among the dead.

At the end of the year, we took our final exam, and thanks be to God, my result was excellent. Since then, whenever I read Psalm 69 I reminisce the horrible incident: "Save me, God, for the waters have reached my neck. I have sunk into the mire of the deep, where there is no foothold. I have gone down to the watery depths; the flood overwhelms me" (Psalm 69:1–2).

## The Case of "Clay"

Shortly after our exams, I visited the school to get my testimonial. When I arrived there, the registrar was not available. I was asked to wait for him. I accepted to wait, and it was not long before one of my friends and former classmate in the school also visited the school. Both of us were very excited to see each other once again after our graduation. Good enough the registrar's short absence afforded us the opportunity to have a conversation. My friend reached for me with his right arm and drew me close to himself: "Come, Clay! Oh, I am so excited to meet you here. I'm not sure when next

I'll set my eyes on you after today. Let's stroll around the school and talk."
We talked about many things that day. When we had gone around the school,
we sat under a large shady mango tree, where we enjoyed the cool breeze.

For want of something to say, my friend said to me, "Uh-huh, Clay, how
on earth did you choose the name 'Clay'? You are the only person I know
who bears the name. Tell me more about the name." I gazed into space
and with a slight smile I affirmed, "A good question! Well, I am—" "Wait
a minute, Clay," my friend interrupted. "I know that you never answer
questions short and straight. You have the habit of explaining things in
a long way. Today, I am not in a hurry. Take your time, but answer my
question." "Are you insinuating that I should give you a short answer?" I
asked. "Unfortunately, I do not have a short answer to your question. Okay,
I'll give you a 'short' long answer.

"My parents gave me the name Clay. I have thought about why the name
Clay, even though I have never asked my parents about what the name meant
for them. I have my own belief about the significance of my name. I think that
the inspiration for the name came from my father, who was a sculptor. When
I was a child, Papa often brought logs of wood at our home. When I looked at
the wood, I saw nothing but wood. But Papa saw beyond the ordinary wood.
With his mind's eyes, Papa could see, hidden in the wood, beauty, the eternal
reality that draws all human beings to themselves. Amazingly, it was after his
artistic touch, his chiseling, shaping, and smoothing of the piece of wood that I
could see what he saw interiorly—the beautiful image shaped out of the wood.
I know that an authentic artist eagerly puts out considerable effort and time to
capture the beauty hidden in nature. A potter pommels the clay with his hands
to create a lovely vessel. A sculptor assiduously works on his wood or stone
until he shapes a beautiful image. A blacksmith laboriously fashions his iron,
hammering it while it is hot, to forge a useful tool. A carpenter tenaciously saws
a log of wood, planes and nails it to form a piece of fine furniture. A painter
steadily and carefully strokes with his brush to create a charming painting.
The varying forms of awesome artifact make us marvel at the skill of human
crafts. If human beings can make beauty shine out of ordinary materials, how
much more does our Creator refine and reshape us to be even more wonderful?
Sometimes, we need to sit back and reflect on the source of beauty? Human
beings have the capacity to make amazing things because God gave us the
privilege of sharing in his eternal wisdom and beauty: '[I] have filled him with

a divine spirit of skill and understanding and knowledge in every craft: in the production of embroidery, in making things of gold, silver or bronze, in cutting and mounting precious stones, in carving wood, and in every other craft' (Exo 31:3–5). So it is that human beings who create amazing things in the world were created by God in God's own image (Gen 2:7), and we are God's masterpiece, the high point of his creative handiwork, wonderfully made to participate in the eternal beauty of the Trinity: 'You formed my inmost being; you knit me in my mother's womb. I praise you, because I am wonderfully made; wonderful are your works! My very self you know. My bones are not hidden from you, When I was being made in secret, fashioned in the depths of the earth. Your eyes saw me unformed; in your book all are written down; my days were shaped, before one came to be' (Psalm 139:13–16).

"Out of awe, some people worship created things: the stars, the sun, the moon, the earth, waters, trees, stones—name them; they choose to worship the creature rather than the Creator. How ignorant they are of the supremacy of God over all nature! How hard of hearing they are who cannot hear the creator speak to them through his creation! They are indeed blindfolded who cannot see the reflection of the creator in nature.

Now if out of joy in their beauty they thought them gods, let them know how far more excellent is the Lord than these; for the original source of beauty fashioned them. Or if they were struck by their might and energy, let them realize from these things how much more powerful is the one who made them. For from the greatness and the beauty of created things their original author, by analogy, is seen. But yet, for these the blame is less; For they have gone astray perhaps though they seek God and wish to find him. For they search busily among his works, but are distracted by what they see, because the things seen are fair. But again, not even these are pardonable. For if they so far succeeded in knowledge that they could speculate about the world, how did they not more quickly find its Lord? (Wisdom 13:3–9).

"All things were beautiful after God created them. As we learn from the Scriptures, God saw that all that he created was good (Gen 1ff); hence, he took pleasure in them all. Now the sin of Adam and Eve marred the original beauty in created things and made the whole order of creation rebel. The result was regrettably unfavorable, breeding all forms of evil: hardship, toil, pains, war, physical deformity, mental conditions, natural disaster, hatred, lust, diseases, and death. But God did not want to leave us to the ugly, debased, evil condition in which sin had thrown us.

"Because 'the vessel he was making turned out badly in his hand,' the Divine Master Potter began again to make a fresh vessel as deemed fit (Jer 18:4). In order to show forth his boundless love, God initiated our restoration through the gift of Jesus Christ. He began to refashion us in order to bring back the lost beauty. He does not abandon us even when through sin we deface the beauty which he puts on our souls. God continues to search for us; he hounds for us. When we allow ourselves to be found, the Lord draws us out of the pit of decay and sin and cleanses us in the ocean of his blood and fills us with the power of his Spirit. He does not grow tired in working on us, chiseling, smoothing off our rough edges, until we shine out with that perfect image, that splendid dignity of the sons and daughters of God. No one is beyond this divine re-creation.

"As a perfect artist, God sees beyond what human beings see. He sees far beyond our weaknesses, our shortcomings, and poverty. The Lord alone knows and sees the beauty hidden in the inside of us and how much he had to work to clean us up.

"Papa understood the reality of God's surpassing power, wisdom, and love at work in me; hence, he gave me the name 'Clay.' My dear friend, let me make a long story 'longer.'" My friend laughed. "The point I am trying to make is that the name 'Clay' signifies that God is at work in my life. How beautifully the Bible describes it that I am the clay and God is the potter, I am the work of God's hands (cf. Isa 64:8). As a potter kneads the clay to model a pot, so is God at work in me to refashion me, to make his image shine forth in a more beautiful way in accord with his master plan for my life. Every circumstance I face, every trial that comes my way, any feeling that I experience, be it joy or sorrow, delight or pain, all are part of the process. The Lord continues to shape and mold me. I'm the Divine Master Potter's Clay!"

I was talking when the registrar's sons ran toward us to let us know that his father had returned. We cut off that pleasant conversation, stood up, and held each other's hand in prayer. I prayed: "Lord, God, you are our hope and our future. You are the Giver of life and of all gifts. Thank you for bringing us together once again. Thank you for the good plans you have for our future. You are our Divine Master Potter. Do not allow sin to harden our hearts. May your Spirit give us the grace to love you with an undivided heart and make our hearts soft and pliable so that you may continue to fashion us into awesome vessels of your choice. We offer to you any pains, struggles, and adversities that you may allow in our lives. Use them to refine us into your fiery instruments for building your kingdom in the hearts of the human race. We open our hearts to you, Lord. Come into us. Live in us. Work with us and for us. In faith and with total resignation to your will, we mean to say 'yes,' Lord, work in us and brand us with the mark of your chosen ones forever. Amen."

## Ample Applications

I graduated from high school with good grades. My desire was to become a diocesan priest but I didn't meet the requirements. Most of the dioceses in the country had their own "minor seminaries" (high school seminaries). Each year, they selected candidates for the priesthood from the graduating students of the minor seminaries. Those who didn't have the privilege of studying in a seminary had little or no chance to be accepted for priesthood in the diocese. Of course, in those days the local church saw what some referred to as "vocations boom." Many young men sought admission for vocations to the priesthood, yet only few were accepted each year. Some of the aspirants who were turned down by the dioceses considered vocations to religious order.

Thus, when I was not accepted in the diocese, I began to give consideration to discern religious life. I hoped to enter into a religious order that year. Having sent dozens of applications to a number of selected religious orders, I waited longingly for favorable replies. Several weeks passed and I did not hear from any of them. I thought the lack of response would be as a result of the then unreliable mail services in my town. Or perhaps the religious communities didn't receive my applications at all. A week later, I finally got two response letters from two different religious orders. Without delay, I anxiously opened the letters. Alas, both were rejection letters! "Well, all hope is not lost," I reassured myself. "I'll wait until the end of the month. Who knows, one of the orders may give my application a favorable consideration." Before the weekend, I received another reply. As though it was an agreement, the reply was unfavorable. One of the religious communities responded that they were not accepting candidates that year. Another said that they had completed their selection for that year. Another answered that I was above their age requirement. Still another replied that they would notify me after they reached a decision on my application, yet they suggested that I took some time to discern with some other communities. They promised to get back to me, but they never did. I spent days visiting a number of religious communities within the country. Sadly, none gave me a positive reply. How distressing and discouraging to suffer disappointments!

If there was anything that kept me on track in those days, it was the grace I derived from the times I spent in prayer. The Lord did not leave me in desolation. The Master Potter stirred my heart and filled me with his Spirit, strengthening me each day in faith and in hope. Thus, I remained undeterred in my aspiration. One year elapsed after I completed my high school examination. At this point, it didn't seem like there was headway, yet I was hopeful that the Lord was able to make a way when it seemed there was no way. I decided to engage myself in life and studies to stay focused on the mission. The words that kept ringing in my heart were, "Whatever you do, wherever you find yourself, keep in mind that you are on mission for the Lord." So I left home for college to pursue educational studies.

## College Course

I was ready to go to college. My brother showed me great kindness. He provided me with enough money to take care of my personal needs. I strove to avoid falling into the temptation of a life of luxury. I wanted to lead a simple life, to help myself live according to the Spirit. I believed that a life of simplicity would aid me in training my body to be subject to the Spirit, to order my life to the impulse of the Holy Spirit. It is true, gratifying the desires of the flesh thwarts spiritual growth. St. Paul exhorts us to walk in the Spirit: "I say, then: live by the Spirit and you will certainly not gratify the desire of the flesh. For the flesh has desires against the Spirit, and the Spirit against the flesh; these are opposed to each other, so that you may not do what you want" (Gal 5:16–17).

In addition, I believed that one who acquires and hoards things more than one needed deprived others of having what they needed. I didn't want to deny others what they need to survive, especially those who were materially impoverished. I strived to be frugal, to avoid being wasteful in the use of material things. I did not obtain from my brother more money than I really needed. I was mindful of my siblings, relatives, and others who also benefitted from my brother's generosity. When I received gifts from some generous people, I would use them for my needs and spared my brother from spending money on me. I wore my older brothers' used clothes and footwear so I did not spend much money buying new things to wear. Nearly all the books that I used were borrowed from the library.

I spent my first two years in the dormitory. Many students lived in that fairly large hall, and it was densely crammed. The walls were lined with metal bunk beds. Students' personal cupboards served as demarcations. Rags, buckets, and utensils littered the dorm floor. The doors and windows were left open all the time. Students uninterruptedly bustled with activities around the dorm as though it was a marketplace. There was no regulated time for anything, no orderliness and quiet. Students did what they wanted to do at any time, whether at night or in the day. Some of the students were "night owls." Night was day for them. They cooked, ate, laundered, joked, prattled, howled, and even brawled through the night. We were frequently disrupted from sleep. One had to learn to put up with the incessant distractions and unruly behaviors in the dorm. Oftentimes I found myself straining to maintain peace within myself. When they disturbed so annoyingly at night, I would simply pray, asking the Lord to grant me the grace of patience.

To give an instance, one night I was ready to go to bed when one of the infamous mischievous roommates named Ochoku sat close to my bed and began to beat his metal plate and hummed a tuneless folksong. The noise was bothering some of us who were in the dorm, but none of us attempted to stop him. We all knew he was drunk and tended to be aggressive. To make an effort to stop him might spark off a fight. I lay down on my bed, clenching my jaw and clasping my bed to calm myself down. Then I closed my eyes and prayed that he might open himself to be found by grace. I also prayed for myself that I might continue to love him. At around one o'clock, Ochoku became tired and went to sleep. He slept for a few hours and woke up around 5:00 a.m. He tied his towel around himself without clothes. He shuffled around the dorms as a drunk, humming his favorite song. At that time, students were preparing for the day. He walked slovenly toward my corner and chanted his plea, "For the sake of Christ, help your brother when he is in need . . . The Bible says that if you help the poor, your reward will be great in heaven . . . Mr. Clay, please help! Help the poor. I have *garri*, but no soup . . . Give me some soup, I beg you, so that that I may eat and live to praise my God." He stretched his arm toward me and begged me to put some soup in his eating plate. With all pleasure, I gave him some soup. Then I said to him, "Ochoku, I hope you'll really praise God as you said." He chuckled and said, "Sure, after eating, I'll praise the Lord. The Lord knew that we couldn't praise him without the 'liturgy of the stomach.' That was why he fed the five thousand people, four thousand people, and other thousands. To help us cheer our hearts, Christ changed water into wine. You know I love wine so much, because I want to honor the first miracle of the Lord. Are you surprised that I know the Bible very well?" I said to him, "Where are you getting all this? Please come back when you finish eating. I would like you to tell me more about this, your interesting subjective interpretation of the Bible."

Ochoku and his group were interesting characters. Some of the students called them "troublemakers." Whenever they saw me cooking food, some of the "troublemakers" would come to keep me company. They would gently sit on my bed, telling me endless stories. They usually shared with me how they loved the Lord and their desire to become "prayer warriors." It might well be that they really loved the Lord. In any case, I knew that once the food was on the fire, what they meant was that they loved the food. Sometimes, they talked about spiritual things in order to sound "religiously correct," to get me engaged while I cooked the food. As soon as they finished eating the food, they would disappear. Their cunning didn't deter me from being friendly and generous to them. I used the time to share the Gospel with them. I didn't mind whether they were truly listening and sharing with their hearts. The Holy Spirit alone knew their hearts. I wouldn't judge them. What I knew was that the Spirit was at work in their lives. I used the opportunity to plant the seed in their lives. To the Spirit belonged the power to make the seed take root and bear fruits.

Life in the school was not easy. Yet the Lord granted me profound peace of mind and fervor to embrace the challenges of daily life. At the end of my second year, my education department was moved to the city campus. The transportation was very costly. Bike transportation to the bus park added enormously to the fare. To cut down the huge fare, I often set off for the school early in the morning walking the four-kilometer distance to the bus park. That helped me save money.

After two months, I rented an off-campus room. It was a poor shack that was in miserable condition. A friend who lived there asked me to share the room with him. It was a small, about 10-foot-by-10-foot shack. The roof had a hole in it. When it rained, water dripped into the room. The wall that was made of rusted metals had some open spots which provided reptiles a thoroughfare into the dark room. There was no constant electric light in the area to light up the room. We had to keep our oil lamp burning. The young man had lived there for over one year and he seemed to be comfortable with the place. He inspired me to live with him in that dark cell. I had a small amount of luggage; hence, we did not have to bother about cluttering the stuffy tiny hut.

On the first day of my arrival, we fixed the leaky roof. But that did not last long. Scarcely had one month passed when a strong rainstorm pulled off some part of the roof. It was around one o'clock in the morning. We were asleep when we felt cold water splashing around the room. We woke and lit our lamp, and alas, one side of the roof was loose and rainwater was fast dripping into the room. The mat on which we lay was already soaked. We could not fix the roof at that early hour of the morning. It was around 2:00 a.m. We placed a bucket at the spot where the water was dripping to prevent the room from being flooded. We sat on our stools leaning by the wall and resting our legs on small chairs. We tried to get more sleep before daybreak but it was difficult for us to sleep under such conditions. I prayed my rosary, commending to God those who had no place to lay their heads. I also prayed for those whose homes were destroyed by natural disasters, floods, hurricanes, tornadoes, or tsunami.

Because the shack was located near a huge drainage system, we had to do battle with mosquitoes. Our room swarmed with mosquitoes day and night. To make matters worse, we had no insecticide to control them. We would cover ourselves with blankets, but after a few minutes, our body would be drenched with sweat since we had no electric fan. During those days of rough sledding, we made St. Paul's words our watchword, "Rejoice in hope, endure in affliction, persevere in prayer" (Rom 12:12). In the midst of the hard life, the love of God which we shared together inebriated our hearts with peace and joy.

I was very involved in the student life in the school. I served in the following capacities: student representative in the college, coordinator of the Young Catholic Student Association, and leader of the campus branch of the Catholic Charismatic Renewal. I also gave talks to the Legion of Mary and the college rosary groups. Our charismatic group made several visits to the local monastery for retreats. It was in the monastery that a friend gave me a copy of the *Imitation of Christ*. It was on that day that I first learned about that inspiring spiritual classic. I used it for meditation each day. Reading lives of saints and meditating with the writings of the spiritual masters greatly helped to fire in my heart the desire to dedicate my life for the priestly ministry.

## A Student-Teacher

On completing my second year in the college, I started my internship in a private school. The school was about six kilometers to my residential area. I commuted back and forth every school day. I usually dressed in my black suit. Teachers were known for dressing in a suit. Some of those who knew me amiably addressed me as "Onye-nkuzi" (teacher). I had a cordial relationship with the teachers and the students of the school. They opened their hearts to me. They were very welcoming, loving, and devout people. Since I left them several years ago, I have never set my eyes on any of them. I may not recognize any of them if I run into them. I may or may not see any of them in this life, who knows? Yet I can still see their faces beaming with warmth and joy. Not long ago, I visited a school and spoke to the students. It was a trip down memory lane. I recalled the days when I was teaching in the school. Those days have passed forever! As a pilgrim that I am on earth, I waved them goodbye one morning and continued my journey. I know that I'm still connected with them in spirit. I keep them in my daily prayers. Wherever they are at present, I commend them to the protection of the Almighty God. I pray that the good Lord may protect and keep them faithful till the end of time.

# The Poor Widow

It was during my internship in Nigeria. The country was going through a hard time. Supplies of gas were limited. Few commercial vehicles were available and the cost of transportation was exorbitantly high. I had to leave early for the school so as to catch the city bus, which charged a lesser fare. On this particular day, I left for the school before 6:00 a.m. Getting to the bus stop, I stood by the roadside awaiting the arrival of the bus. I was silently praying my rosary. Soon I caught sight of a woman on the sidewalk. She was pulling a log of wood for her son to sit on. For some reason, I walked toward them and greeted, "Good morning." With a grin, she politely responded, "Good morning, sir." "How are you doing?" I asked. She answered in the local language, "I thank God that we are alive to see another day." Without hesitation, she began to relate her story. She was widowed five years at that time. Her brothers-in-law had dispossessed her of her husband's property. She had nothing left to meet the needs of her five children, including the seven-year-old boy with her, named Lewechi, who was blind.

She reached for her son, and turning her son's neck, the woman said to me, "See his face. He lost the two eyes from measles when he was a baby." With eyes bathed in tears, the woman said, "It makes my heart bleed that each day I bring my son here, sitting all day long to beg for alms." She wiped her tears and continued, "Yet, I trust that the Lord has not abandoned us. He sees my many tears." She was still sobbing when the city bus arrived. In a hurry, I thanked her for sharing her story with me, promising to meet with her soon. I bade her goodbye and hopped into the bus.

When I went onboard the bus, thoughts of the woman with her son could not get off my mind. I shared with one of my colleagues about my experience that morning. Surprisingly, he knew the woman. He told me that she worked as a porter in a local bakery. The son always sat by the roadside by himself begging. The young man affirmed that the poor widow had passed through serious abuse and neglect from her brothers-in-law. She had to struggle very hard to support her family. The son who begged for alms on the street received considerable amount of money and food stuff, which helped in taking care of the family's daily meals.

It is true that some beggars disguise themselves as sick, homeless, or handicapped with the intention to get the people's attention and sympathy.

A friend once told me of certain parents who, due to greed and sloth, turned their children into street beggars. Begging for them generates more money for the family than taking up a job. With this in mind, when I first saw the woman with her son from a distance, my first impression was that she might be one of those who feign illness or disability to get people to give them alms. I thought about how some exploit innocent children for the sake of money. But this woman's case was not as I had thought. How prejudiced and judgmental I was! She did not decide to turn her son into a beggar. It was rather as a result of the unfortunate condition that made begging an unavoidable option for them. My heart was pierced with compassion as I gazed at the young boy who could not see the beauty of creation. Who wouldn't have sympathy for the poor lad who had to sit there by himself asking for alms all day long, come rain or shine? It struck me even more deeply when the woman told me her sad story.

As I reflect on my encounter with the poor widow and her son, I think of Christ's presence in the lives of the poor. I recall Christ's own words in Matthew, "Amen, I say to you, whatever you did for one of these least brothers of mine, you did for me" (Mt 25:40). I can see myself among the audience to whom St. Caesarius of Arles addresses his sermon when he asks, "What kind of people are we? When God gives, we wish to receive, but when he begs we refuse to give. Remember, it was Christ who said: I was hungry and you gave me nothing to eat. When the poor are starving, Christ too hungers. Do not neglect to improve the unhappy conditions of the poor . . . Christ hungers now . . . it is he who deigns to hunger and thirst in the persons of the poor."

Many of the saints have wonderful insights into our relationship with serving the poor. Mother Teresa of Calcutta teaches me how I can identify Jesus among the people. She says that I need the eyes of faith to be able to see the Lord in the frail and impaired bodies of the needy who are Jesus in disguise. She expresses clearly that I need Christ's hand to hold the bodies of the poor who are pierced with pain and plight. In another place, the blessed woman says that it amounts to loss of faith when I do not acknowledge that the poor who lie helplessly in the streets are my "brother or sister." St. John Chrysostom's counsel concerning the poor, as well, flashes into my mind. The holy man exhorts me to clean the poor if I say they are dirty, to give them clean clothes to wear and have them dine with me. St. Chrysostom advises that I should not delay in work of mercy for Christ comes to me in the disguise of the poor. I cannot help pondering the exciting words of Gregory of Nyssa who enjoins me not to look down on the poor, but to see them as precious persons created in the image of the Lord. They are "heirs of future blessings, bearing the keys of the kingdom."

In our own time, Pope Francis is right when he says that we can learn much from the poor. In their difficult struggles, the poor keep the faith and "know the suffering Christ." Truly, I learned my lesson from the widow. It is exciting to note that the woman's trials and challenges would not tempt her to lose her faith in God's presence and merciful love. "Yet, I trust that the Lord has not abandoned us. He hears all my many tears," she said. Here the words of Psalmist come to mind, "Though I am afflicted and poor, my Lord keeps me in mind. You are my help and deliverer . . ." (Psalm 40:18). Like the Psalmist, the woman rests her hope in the Lord. She accepts her poverty with patient resignation to God's will, trusting that the Lord has not abandoned her and her family. She was convinced that despite the darkness of the moment, the Lord is at work in her life and in her family. Indeed, the compassionate Savior hears her many tears! How my little faith had inclined me to seek consolation somewhere else when things did not go my way! Now I have learned to wait on the Lord. When I experience any adversities, I remember that God has a plan for my life and is working for my good.

But it is not enough for me to have an abstract kind of faith in God. Faith without mercy is really a mess. We are called to be merciful. I see mercy as love's healing balm touching the core of our hurts. My Christian faith calls me to exercise the acts of mercy to my neighbors

I realize that the poor widow wanted me to listen to her story. Ah, I wish I had not been in a hurry at that moment! The Spirit constantly stirs up my heart to be more attentive to the needs of my neighbors: the suffering, the sick, the oppressed, those feeling lonely, and those on the fringes of society. I am called to listen to their stories, to be close to them, to be a sign of Christ's visible presence to them, to serve and to share my resources with them without taking advantage of them. As Christ says, whatever I do to the lowly ones I do to him. I may not be able to supply their material needs but love and care do not run dry in the hearts of the people of faith, in those who love Christ. Some persons' needs are not necessarily the material gifts that I may offer them, but rather my listening ear, my care, my genuine smile, my accompaniment, my words of cheer and encouragement. Mother Teresa of Calcutta had this in mind when she insightfully remarked that poverty is not only about hunger, nakedness, and homelessness. She described as the greatest form of poverty, "the poverty of being unwanted, unloved and uncared for." The holy woman called us to begin addressing this form of poverty right from our homes. Surely, it is not too late for me. And so I ask that the Lord may make me a missionary of his love and mercy.

I know that in some occasions in the past, certain preconceived ideas had prevented me from giving myself in solidarity and care for certain persons. Accordingly, when I first saw the woman with her son, I thought of exploitation, laziness, greed for money, corruption. Christ does not want me to stereotype anyone or relate with others in a judgmental manner. Such attitude damages true love, basic trust, and life-giving concern for one another, which we should enjoy as children of God. When someone begs for alms, instead of judging the genuineness of his or her neediness (which is sometimes hard to determine), I should see in them the face of Christ. The act of begging in itself is a state of neediness. I should look at the person begging, even those who are deceivers and impostors, with the eyes of love. They too need my love; they need my prayer so that they may be open to the grace to improve and behave with honesty and integrity as God's children. When I love others unconditionally, then the Spirit will help me to offer the right help at the right time, and this may be moral or spiritual or material assistance. Christ looks at every person with the eyes of love and seeks to help the individual share in his boundless merciful love, freedom, peace, and joy.

The author of the Letter to the Hebrews reminds me to "keep doing good works and sharing" what I have received from the Lord, for "God is pleased by sacrifice of that kind" (Heb 13:16). My vocation as a Christian is one of communicating Christ's love, touching lives in joyful, generous, transforming services of charity. When I listen to my neighbor, when I express a genuine sympathy for his or her plight, when I forgive hurts, when I share with him or her the gifts the Lord has entrusted to me, I live and offer the Gospel to the world. No better way to live the Gospel than to share what I have with my neighbor for the sake of Christ. My love for the Lord should move me to give to the needy. In giving, I am sharing in their suffering and, of course, in Christ's suffering, for, as St. Paul says, we are members of Christ. Christ is our head in our mystical, mutual connection with him (cf. Rom 12:5).

No one who encounters Christ remains the same. The growth in my personal relationship with Jesus Christ has transformed my perception and relationship with my neighbors. Each morning, Christ invites me to open my heart so that he may breathe into me a fresh breath of his love. The Spirit of love sets me on fire with God's love and mercy to relate with others in a more healthy and holy way, free from prejudice, discrimination, duplicity, and selfish interest. I strive daily to be more and more disposed to the Spirit who works in us in reaching out to others to invite them to a life-changing encounter with Christ. We know that Christ showed great care for the poor and the suffering. I, too, am called to love and care for them, to serve and to share with them the joy and consolation of Christ's presence in their lives.

Every morning, I pray that the Lord may show me how he wants me to serve him in my neighbor. At the end of the day, I spend some time to do an examination of conscience to see how I have shown love or have failed to exercise mercy in the course of the day. I pray always that the Lord may make my heart like his so that I may be more concerned and attentive to the needs of others rather than being selfish and biased, to be more tender and caring rather than being hardhearted and neglectful, to be more compassionate and sensitive to the sufferings of others rather than being indifferent, to be more humble and respectful rather than being arrogant and scornful, to be more merciful rather than being vindictive and spiteful. I beg the Lord to open my eyes of faith to see him in those around me, most especially in my suffering brothers and sisters, for unless I begin to see Christ in my brothers and sisters, I will lose sight of the Lord.

## Moving Words

On another occasion, I stopped by the road to see Lewechi, the boy who was blind. I brought some gifts for him. He had not eaten that morning because no one had given him money or food to eat. My heart was greatly moved when he told me that he wished he could see the beauty of nature. I felt at a loss for words to console him. I drew him into my arms and said, "It is hard to imagine how you feel. I wish I could lend you my own eyes to see. I'm here for you." I gave him some of the stuff I bought. I stayed with him for a while, holding his hands and praying in my heart. Then I assured him that I would be visiting with him.

As I walked away to catch the metro bus, a rather small white bus drove toward me. Reaching where I stood, the bus conductor shouted out the name of the town where they were going. But I didn't hear him well. I guess it was because thoughts of the blind boy so engrossed me that I didn't think of where the bus was going before hopping on it. Soon after the bus zoomed off, the bus conductor asked me for the fare. "How much?" I inquired. "One hundred naira," he replied. I was taken aback. It was four times the fare that we usually paid for my destination. "Surely I have boarded the wrong bus," I thought. "Please, where are you going?" I asked. The bus conductor pulled a face and retorted with a snobbish tone: "Where are you going yourself?" With a soft voice, I told him my destination. "It is your cup of tea," he replied harshly. He continued, "I told you clearly where we are going and you boarded our bus. Whether you are going with us or alighting here, you must pay me." "I'm sorry that I didn't understand when you said it. I'm sure that I was distracted by something else. Please let me get down here," I appealed. The driver jammed the brake and put the van to a stop. "Let him alight," he said to the bus conductor. "No! I can't allow him to go without paying me my money. No reduction! No negotiation! I can't find any other passenger that would take the seat. It is his fault, his fault! not mine. I can't eat excuse. I need money, this is my business." I tried to apologize to him, but he was not willing to listen. "Let him alight! We all can make the same mistake," the driver said. "Why don't you listen to your driver?" one of the passengers questioned. Raising his arm, the bus conductor pounded on the bus, yelling, "I'm ready to fight with anybody right now! Let no one dare to provoke me! If you talk nonsense, I'll break someone's head right now." Almost all the passengers angrily let him have it; some cursed and wagged fingers at him. Some berated and derided him. Some called him names. The bus conductor turned to me and began to hurl insults, "Poor man! See how you dressed as an old, retired headmaster. You forgot yourself because you were looking at women."

He said many scornful things against me, but I did not say a word to him. See how the Lord loves his children! Didn't I deserve such embarrassment? Whenever I am infected with a virus of pride, the Lord gives me a high dose of humiliation to cure me. The Lord shakes me up when I feel too relaxed. He pinches me whenever I feel too comfortable. All are a sign of his infinite love for me. My Divine Master Porter disciplines me because he loves me so much (Heb 12:6).

Wait a minute, was I prideful? I didn't intend to be haughty. Even so, it is easy to get caught up with a sense of flamboyant self-importance in a such society where many youths are poor and jobless, where many are uneducated, where many toil hard in manual labor to make ends meet, where many youths in tattered clothes labor strenuously on a daily basis transporting goods on their heads or with wheelbarrows, peddling peanuts and bananas, which in their state of impoverishment barely supply for their livelihood. May the Lord deliver me from the spirit of egotism and pride! The Lord gave me the grace to endure the insults. I recalled that King David endured his own gross insults. For my sake, Christ bore the stigma and revilement of his persecutors. The Lord gave me an example to follow: he returned insult with love and endured the pain of his passion with perfect surrender to the will of his Father. The Spirit worked in me in a way that those mere words couldn't cast me down or steal my peace. I prayed: "Lord, may you always grant me your heart to love and to endure patiently any temptations and trials that may come my way."

At some point, the bus conductor listened to the driver and calmed down. The driver also pleaded with the passengers to let go. Then they drove off. I stood there for a while waiting for another bus. It was usually difficult to find a bus or ride along the road. God was so gracious to me that I did not wait very long before a goodhearted young man pulled up and offered me a ride. Even though I got to school rather late that morning, we had a great time in class. Praise God!

## The Sermon of the Insane

One day I attended Mass at a parish close to our school. I remember that the Gospel reading that day was about carrying one's cross: "Whoever does not carry his own cross and come after me cannot be my disciple" (Luke 14:27). In his sermon, the pastor posed a rhetorical question: "Who among us has a life free from problems?" One woman was sitting by herself in the back row of the church. She raised her two hands to respond to the priest's question. The congregation started to murmur because they knew that the woman had a mental condition. The pastor did not know who she was. Drawing closer to her, the priest discovered that she was barefoot and her dress was old and torn. It was apparent to the priest that the woman was not sound in mind. The pastor asked her to share with them what she thought. She sprang from her chair, with hands on her hips and eyes wide open. She swung her right arm to the direction of a crucifix suspended over the altar. Then she exploded her response, "Look at the kind of question you are asking me. Here is he who carried all my problems! Have you forgotten our Redeemer, eh?" The pastor could not hush her as she kept on muttering and murmuring.

Some of those who were present at Mass that day dismissed the woman's words as nothing but nonsense, a mere manifestation of her insanity. But could the Lord mean to speak to us through that woman? Most probably. Now think about this. Some of those whom we see as insane are teaching us true wisdom. Some whom we regard as in slavery are teaching us how to be free. Some whom we consider as mourning are teaching us how to rejoice. Some of those we look at as dying are showing us how to live. Some of those we conceive as lost are pointing to us the way home. Some of those we evaluate as poor are directing us to the bank of incorruptible treasure. God can speak to us through any person, even those we may consider as the "scum of the earth." Remember the humble faith of the Gentile woman who some regarded as a "dog" (cf. Matt 15:26). Think of the unflagging faith of the blind beggar Bartimaeus; some rebuked and tried to hush him up (Mark 10:48). Even though she had a mental condition, the woman in the church understood that Christ bore all our illness and carried to the cross all our cares and troubles. The Psalmist trusts that God supplies all his needs, "The Lord is my shepherd; there is nothing I lack" (Psalm 23:1). Don't you lack something? It is commonly believed that there is no life on earth without some sort of problem. As human beings, we have both spiritual and material needs. Some people are blessed with plenty of material things while some don't enjoy such an advantage. Some people are blessed with good health while others suffer certain illnesses. Some rejoice now while some are mourning.

We know that Christ did not promise his followers in this world perfect health or wealth, or a painless life or human acclaim. He didn't assure us that life would be easy and comfortable for us. On the contrary, Christ invites us to carry our inevitable "crosses" and to be ready to face possible persecutions if we are ready to be his disciples. No one can claim to have the answer to the why of the "crosses" of life, especially for those who have a relationship with the Lord. Yet people of faith trust that in the midst of their daily crosses Christ is at work for their good. In this light, they connect their daily struggles and challenges (crosses) with the cross of Christ. It is beneficial for the sick to pray for healing. It is in order of faith for the poor to pray for material blessings. It is a sign of trust in God for those who hurt or feel the weight of their afflictions to ask the Lord to remove them. However, firm faith is made manifest in our inner surrender to the will of God in all circumstances, whether or not God directly grants what we ask him in prayer.

The Bible assures, "My God will fully supply whatever you need, in accord with his glorious riches in Christ Jesus" (Php 4:19). Our Lord Jesus can do all things. He can grant the poor abundance of their material needs. He can grace the sick with his blessing of physical healing. He can save us from certain death. Apparently, we know that some faithful Christians suffer and die of poverty, hardship, sickness, imprisonment, and persecution. The first disciples of Christ suffered and/or died for their faith. Some were devoured by wild beasts. Some were tortured and beheaded. Some were stoned, burned at the stake, flayed or skinned alive. Why didn't Christ save them from death? Who knows? Now think about this: Lazarus was raised from death but he later died anyway (John 11). Peter's mother-in-law was healed from illness but she later died anyway (Mt 8). Peter was miraculously rescued from prison, from the clutches of King Herod, but he was later martyred anyway (Acts 12). Solomon was blessed with material riches but he died and the wealth wasted away anyway (1King 10).

Are human beings meant to live forever on earth? I'm sure we all know the answer. Do we think that the pleasures and happiness of this world will be endless? Of course not. Recall the words of the Bible, "All flesh is like grass, and all its glory like the flower of the field; the grass withers, and the flower wilts . . ." 1 Pet 1:24). If material things are liable to decay and human beings subject to die, in what way do we believe that Christ supplies all our needs? Don't you think that there must be something more than material needs that Christ offers us? Christ comes to give us lasting treasures from his riches in glory. He comes to give us his peace in the midst of the world's warfare, patient endurance in times of afflictions, consolation in the moment of sorrow, inner peace and joy in the face of adversity. The Lord comes to imbue us with the fire of the Holy Spirit so that we may be steadfast in faith, fervent in hope, and boundless in charity. The Savior comes to offer us victory over death.

Without Christ we would be living dead, alive in the body but spiritually dead. He is the remedy to heal the sting of death. Thus Christ supplies our fundamental need: life. He is life. In his glorious kingdom are the treasures of life. I affirm with St. Paul that nothing (be it persecution, famine, nakedness, sword, death, creature) can sunder me from life or love (cf. Rom 8:35–39). Christ invites me to carry my daily cross with love and joy, following and uniting it with his own saving cross. In Christ, "my yoke is easy, and my burden light" (Mt 11:30). When my cross is easy, I can rightly say, like the woman in the church, I have no problem. Grace gives me the power to say that I have no fears and worries as long as I am united with Christ. I rejoice in him who has poured upon my heart abundant grace (Jon 1:16). To have the Lord is to have all things, to lack nothing. When one knows the solution to one's problem, doesn't one say, "It is nothing to worry about"? Christ, who is the answer to all problems, is always with me. I do not allow myself to be weighed down by those trials that seem insurmountable. I do not give in to the spirit of despair.

My Lord Jesus Christ is the "answer" to those things that present themselves as problems. I have learned to cast all my worries upon the Divine Master Potter, because he is always there for me (1Peter 5:7). Even in tribulations, I can confidently boast that I have no problem, for Christ has carried my entire problems to Calvary. I have surrendered my life to the Lord, "I live, no longer I, but Christ lives in me; insofar as I now live in the flesh, I live by faith in the Son of God who has loved me and given himself up for me" (Gal 2:20). I have learned to speak to people about Jesus with a joyful heart instead of a heavy heart, for mine is a vocation of joy. I strive to rejoice always even when things don't go my way. When someone asks me how I am doing, instead of recounting a litany of woes I'll testify to God's loving presence and goodness in my life. Instead of saying, "I'm horrible," I'll say, "I'm healed." Instead of saying, "I can't complain," I'll say, "I can express my praise to God." Instead of saying, "Things are hard for me," I'll say, "God hears my prayer."

I pray to you, my Master Potter, redirect my steps when I begin to drift away from you. Shake up my heart when I begin to be attached to created things. Jiggle me when I begin to forget that you bore my infirmities. Pinch me when I begin to cling to the pleasures of this world. Charge me up with the fire of your Spirit when I begin to grow cold. Inebriate me with your joy and peace when the world offers the cup of bitterness and sorrow. Flood me with the river of your consolation when I walk through the world of dryness and desolation. I pray you, Lord, open my inner eyes to see your abiding presence when I am rocked and tossed by waves of tribulations. I beg you, Lord, with your sea of faith, drown all my fear and anxiety. I trust you are always with me, and so I have no problem!

## The Horrible Hour

The year flew by very quickly. I finished my teaching practice successfully. I returned to school to complete my last academic year. When I came back to school, I found that our little shack was falling apart. My roommate and I made every effort to fix it but it did not work out. It needed to be demolished and rebuilt. The poor house owner had no money to take care of that. So we had to find a new accommodation. Within a few days, my friend and I found a good room to rent. It was located in a quiet environment. The room was not spacious but it was a little larger than the former room. We did not have a bed. We had a thin mattress which we leaned against one end of the wall during the day so as to have a workable space in the room. We had lived in the room for two months and the daily routine of student life was progressing well.

One lovely night, we retired to bed rather late. We had spent long hours of the night puzzling over certain hard homework. We had barely fallen asleep when suddenly someone banged on our door. It was around 2:00 a.m. "Who is disturbing us at this late hour of the night?" we wondered. We suspected that it would be the local vigilante group. Every resident around that street paid a monthly security fee. Those who could not pay their levy at the end of the month were charged late fee. The vigilante went door to door to collect the levy. We had paid our security fee for the month. We thought that the security had no reason to disturb us at that hour of the night. The striking was getting violent and terrifying. I fretfully rose from the mattress to answer the door. As soon as I opened the door, one of the men pointed a gun at me: "Bring the money or I shoot you now," he ordered loudly. As I saw the gun, my heart missed a beat. I shouted,

"My Lord Jesus, save me!" Obviously, they were not vigilante men. I had watched some movies on malicious operations of armed robbers. I had dreamed about them. I had heard stories about them. Even though I had never had an encounter with them, I knew that they carried death-dealing weapons, ready to crush any person at any time. They shoot without sorrow. They maim without mercy. They loot without lenity. "Is this a dream or a reality?" I imagined. Oh, it wasn't a dream!

With my arms raised and my head cast down, I toddled back to the room and lay face down, pleading for mercy. Unfortunately, bandits do not know the language of mercy. They can spare one's life only when one acts fast to their demands. The room was dark but one of them was pointing his flashlight at us. I closed my eyes. My heart raced. My body trembled. Cold sweat rushed over my body. By this time my roommate had already gone into a spasm of fear, wincing and wailing, "We love you! Please don't kill us. Have mercy! We are your brothers!" He was so scared that he almost emptied his bowels. "Don't waste our time!" one of bandits threatened. I directed them where I kept the little money I had. "The money is there in the drawer," I said in a wobbling voice. I felt apprehensive that they might be enraged with the little amount of money in the drawer. One of them quickly pulled out the drawer and grabbed all the money and put it into his pocket. Perhaps he thought that it was a large sum since the money was in small fraction of currency, about forty notes of ten naira. One of them turned to my roommate and kicked him heavily on his back, roaring, "Hey, bring it. Don't waste my time." My roommate quivered and pleaded, "Have mercy, I love you . . . Please! Please! Don't kill me!" One of thieves, who was holding a beer bottle which he stole from our landlady's refrigerator, yelled furiously, "You dumb! Do you think we are playing here?" Like a shot out of hell, he smashed the filled beer bottle on the head of my roommate. Poor guy! He lay still as one in a traumatic coma. He neither screamed nor shook his body. The stunning blast sent chills down my spine. It struck more fear into my heart. "Is he dead? Is his head crushed? Are they going to kill me also?" I recoiled, waiting for my own share of the blow. I kept still praying in my heart: "Jesus, my Savior, save us!" I asked St. Michael to defend us. In a flash, there was silence in the room. "Where are they?" I wondered. Within a second, they started banging at the door of our neighbor. They had left our room. I opened my eyes, but the room was dark. I could not see my roommate. I stretched my hand to reach him. I felt his pulse and found that he was still breathing. I did not want to light up the room yet to avoid stirring up the robbers' rage. I pressed my palms down on his head to cover the spot where I felt the blood was oozing out. I softly called him by name but he did not respond. I felt he was unconscious. I called the fourth time, and he answered with a weak voice. I was happy to learn that he was regaining himself. I was praying with him when I heard a siren sounding toward our street. Someone had notified the police. Hearing the sound of the siren, the bandits took to their heels. I could hear the sounds of heels.

As the police officers alighted in front of our house, one of them shouted, "Hey, don't move! If you move I shoot!" They didn't see anybody. They were trying to scare away the bandits. We felt relieved that the police had come to intervene. Some of the residents who hid in the bush emerged. I got up, groped in the gloom of the room as I searched for my flashlight. I flashed the light on my roommate's head, and, thanks be to God, the wound was rather small. I slightly opened my door and looked outside and saw that almost all the residents around our quarters had already gathered at our front yard, each narrating his or her bitter encounter with those unwanted visitors. I recounted our own ordeal. A nurse who lived next door bandaged the head wound of my roommate. Neither of us was able to return to sleep that morning.

## Exciting Trip

One weekend, exactly one month before my graduation from college, I went to visit with my family. I boarded a bus, and everything seemed to be going well. After riding halfway, our driver jammed on the break and stopped our bus. A crowd of people were standing along the road. Two vehicles were involved in a ghastly automobile accident. A truck collided with one commuter bus. Several people died. Some human body parts littered the road. I sighted one man whose skull was severed and the brain was disgorged. A dead body was laid by the roadside. Blood flooded the road. Some badly crushed bodies were seen piled at the west end of the road. Some persons were weeping and wailing uncontrollably. My fellow passengers were also in tears. One woman who was sitting beside me cried loudly, *"O Chi mu-o-oh* (Oh my God)!" But who would not be moved beholding such a horrible scene? One glance at such a terrible incident was enough to move even the cold-hearted to sigh with sorrow.

There was heavy traffic as many travelers alighted from their vehicles to help rescue those who were trapped under the truck. If not by the grace of God, I could have been one of those poor souls who lost their lives. How I need to stay awake for I don't know the day when my own journey on earth will come to an end! (cf. Mat 25:13). I don't know the day and the hour. Only the Divine Master Potter knows. He does not want me to be about the business of determining the day, but rather, to occupy myself with the preparation for the day. I commended to God the souls of those who died in the accident.

On the next day, I set out for school. Shortly after getting to the bus stop, a new luxurious bus pulled up. I thought it would be a good ride, and so I went aboard. Within a short time, the bus was filled with passengers, and the deafening sound of the motor horn signaled our departure. Gradually and patiently, we galloped along the potholes of the narrow streets. When we got to the main highway, the driver made a burst of speed. He was going so fast that I became upset. I could not endure it, hence I shouted out my warning, "Please, driver, take it easy! Slow down! It's better to arrive late than to stop on the way." The driver turned a deaf ear to me and went ahead at top speed. I looked around, and no one seemed to be worried about it. I wondered if my fellow passengers were comfortable with the apparent overspeeding. "Am I suffering from tachophobia (speed phobia, fear of speed)?" I wondered. Then I thought that it might be because I witnessed an accident the day before. I tried to calm down but I could not. The speed was very frightening to me. I called out again, "Driver, easy!" Then I signed myself with the sign of the cross and kept quiet. One woman sitting at my side spoke up, "Driver, can't you listen? It seems that you are drunk!" The bus conductor hushed her, "Madam, shut your mouth. Don't disturb the driver!" The bus conductor and the woman were having words when the bus suddenly went out of control and veered into a bush.

Some of the passengers who were asleep were shaken up. Some of us frantically burst forth into ejaculatory prayer, "The blood of Jesus . . . my Lord, save us . . ." The driver made a zigzag maneuver to control the bus in the shrubs for about two minutes. Eventually, the bus got stuck in the swampy soil. As soon as the bus came to a halt, all the passengers jostled their way out; some jumped off through the windows. Some of the tough guys pressed their way to unleash their rage on the driver. I tramped the swampy bush to the road without turning my back. I could hear the passengers and the driver brawling. I could hear sounds of heavy blows and blasts. I moved ahead without turning back, thanking my Lord for delivering us from the trap of the evil one. When I got to the road, I boarded another bus and continued my journey. I made it safely back to school. Praise God!

## Saved by the Second

One of our professors in college was very strict about time. There were many students who registered for his course each year. His class began by 9:00 a.m. every Wednesday. He expected the students to be seated before 9:00 a.m. He locked up the doors at nine o'clock on the dot. Thus, those who got to the class a minute late knew that they had missed the class for that day. I had been accustomed to being in class at least five minutes early. But one day, something unusual happened. I don't remember what it was, but it actually delayed me that day. As I was walking down the street, I noticed that I had two minutes to get to the hall. "Hurry up, Clay! We are late!" shouted one of my classmates who was rushing down the lecture hall. In all haste, I raced to catch up with him, and the two of us ran as fast as our legs would carry us. We were roughly just a few steps away from the class hall when the professor stooped to unhook the door in order to close it. He had a hard time removing the hook, and that was to our advantage. My classmate got to the door before me and hurled himself into the class. I reached the door at the time when the professor was closing the door. I squeezed myself behind him, and his fat buttocks helped to push me into the classroom. Wow! a second more, I would have been locked out of the class! I sat down and tried to catch my breath. I breathed in and out to calm myself down.

That was a lesson for me. Some will narrowly enter into the gate of heaven while some will narrowly miss it. God forbid that I miss the gate to life. I strive daily, by the grace of God, so that I may enter heaven, not narrowly but at the right time. This is my goal.

# A Hearty Farewell

I had my last exam for the Nigeria Certificate of Education program. On the last day, we organized a farewell party for our beloved professors and students. I delivered the farewell address. It was great. All the professors were very delighted with us. They testified about our hard work and generous service to the school. They offered us some keepsakes. I received plenty of gifts that day.

After the luncheon, I asked that all the students stay behind so that we could exchange our contact information. When the members of the staff took leave of us, the graduating students gathered at the rear of the hall. I stood and addressed them in these words: "We have already given the farewell address, but permit me to add a few words particularly for us graduating students. Today is remarkably a day to say goodbye to one another. It is the last day for us to share together as students in this college. We have lived together as brothers and sisters for the past three years. We have had a great, blessed time. We have accepted and loved one another. We have studied together, collaborated, and supported one another. We will never have a time like this anymore in this world. Though we may meet again, it will surely never be as students of this college. We are going away into another phase of our lives. Our vocations and vacations may take us to different parts of the world. Who knows, today may be the last day that some of us will set our eyes on some of us sitting in this hall until the glorious day of the resurrection. I don't mean that we are leaving here to die soon. May the Lord grant us the grace of long life! In any case, there is a kind of death that we shall face tomorrow—death of this present time. Time once past cannot come back. Our today will never be regained tomorrow. Tomorrow, we'll begin to reminisce our happy moments of today. Yes, tomorrow, the memory of today will haunt our thoughts. It will be a time when we shall wish that our past fun and fancy could be relived, when we shall remember our beloved friends, when the love and friendship we enjoyed will make us nostalgic with the twinge of pain that comes from knowing that the moments would never return. When that time comes, let us replace that yearning with the contemplation of the divine consolation, God. The teacher is right when he says, "There is an appointed time for everything, and a time for every affair under the heavens" (Eccl 3:1). This is the time for us to bid bye to this college, to our friends, to our schoolmates, teachers, well-wishers, and one another. May we always keep in mind that we are on pilgrimage on earth, and that each place we find ourselves is a transitional stage in the course of this solemn journey. We are called to sanctify each moment by our life of faith and charity, staying focused on the path of life, on Christ.

"As we bid goodbye to one another, and as our life's journey take us to any place, may we stay close to one another in spirit, united in the heart of our blessed Lord as we pray for one another. I invite you now to kindly turn to someone and say, 'I love you. May the peace and joy of Christ stay with you wherever you'll be tomorrow.'" With warmth, we bid farewell to one another. As the exchange of greetings progressed, it was obvious that some of us were overwhelmed with emotion. Most of the students hung their heads in tears. Some held each other with holy embrace. A couple of months after our graduation, I got word that one of my classmates who graduated with us had peacefully gone to the Lord. May God rest her soul! I have lost contact with most of my classmates, but I remember them with great affection and my prayer is with them.

## Discerning out and Discerning In

When I graduated from the college, I was not sure the next step to take. I had no doubt that the Lord was taking me somewhere, but I was not sure where and when it would be. The desire to serve God and his people in the priesthood was still burning in my heart. I visited some religious communities to discern my vocation. My applications met with the same old story: disapproval, denial, rejection, disappointment. No! it was not a disappointment but a process of appointment. I had planned on pursuing a course in university when I received a letter from one of the religious communities. The vocations director asked that I teach in their school as part of my discernment with the community. I accepted the offer and began teaching in the school that year. At the end of the year, I was accepted to begin the initial formation program (postulancy). The religious community had a great apostolate, yet I felt that God was calling me somewhere else. I decided to stay a little bit longer to pray about it to have some clarity that the feeling was not coming from any negative spirit or from impulse of nature. As the days passed, I experienced more and more desolation.

During my quiet time one evening, I asked the Divine Master Potter, "Lord, I thought that you brought me here. Why do you deprive me of joy and consolation in this place? If this is a temptation, please give me the grace to overcome it." I listened to hear what the Spirit would say to me, but throughout that night I did not get any word from him. Did he turn his back on me? I did not think so. The Lord spoke to me, but the noise within me kept me from hearing the Lord. I didn't spend much time with the Lord. My heart was preoccupied with thoughts of the future, what to do next. And so my prayer was hurried. I hid this inner conflict from the vocations director. I didn't know what really kept me from consulting with him. Perhaps it happened that way so that things would fall into place to fit into God's plan for my life. I continued to pray and do penance. I understood that the devil could manipulate situations in subtle ways for his purpose. I consulted with my spiritual director. He spoke to my heart. The Spirit spoke to me through the priest to clear the air.

After four months with the community, the time finally came for me to go forth on the journey process. I spent the eve of my departure in prayerful vigil for the will of God. In the morning, I met with my novice master and made known to him my intention to leave the community. After some hesitation, he allowed me to go.

It was so hard for me to say goodbye to my brothers. As I boarded the taxi and was about to depart, I had mixed emotions. I felt a twinge of fondness remembering the fraternal spirit we shared together. I also felt the melancholy of saying farewell to such spirit-filled brothers. I knew I was leaving the community but had no idea of what to do next. I was going back home to begin the tough journey afresh! Shortly after my arrival, a priest friend referred three other aspirants and me to another religious community. In accord with God's plan for my life, we got word that the authorities of the religious community cancelled the meeting with us. How true it is that "the human heart plans the way, but the LORD directs the steps" (Pro 16:9).

## Via University

After praying and listening to the Spirit, I went to university to obtain a degree. My admission into the university worked out quite smoothly. I began my studies for a bachelor of science degree. The university was held in esteem, especially for its moral excellence. Many parents and relatives sought admission in the school for their children and loved ones. As a result, the university saw a significant increase in enrollment. There was ongoing demand for expansion of the infrastructure, especially living quarters. I arrived at the time when some new dormitories were under construction. The available ones were temporarily overcrowded with students. I was assigned to a small room with over ten students. I had been used to living with people of different personalities, attitudes, and characters. I had learned to put up with certain disgusting behaviors of some students. We had some who deprived others of their possessions. Some took pleasure in messing up the rooms and the environment. Some exposed obscene images on purpose. Still some students were very noisy; they didn't like to be silent for a moment and they would not want to create a quiet environment for others.

There were, however, some students who remarkably touched my life. I think of their modesty, simplicity of life, humility, devotion, openheartedness, and fervent faith, which were few of the virtues that distinguished them. God also graced me with wonderful professors and friends and course mates. Some of my friends were female students. They were wonderful people who truly loved the Lord and strove to grow in their relationship with him. By the grace of God, we maintained a loving friendship. It was uplifting to have such brothers and sisters who loved the Lord and lived in the Spirit.

I confess that on some occasions I battled with strong fleshly temptation in the school. I believed that the Lord allowed this to be a constant reminder of my humanity and need for his grace. I remember one evening when the wave of temptation almost swept over me like a surging tide. I prayed and whipped myself to tame the flesh. I called my prayer partner and shared my feeling with him. We prayed together and went for a walk. We talked about spiritual things as we walked along the narrow path. When I returned, I felt a deep calm within me. The storm was over. The Spirit took captive the natural impulse which stormed to incite me to act against purity. It was in that period that the words of this prayer came to me: "My loving God, it is your will that I serve you with an undivided heart. Many a time, the desires of the flesh buffet my heart to pull me away from you. Grant me your grace always so that I may be able to overcome the temptations of daily life. Set my heart free from any unhealthy and unholy attachment that tends to divide my heart between you and the world. Create in me a heart that is ever pure, ever humble, ever faithful, and ever submissive to your holy will."

## Formal Fellowship

After my first year in the university, I was chosen to serve as a hall representative. I was in charge of the students living on the first floor of one of the dorms. I moved to a small room. I gave my close friends access to the room. They kept their important stuff there for security reasons. I also served in the following capacities: department student representative, president of the Patrician Forum of the Legion of Mary, and coordinator of the Catholic Biblical Movement. It was a humbling experience to serve in those areas. Without the support of the gifted friends who were always there for me, and without the grace of God, I wouldn't have been able to carry out the responsibilities effectively.

In the course of my studies in the university, the fire of zeal for the sacred service did not go out. It burned, rather, with great intensity. Each day the Spirit whispered to my heart, reminding me that the call to follow Christ is a call to love as Christ loved, and to serve as Christ served. After our last exam in October that year, we gathered to say goodbye to the school. After a short prayer, I reminded the group that the gathering would be our last one in the school. Before the meeting, I had packed my luggage, ready to leave, to begin another phase of my pilgrim journey. We sang together, "I know there is another fellowship in heaven . . ." Many of us were in tears. It was a warm and heartfelt goodbye.

Many years have passed since then and I have never set my eyes on or heard from most of my dear schoolmates. The other day, I sat on a desk stool in my hermitage thinking back on our last farewell in the university. You could imagine the nostalgic vibe this gave to me. I recognized it, yet I did not allow my heart to dwell on it that long. I understood that everything that is given to the human race in time would pass away with time. I miss my beloved friends! I don't know where they are right now. Wherever they are dispersed across the world, I commend them to the protection of the Almighty God. If I am not graced with the opportunity to meet them again in this life, I am looking forward to the eternal fellowship and communion in heaven where I will reunite with them at the end of time, never to part anymore.

# Falling in Affection

Uredi was my schoolmate in the university. She was lovely, smart, cheerful, and modest. Above all, she was such a devout and faithful soul. She had all the good qualities that a Christian gentleman would want in a wife. I first met Uredi in a Catholic organization in the university. She made an impression on me. I admired her greatly. Of course, my desire for celibate life neither blinded me from recognizing beauty in women, nor blotted out my natural impulses. I did not reveal my innermost feeling for Uredi. I didn't give her special attention. I didn't want to involve myself in a special friendship, partly to avoid the temptation of distraction from my prospective vocation, and partly to avoid being entangled in an unholy relationship that would be difficult for me to extricate myself from. At that time, I had no idea that Uredi had a special love for me.

Upon graduation, I accepted a job offer in the university while awaiting God's time. I had a small office in the university library. Once in a while Uredi would stop by my office to say hi! One afternoon, Uredi paid a special visit to me. It was during the time when I was preparing to enter religious life. I had sent my resignation letter to the school. I thought it was a good time to let Uredi know about my desire to become a priest. I thought that she would be enthused to learn about this. I said to her, "I have good news for you." She smiled and said, "Okay, tell me." "Well, not right now." "No, don't put me in suspense. Tell me right now to put my mind at ease," she said with a tone of curiosity. "Guess what?" I quizzed her. "What? I can't guess, please tell me now or never. Don't give me a hard time with a tough question." I cleared my voice and said, "Praise the Lord for me. I have been accepted to begin my formation to the priesthood. I'm leaving for the city next month."

Uredi made a face, looking downcast in a strange sort of way. She kept silent for a while. Then she glanced at me with her eyes fogged with tears. "You must be kidding me," she muttered. "No, I mean what I am saying," I tenderly replied. I reached into my bag and showed her my letter of acceptance. That was like the "straw that broke the camel's back." She felt completely crushed. "So you mean to leave me?" she sobbed. Tears streamed down her eyes as she looked intensely at me. It was a strange drama to me. "You have greatly touched me by your tears. Yet I'm not sure what is going on here. Could you help me understand this strange reaction of yours?" I pleaded. She glanced at me and reproached, "Do you mean that you don't know what you want to do to me?" She kept silent and then continued, "I had been praying that God might join us together for life. I concluded the novena prayer today. I came here straight from the chapel, and here you are now telling me this heart-rending story."

I hung my head, bewildered and confused. I wondered how the idea of marriage came into her mind. We had never talked about friendship. We had never discussed courtship. We had never been on a date. We had never been into any intimate relationship aside from being together in our prayer meetings. "Well, I'm very sorry! I didn't mean to hurt you. You didn't tell me that you had marriage with me in mind. You have prayed to the Lord. Could we say that this is God's answer to your prayer? Who knows?" I asked rhetorically, adding, "I had no clue that you were having a novena. I would have joined you in the prayer." She stared at me and tried to blink her tears back. Then she sighed and said, "So you are waiting for me to say it to you? I have been here with you for over three years, but you never said 'I love you' to me." She blinked at me in a scornful manner and turned her head away. She wiped her tears away with the back of her left hand.

Who can quench the fire that the Lord lit in my heart? My vocation is from above and my response is an unwavering, definitive yes. No sentiment can reverse it. No emotion can move it. I will not compromise it to any passing alternative. I have decided to give up the beautiful gift of conjugal love for the sake of the kingdom of God. I tried to console her, but it was too early. The wound was still fresh. She needed some time to heal. Her emotion was running high; she needed some time to calm down. She wished I could change my mind. And so she argued, "Holy orders is a sacrament as well as marriage. Each of them is a holy path to paradise. We can live together and still serve the Lord and his church." "You are right, dear Uredi. Remember that the two sacraments are different callings. The Lord calls each person to a given vocation; some to married life and some to consecrated life. When one discovers his or her calling, one is expected to say 'yes,' responding with joy and resignation to God's will. I would have loved to marry you if it was good to escape from God and turn down his invitation for the vocation. Knowing how you loved the Lord, I trust that you would not want me to rob God of his chosen instrument for the mission. Pray for me and accept me as your brother and friend." She stood and left.

I called her on the phone a couple of days later. She answered, thinking that I had changed my mind for her. No, I called to bid her goodbye. She hung up the phone on me, never said a word to me. I could imagine the deep wound in her heart. I didn't want the sentiment to overwhelm me. I commended her to the loving Lord and set my heart on the sacred mission. We lost contact for a long time. Today she is happily married and I have been chosen, consecrated, and set apart for Christ forever. "Some are incapable of marriage because they were born so; some, because they were made so by others; some, because they have renounced marriage for the sake of the kingdom of heaven. Whoever can accept this ought to accept it" (Mt 19:12).

## The Accuser and the Advocate

During our graduation, I received a scholarship award for moral excellence. Certainly I was not the best behaved among all the hundreds of students graduating that year. God rather graced me with the award to challenge me to keep faith with him. Upon my graduation, I was offered a provisional job in the university. I was initially uninterested to accept it. But after some consideration, I ultimately took up the job. A few months later, in response to my application, I was invited to study as a seminarian for an archdiocese in the New World. My travel was hampered by the difficulty I had in securing a visa. I went to the consulate a number of times, but each time the authority denied me a visa. I had no doubt that the Lord was calling me for a special mission, even though the prospect seemed bleak at that moment. I anticipated that hardship, disappointment, and trials were facing me along the way. I kept waiting patiently for the Lord. I kept persevering. I kept trusting in his unfailing promises, for I believed that I needed "endurance to do the will of God and receive what he has promised" (Heb 10:36).

During the bleak moment, a lot of advice came from my friends and acquaintances. Some wanted to fix the problem for me. In trying to do so, they ignorantly gave the wrong advice. They are not to be blamed anyway.

Without the illumination of the Spirit, one cannot understand divine wisdom and the paradox of Christian life. How could one comprehend the mystery of the necessity of the cross in discipleship, that to be free in the Savior one must be his slave, that to be alive one must be prepared to die, that to share in Christ's peace one must engage in spiritual warfare, that to gain lasting treasure one must be disposed to lose the temporal one, that to win one must allow oneself to be defeated, that to succeed one must be ready to face failure, that to rise up a fall is inevitable, that to be elevated one must be prepared to be humiliated. Jesus Christ taught me how to live. His life on earth was a paradox par excellence. He took upon himself a human body so as to enable the human race to share in his divine life. The Lord chose to be poor in order to enrich me with his treasures of grace. He carried the cross so as to remove my curses. He was humiliated so as to elevate me to the dignity of an heir of the kingdom. He fell several times under the weight of the cross so as to raise me up to himself. He was crucified to set me free. He died to destroy death forever and win life for me. Without the eyes of faith, one will see and judge things based on one's personal value judgment, feelings, emotions, and rationality. Think of St. Peter who impulsively wanted to discourage the Lord against the mission of the cross. (cf. Mat 16:22). He did not speak in accord with the holy will of God. Without knowing it, Peter's words were in line with the will of the adversary, the opposing spirit.

Some of my friends saw an enormous cross in my way and wanted to talk me out of it. They didn't see the Christ of the cross. They were oblivious of God's plans for my life. Some advised me to change my mind against the mission. Some said that the disappointments were a sign that God did not call me. The more they tried to dissuade me, the more the desire burned in me. They were not able to convince me to give up. As time went on, through prayer and movement of the Spirit, I came to discover that some of the words I received and some of the thoughts that popped up in my mind were from the negative spirit.

You know that the old serpent takes advantage of the limited human vision and wisdom to sneak in with his deception. Remember the old serpent entered the "garden" with his falsehood and deception. He urged Adam and Eve to stray from the path of life. The father of lies came into the garden of many hearts to present reasons why I should discontinue my aspirations for religious life. The false spirit argued that I had been disappointed several times, but the Spirit of Truth rebuked him and declared that I was disappointed in order to be appointed. The liar contended that all my disappointment was a sign that I was not called, but the voice of the Lord who calls resonated, lambasting the enemy that all the trials in my life were signs that I was called. The accuser said that I was rejected because I was not qualified, arguing that priesthood is for those who are more intelligent, smarter, and more creative than I am. But the blessed advocate vouched that I had been chosen to be qualified. The fiendish voice howled that I was not chosen because I was a sinner. The Spirit interceded that the Blood of the Lamb was poured out to purify me. The enemy said it was better for me to have my own children. The Spirit answered that the Lord had made me a spiritual father of many children. The false spirit asserted that I could do better in another occupation than being a priest, but the Spirit of Truth assured me that the call was not a plan I had for myself. Rather, it was a call from the master of the sacred vineyard. It was the Lord of vocation who chose me from the womb to be his instrument for the mission of bringing his love to the poor. Again, the spirit of despair whispered that it was better to lose all hope, because it was impossible to get there. The Spirit of Hope promised me that my future had been blessed, urging me to hold firm to hope, for time and age is subject to God. "Everything is possible to one who has faith" (Mar 9: 23). The liar said, "If you don't get what you want in this last chance, you are just a failure." The Prince of Peace said to me, "My son, I'm the master of time. Rejoice at all times. Wait for my time. I'll do it in my time." The fiend said that there were already enough workers in the vineyard, that the vocation is outmoded, and many who realized the trends of modernity have left the priesthood. The master of the vineyard said that laborers were few, and those who endure to the end will receive the crown of glory. The word of the serpent stated, "You are running short of time! You are getting old. Priesthood is more enjoyable in youthful age. Get the desire off your head. Forget it, and find something better to do with your life, something else that can give you pleasure and joy. Be useful for yourself and enjoy your youth, for tomorrow we die." The word of the Spirit of Truth came, "You are getting close to the appointed time. Do not relent. Prepare for the great mission to which the Lord has called you. Love the Lord above all things.

It is in accepting your vocation faithfully and joyfully that you will find true peace and joy."

## Dad's Death

It was during my final year's examinations in university. I got word from home that Papa was ill. That weekend, I hurriedly set out for home to see him. When I arrived, Papa was lying in bed critically sick. I went into his room and threw my arms around him. His body temperature was high. I felt apprehensive because his health was apparently failing him. I called him with deep emotion, "Papa!" He was weak to respond, and his voice was fading away. Papa had always tried not to be the cause of anything that would upset us. This time, he could not cover up the seriousness of his sickness. He made an effort to raise his feeble arm to stroke my face. He was drained of energy to do so. He was severely hurting all over his body. I helped him to raise his arm around my shoulder.

He gently stroked my neck and said, "Clay my son, why did you leave your studies to be here?" "Because you are not well, Papa," I answered. He sighed and said, "Oh, it is not too serious. You shouldn't have troubled yourself to be here. Go and find something to eat in the kitchen." I knew Papa was just trying to console my distressed mind. Tears fogged my eyes and my nose started running. I tried to sniff back the mucus in my nose. "How can I have an appetite to eat while you yourself have not eaten since last night?" I sobbed. He sighed and said, "Do not worry about me, my son. I'll be all right. Put your trust in the Lord." I replied, "I can't help worrying about you, Papa. I hurt because you are hurting; I want you to get well soon."

I was still standing by Papa's bed when my two older brothers arrived from the city. "Papa, we have come to take you to the hospital," one of my brothers said. Papa seemed to know very well that his end was near. "Oh, no, no! I'm not going to any hospital," Papa objected. All the members of my family who were present that day urged Papa to go to the hospital. "I have told you that there is no need to go to the hospital, but if you insist that I go, then do me a favor and summon the family members here. I would like to speak to you before leaving for the hospital," Papa requested. I made haste and called together all our family members and relatives who were available that day. "Papa, everyone is here," I said. He signaled that I help him sit on the bed. I sat by his side, holding him with one arm to help him from falling.

Papa cleared his voice and slowly began his stirring "sermon," punctuating his words with a sigh and silence. "When one goes to the hospital, two things are involved: either the person comes back alive or the person comes back dead. In any case, people of faith are ever open to accept whatever God wills. You want me to go to the hospital, but I would have preferred to stay back. Well, if I come back alive, praise God. If I come back dead, praise God also. Those who trust in God are not overwhelmed by fear of the unknown. In all things, we ought to give glory to God. I beg you, learn to forgive one another. Remember always to live in peace. Live in love, work and dine with love. Be quick to forgive anyone that offends you. Put your trust in God. I'll say it again, be ready to welcome any situations with joy and resignation to God." Turning to me, Papa said, "Clay, my son, God has a special plan for you. Keep your faith alive. The Lord will never fail you."

Papa also spoke to some other individual members of my family. As Papa addressed us, some of my family members were in tears. "Papa, I don't know the meaning of these strange words of yours. Is something going to happen to you?" my sister sobbed her question. Papa didn't respond to that question.

My brother and I helped to dress Papa up. We drove to the city hospital. We arrived there late at night. My brothers returned to their homes in the city while I stayed back to take care of him. I stood by Papa's side praying my rosary. Now and then, I stroked his hand to soothe his pain. Papa sighed and shook his head. He muttered and gurgled as he tried to say something to me. I could not understand what he was saying. I was sure he was very worried about me. I had spent the whole night standing beside him. I thought he was trying to ask me to sit down and have some rest. "Do not worry for me, Papa. I am good! I am praying for you," I comforted him.

Before the doctor could see him that night, his breathing had become seriously strained. He was terribly weak. As I listened, it was as though his breath was echoing, "Now . . . ready . . . going . . . now ready . . . going!" Perhaps his breath was singing the music of summons to eternity. I believed that the angels were at the gate ready to open the gate of everlasting life for him. The heavens were resounding with joyful welcome songs of the saints in glory. Our blessed Lord was ready to embrace him, to guide him with the mantle of eternal peace of paradise. Papa was placed on a respirator to help him breathe.

At exactly 7:00 a.m., I stepped out of the room to brush my teeth and clean my face. When I got back, I could no more hear the sound of Papa's breathing. He was lying motionless with a sort of serene look on his face. "Has he fallen asleep?" I wondered. I touched him and discovered that there was no sign of life in him. He had passed in peace to paradise! Ah, just a few seconds after I left the room, death swooped swiftly upon him like a bird of prey and snatched him away. Papa was waiting for me to step out of the room. Like a flash, Papa's spirit flew back to his Creator! I held my gaze steadily upon Papa's lifeless body. I was overwhelmed with sorrow. I put my arms over my head in great agony. I cried, "Papa, you have played tricks on me! You had waited for me to step out from you so that you would breathe your last." I wept bitterly that morning. I called to mind Papa's words to us before we left for the hospital. I remembered particularly his words that we should be ready to surrender to God's will in all situations. I had no doubt that Papa had gone to the Lord. When I reached home that day, I leaned on the wall of our house and gazed into space. Then I began to pour out my heart to the Lord, "Lord, you know that I love Papa, yet I know you love him more than I do. I love him not so much because he was my father as that he was a treasure to the family. Papa's heart was full of love. You are love. A heart that is filled with you is a heart of lasting treasure. Now the words of St. Paul make more meaning to me: '[W]e hold this treasure in earthen vessels . . .' (2Cor 4:7). Alas, this precious pot that holds the treasure has been broken, and you have taken away your treasure. Papa has passed to life. He is not dead! That which is lost in your care is that which is truly gained. Papa's soul is in your safekeeping, and I hope to meet him again in the holy city, the treasury of an unending life and happiness. Lord, may you grant Papa eternal rest."

Papa was my model. He was such a humble, generous, faithful, and devout Christian. I missed Papa's humor, his wise counsel and encouragement, and his great artistic gift. I loved to watch him work on wood with his sculptural skill. I missed Papa's deep affection for the family, his unique way of bringing the family together. I missed his loving smile, warm embrace, his companionship, the melody of the flute that he used to play, his exciting whistling, his folktales and histories which I didn't grow tired listening to. Papa taught us with the language of love. He didn't only teach us the faith, he also witnessed to it by his exemplary life. He proclaimed Christ to people and also bore the heart of Christ. He spoke about justice, lived it out and stood for it.

Soon after Papa's death, we held a Christian wake. After the funeral Mass, the family bade Papa farewell as his body was lowered into the grave. Some of my family members were given a shovel to throw dirt into Papa's grave. Who will not mourn when someone so dear to him dies? I knew I would miss my beloved papa for the rest of my life. But the hope of being with him on the last day radiated deep within my heart. Papa was a great support to me, especially in my vocation. I wish he was alive to celebrate with us the fulfillment of the vocation. Papa had no birth certificate. The older folks estimated and put his age at eighty. I bade goodnight to my loving father until the daybreak of our eternal glory, the resurrection morning when we will meet again to part no more.

## The Appointed Time

After my graduation from the university, days went by speedily. Months flew by quickly, and years passed away swiftly. My desire to the priesthood was not yet realized. I was, however, hopeful that one day the Lord would set me en route to my vocation proper. Each day the Spirit whispered within me that the Lord was leading me somewhere. But I didn't know where he was leading me and when it would be. Some days I couldn't feel the consolation of Christ's presence. I felt like one in a long dark tunnel without any glimmer of light at the end. One evening after a private retreat at the monastery, I reflected on Peter who had toiled all night long fishing without a catch. We know how Peter's story ended. At a time when a professional fisher would consider a wrong time to fish, Jesus came on the scene and ordered Peter to cast into the deep for a catch. It was then that Peter caught an incredible amount of fish. Like Peter, it seemed that I had labored fruitlessly for a long time. I had walked a long distance without getting somewhere.

One morning, I had an inkling that the appointed time was near, a time for my special divine visitation. I prayed for the grace to keep faith with the Lord, to stay pliable like soft clay in the hand of a potter. "Like clay in the hands of a potter, to be molded according to his pleasure, so are people in the hands of their Maker, to be dealt with as he decides" (Sir 33:13). The Divine Master Potter designs not by manipulation but by declaration. The Lord says it, and it comes to be. During my meditation one evening after I returned from the monastery, I began to sing the words of this song: "Lord, do the wonder in my life that I may not wander away. Continue to mold me into a precious vessel of your choice. Let the stronghold of peace and joy hold me firm in your palm. In hard times, deepen my faith in you. When I am weak, be always there to strengthen me. When I fall, pick me up and cleanse me. When my courage ebbs away, refresh and fill me with fortitude and inebriate me with joy. When I fall, pick me up and cleanse me. I pray you, joy so wonderful and peace so consoling! Come into my heart with your fresh fire. Come with your healing breath. Come and make my life resonate with the symphony of your peace and joy. Teach me to sing and dance your sweet, joyful song in all situations. Lord, continue to work in me and through me to comfort those who are sorrowful, to feed those who are starving, to bring back home those who are wandering, to light up the way to those in darkness, to lead the blind to the way, and to bring your freedom to those in chains. May your spring of life burst forth to quench the thirst of those in waterless land and to revive those who are spiritually dead. Let all people, especially the suffering relish your irresistible sweetness. Make me a humble messenger of your peace, love, and joy. Set my heart to sing you an unceasing song of joy every moment of my life."

I don't remember the tonal pattern I used in singing the song, but I knew I sang it with great passion. Two days later, I received a reply to the application I wrote to one religious community one year before. The vocations director had sent me an application form with an outline for a long essay. I completed the paperwork and mailed them to the vocations office. The vocations director and I had a series of correspondence for some time. At long last, I was invited to the community for an interview. For some reason, it didn't turn out well. Not long afterward, I met a friend who acquainted me with another community in the city. I decided to go and check it out to see if it was for me. After spending some days there, I felt greatly attracted to their spiritual orientation, their material simplicity, and evangelization apostolate. I cherished the solitude. The community was located in a quiet place that fosters communion with God. It was located in a place free from the world's noise. In that place, one could listen and hear God speak to one's heart.

After he received my application and paperwork, the vocations director invited me for a two-week retreat. In the same period of time, I also received an invitation for an interview with another religious community. My prayer partners and I offered prayers to seek God's will. Upon completing the discernment retreat, the vocation director presented me with an acceptance letter indicating that he had received me into that religious order. The appointed time had come! And so I terminated my job with the university because the zeal for the mission spurred me to do.

## Severe Seduction

I was preparing to leave home for the religious community. The lord of lust plotted to push me into a cesspool of fleshly sin. I was on a trip to a city in Nigeria. I had planned to pass the night with a friend of mine who had a home in the city. He had a fiancée whom I met during my last visit with him. My friend had told her to prepare a good dinner for me. She wanted to give me a warm welcome in her own way, so she secretly invited one of her classmates to visit with her that evening. I arrived at my friend's house before evenfall. The three of us were having good conversation in the sitting room.

Soon, her friend from university arrived. Evidently, my friend's fiancée had thought that she could give pleasure to my heart by making me eat from the "forbidden fruit." I was shaken up greatly when I saw her charming friend walk into the house. She was such an attractive girl. Her seductive outfit particularly gave her away as a girl of loose morals. She might have felt noticed and admired when her eyes caught my sidelong glance at her. I greeted her. With an invitingly amorous look, she smiled at me and responded with an appealing soft voice. My friend's fiancée introduced her to us. She stood before us trying to catch her breath, panting heavily as though she just returned from a marathon race. She wiped her neck with her handkerchief, pulled a face, and said in a low voice, "I'm a kind of tired." "I'm sorry, sweet babe. It's really a long walk," my friend empathized. He offered her a seat, "Sweet babe, please have a seat. Take some glasses of cool wine to cool off." She swaggered straight toward me and plopped down into the seat where I was sitting. "My goodness, what is she up to?" I thought. I wondered why she wanted to share a seat with me while other seats were unoccupied. I held myself firmly, pretending not to mind her. I scooted over to the right and turned my eyes to the television, as though I was very engrossed with the television program. For want of something to say, I said to my friend's fiancée, "Give her a glass of water to drink first before giving her wine." "French do not care for water when wine is available," my friend teased. We burst out laughing. Then I argued, "But she is not French. She is a Nigerian lady." "Sweet babe, don't mind Clay. Those who don't drink wine do not know the value of wine. Wine brings strength and joy to the heart, and drives away pains. Drink enough to drown the pain of the long walk," my friend joked. Then I digressed, calling their attention to the program on the television.

Before long, the girl began to play some sort of drama. Again and again she stroke over her long attachment hair and flashed her manicured, red-painted fingernails. Her miniskirt was visibly exposing her thighs, and her top wear was made in a fashion to display her bosom. Over and over again she waggled her legs. At some point, I felt unease. My vital sign was running high. The lure of fleshly desire impelled me to leer at her, and this at once gave me a twinge of conscience. I knew that great temptation is looming. The lure of the eyes and the pull of passion were becoming strong. Unless I stayed awake in spirit, I would surely fall into this apparent seduction. If I relied on my own power, it would cause me a deadly slide into sin.

So the Spirit whispered in my heart to escape from the occasion of sin. I excused myself and went to a hidden end of the property and spent some time there in prayer. I prayed for the grace of the moment and listened to what the Lord would say to me. His words echoed in my heart, reminding me that my body is a temple of the Holy Spirit and that I had been called for a special mission. The inner voice asked me to choose to use my body not to satisfy the fallen nature, but to give glory to the Lord (cf. 1Cor 6:19–20). After that prayer, I felt the presence of grace in a more powerful way. My body became calm, the door of lust was instantly shut. I experienced deep peace within me. The Lord granted me the grace to obey the voice of conscience. Yet the war was not over.

When I returned from my prayer, I went into the room where I was assigned to sleep. I saw the girl lying on the bed in a highly seductive manner. She looked at me and beamed a deep, inviting smile. She didn't care to cover her bare body. I remembered the teacher's warning against the cunning of a harlot, "So now, children, listen to me, be attentive to the words of my mouth! Do not let your heart turn to her ways, do not go astray in her paths; For many are those she has struck down dead, numerous, those she has slain. Her house is a highway to Sheol, leading down into the chambers of death" (Prov 7:24–27). I recalled Samson and his mistress Delila. She disguised herself as a friend, but was actually ready to give Samson a venomous kiss. Grace hastened my heart to excuse myself. I got out of the room. I could hear within me two voices. The spirit of impurity was urging me to enjoy the forbidden apple while the Spirit of the Lord was inviting me to stay pure with Christ. I tried to reach my friend to let him know about this, but he and his girlfriend had already locked themselves in. I got one thin mattress from the room and used it to make a bed in the living room. I covered myself with a blanket. Sleep escaped from my eyes. The voice of the old serpent kept coming to me, but the power of God was with me. The father of all lies said, "No one will know, go and make love with her." The voice of conscience said, "God sees you, you can't hide from him. Do not defile yourself." The voice of the tempter came to me as it did in the Garden of Eden, "Enjoy yourself and eat from this 'apple.' Tomorrow you may go for confession. It won't change you. You will still remain who you are." The Spirit of the Lord said, "You defile the temple of the Holy Spirit if you give in to the lust of the flesh. Beware, this pleasure may ruin your life and cause you lifelong regret and agony. Do not listen to the voice of the negative spirit." I clung to one of the chairs in the sitting room, rebuking the voice of the enemy of truth. Later that night, I fell asleep.

When I woke up, it was already morning. I praised God who saved me from the temptation. I realized how weak I was. Were it not for the power of his grace, I would have fallen headlong into the mire of impurity. I had time to speak with the girl that morning. She was still lying on the bed when I entered the room. Sitting on a chair near her bed, I called her, but she feigned sleep. I called her the third time, and she responded in a soft voice without looking at me. I pleaded with her to sit down for a chat. I said to her:

When I first saw you yesterday, your beauty blew me away. Yet, I wondered whether you really realize how stunning you are, how God adorned you with such a dazzling natural glamour.

You are beautiful, not necessarily because of your attractive appearance, but because of your identity as a daughter of God. The Lord created you in a wonderful way and made your body to be His **sacred** temple. St. Paul teaches us that our body is a temple of the Holy Spirit (cf. 1 Cor 6: 19). What is more worthy of esteem than a sanctuary of God? Are we not supposed to treasure what is precious? Shouldn't we treat with reverence what belongs to God?

Our beauty shines out more brilliantly when we seek to love and serve God with all our whole self: soul, heart, mind, and body. Think about this: in fifty years to come, your radiant body and mine will not remain the same; the "incision" of age will visibly dim our bodily beauty; even so, if we fear God, if we love with our whole heart and obey His commands, He will robe us with the garment of unfading beauty.

God wants us to take care of our body and soul and keep them holy for His glory. To keep the body pure is to revere the temple of God which we have become by grace; to revere it is to appreciate its beauty; to appreciate its beauty is to recognize our dignity as children of God. When we make room for the Lord and keep our body pure, we breathe in inner peace and joy of his divine presence in our lives.

We don't want to separate any part of our body from our spirituality. We don't want to seek to gratify the desires of the flesh in a manner contrary to our call to holiness.

The Lord gives us our sexuality for some purpose: so that when we get married, we may participate in His ongoing work of bringing new lives to the world; and also so that we may express our love by sharing the gift of our body with our spouse to deepen and strengthen our intimate bond.

You and I are not married. If we do something that is supposed to be exclusive and proper for spouses, we are cheating ourselves. Such an act will deface the luster of our beauty; it will make us ugly on the inside. The pleasure which we may feel in doing such a sinful act will swiftly fly away leaving our hearts miserably bitter and broken. Surely, it does not profit us to indulge in the fun of it now and afterward suffer a life-time internal pressure and torture.

Because of promiscuous life, some have been gripped with guilt, devastated with addiction, ravaged with rage, crippled with confusion, bedeviled with despair, and afflicted with the feelings of emptiness, low self-worth, and insecurity. Some people have lived to regret their unholy sexual behavior because it did not give them the peace and joy for which they yearned. Some are seriously hurting because in their lack of self-control, they contracted deadly sexually transmitted diseases. Still, some have sought to destroy themselves or other person's life, for they are wracked with severe emotional pains of unplanned pregnancy.

Worst of all, if we make love outside marriage, we act against the Lord's command of chastity. Unchaste life stains the splendor of our soul; it breaks apart the harmony and beauty of the gift of the human sexuality. If I sleep with you, it means that I don't love you; it means that I'm acting out of lust rather than love. To do such a thing amounts to trashing a treasure, defiling a temple, and staining the beauty of our body. You are not a "sexual object" for me to use to satisfy my carnal desire. No, you are an awesome daughter of Christ, and I should treat you with genuine respect and love which you deserve.

I would encourage you to save your sexuality for your spouse and use it to the glory of God. The "love of your life" deserves a gift of love, a gift of your whole self. Who would want to give to his or her beloved a broken and unwholesome gift?

Anyway, I know that God is merciful. The outpouring of His grace is ever powerful and ever overflowing in our lives. No matter how far we may have fallen down the scale of morality, no matter the degree of our brokenness, the Lord is ready to accept us as we are, if only we can turn away from the way of the world and turn to him. If we can raise our hearts and cry out to him to save us, the Lord will hear and lift us up from the sludge of sin; He will heal any part of us that is broken and make us whole again, so that we may radiate with the enduring beauty that brings a lasting joy.

The girl listened to me, casting her head down in shame and self-pity. I could see tears flowing down her cheeks as I talked about our Christian call to decency and purity. When I said bye to her that morning, she said to me in tears, "Thank you, pray for me." I was happy that I planted a seed in her; hopefully, God would take care of the growth.

I prayed my prayer: Lord, I believe you died and resurrected that I might have life to the full. I believe you live within me each day in all of your resurrected life and life-giving power. I believe by the power of your resurrection you have given us the grace to triumph over sin, adversities, sickness, pain, and the darts of the evil one. No matter how hard life may be, may I live daily in the joy and power of your resurrection, awaiting the glorious morning when the perfect joyous life you promised us will break forth for all eternity. Amen.

# The Beginning of the End

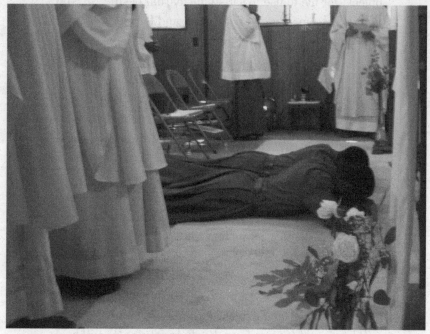

Br. Clay with his religious brother lying prostrate on the day of
his profession of Vows; he has emptied himself of all but total
and perpetual self-oblation to the Divine Master Potter.

In June of that blessed year, I entered a religious order. We were
eleven men in the batch. The initial formation period was two years: one
year postulancy, and one year novitiate. Upon completing the two years,
the candidates proceeded to the seminary for onward formation to the
priesthood. The general life in the community was very rigorous and
austere. We received intense and intensive formation in religious and
monastic spirituality, with strong emphasis on the evangelical counsels:
poverty, chastity, and obedience. We worked vigorously in manual labor.
We cooked our food and hewed firewood for cooking. We worked hard on
our farm to support our meager food budget. We cut grass, built roads, dug
trenches for construction, carried bricks on our heads to building sites to
cut down the high costs of construction. We fetched water from springs and
sometimes from the public water system in the village. We visited homes
to share the good news to the villagers.

Each day, we arose by 4:15 a.m. We spent long hours in prayer and spiritual exercises. We kept no personal fund or bank account. Our hermitages were very small and the rooms were stark, with a few simple items we needed. We slept on wooden tables. Our food was simple and sometimes monotonous, insipid, and insufficient. We were allowed to visit our homes once a year, spending not more than two days with our families. Notwithstanding the demand of daily sacrifice in the life, I embraced the formation process with joyful zeal and passion. I was involved in the community life, doing all that I needed to do with the spirit of self-giving love. How true it is that love makes any sacrifice light! My unfading love for the vocation and my zeal for the Gospel urged me on. When our two years of initial formation program were nearing their end, we were looking forward to beginning our studies in the seminary. But providence had its own plan.

One fateful evening, just a day after our community's central chapter was held, our community bell began to toll. We had no idea that it would be a bell of startling, unpleasant news. It was usually our traditional signal bell for meeting, class, meal, and prayer. Given the time of the day, we thought it was the time for catechism class. All the brothers in the novitiate unsuspectingly grabbed their notebooks and writing materials and hastened to the conference hall. Beginning his address, our superior cleared his voice and then hesitated a little bit. He looked downward, fixing his gaze on the floor for a while. It was puzzling silence to us. It surely signaled an unpleasant atmosphere. Everyone was calm and still. No one talked or moved unnecessarily when the superior was present. We were kept in suspense, wondering what it was that seemed hard for him to speak about. We sat silently, anxiously awaiting to hear what he would say to us. I can still see how we sat there quiet and attentive like disciples who listened to the instructions of their rabbi.

After a long pause, our superior started out his sermon: "You know that religious life is a sacrificial life. How much more so ours with the tonalities of victimhood and childlikeness. We want to have ample time for proper discernment and formation. When one properly discerns his vocation in life, one embraces it happily even in all adverse situations. One will be confident to face any challenges in the vocation journey. The more one loves his vocation, the more one has the joy and enthusiasm to live the life no matter what. Of course, none of us were born into this life. We need to learn to grow in the spirituality of the life. Personally, I have been in the community for nearly twenty years. I must confess that it has never been an easy journey. I need the grace of God to press on daily, to carry out its daily demand of self-giving and self-sacrifice. I have said this before, and I'll repeat it: religious life is a lifetime commitment, and thus, there is no need for hurrying, unless one has some ulterior motive. In the beginning of our foundation in this country, we had some brothers who came with the intention to use our community as a stepping stone to priesthood. Our primary call in this life is not priesthood but religious life. Let it sink into your minds: we are not here simply to become priests. Rather, we are primarily here to become religious, to pursue holiness, to live out our charism. We have to begin right now to form good religious habits that will form our character as religious tomorrow. If we don't get this now, we'll miss the whole point of our call in this community. I assume that you all have willingly chosen this life. It is my hope that you will not be agitated by any decision of the central chapter insofar as they are meant for our common good, for the good of our community and for your own spiritual interests. What I am about to make known to you may be 'good news' to some and 'bad news' to some others. It will be good news to those who are truly called in this life, and bad news to those who have their own personal agenda that has nothing to do with genuine interest for our religious community. Now here is the news: our central chapter has decided that from this time forth, the initial formation will be three years, and this takes immediate effect. This means that those of you who are in their second year will have one more year to complete their initial formation before they proceed to seminary studies. We are not sending any group to the seminary until next year. I hope this is clear to all of you. If you have any questions or comments, feel free to ask now."

The news banged in our ears like a bombshell. The hall became restive as a turbulent sea. Almost spontaneously, all of us turned our heads and cast a look at one another in dismay. Some murmured. Some muttered. Some changed their seats. "Is this a dream?" I shook my head to see if I could jolt from it. Alas, it was not a dream. It was reality! One of the brothers raised his hand to air his view. "Before our admission, we were told that the initial formation was two years, and now we are at the verge of completing our novitiate, hoping to be in seminary this year. It doesn't sound right to begin this new extended period of initial formation with our batch." Another brother said, "Frankly speaking, I can't continue in this life if the community adds another year for us. I am ready to quit." Each of us in turn presented reasons why we should be allowed to go ahead to seminary. The judge had hit the gavel. The decision had been made. The authority was not open to change it.

We had to make our individual decision in that regard, whether to stay with the community or to drop out. It was really a time of violent storm in our vocation voyage. More than half of our number would be snatched away by the storm. By the grace of God, I was one of the two that the tempest could not throw overboard. The Lord opened my inner eyes to see the star leading me to the way. Despite the challenges, I was confident that I was on the right track to the vocation journey. The raging vocation wave was serving its purpose, tossing me safely to the shore of God's mission field. We went along through the remaining year pretty well. At the end of the three-year initial formation, I took my vows and received the habit and the constitution of the community.

Br. Clay walks to the reception hall after making his Vows, joyfully contemplating the precious gift of his vocation. "I keep the Lord always before me; because He is at my right hand, I shall not be moved" (Psa 16:8).

# The Tick-tock in the Solitude

(Br. Clay in the Solitude). Lord, you have drawn me away from the deafening world's noise. You have invited me into the woods for a heart-to-heart with you. Speak, Lord, for my ears are attentive to your word. I can hear you speak directly to my heart. I can hear you speak your glory loud and clear through your creation. I hear the symphony of the heavenly bodies (the moon, the stars, the sun, and the planets) in cosmic worship dance to you, the Maker. I hear the orchestra of the trees declaring your glory. I hear the melody of the birds singing praise to you; I hear the cascading spring water intimating your grace flowing into a thirsty soul.

The Lord never ceases to draw me closer to his sacred heart. His gentle whisper constantly echoes in the depth of my being. The Lord has spoken to me in various ways. He speaks to me through nature. As the Psalmist says, all creation is telling the glory of the Creator (Psalm 19:1). God speaks to me through my fellow human beings, through the Bible, and through the Church, "the pillar and foundation of truth" (1 Tim 3:15). I can hear and understand what the Lord says to me, especially in a place that is peaceful and quiet. The religious community was located in a quiet setting, in a place hidden from the world's noise. The solitude brings a silent spiritual climate that fosters contemplation. It was a place naturally decorated with luxuriant greenery. The lush palm trees which provided home for myriads of birds fascinated many who came to the community. Once in a while, I listened and prayed along with the sounds of the birds as they chirped with varying melody, as though they were in adoration to the Divine Master Potter. Besides the welcomed nature's intermittent interruption of the solitude's quietude, I heard certain sacred "noise" that awakened my consciousness of time. The other evening, I was deeply immersed in meditation in the hush of the solitude's chapel. Soon, a noise intermittently chimed in: "*tick-tock, tick-tock, tick-tock . . .*" The sound went on and on. What was making the sound? I wondered. I opened my eyes to see if I could find the cause of the noise. Ah, it was the ticking of a clock hung above the front door of the chapel. "Surely it is saying something to me about time," I thought. "Oh yeah, time has meaning for us pilgrims. It is a gift to be treasured and used well," I affirmed. In this light, I tried to read meaning out of the ordinary ticking of the clock. When I felt distracted by this thought, I made an effort to return to meditation. At an instant, another thought sprang to my mind: the clock was telling me "now's time." It was reminding me that now is the right time to seek God in spirit and in truth. Each passing second, each passing hour, day, or year is a grace and warning to me. I should cherish and sanctify each time with good works and self-giving love. Having affirmed it, I began to meditate along with the sound of the clock. The *tick-tock* melody formed a background and gave me a mantra for meditation: now is the time. Now is the time for grace, a time to give all in order to have all.

## The Flickering Light

In the beginning of my religious life, one of my challenging experiences was how to stay recollected in my holy hour. In those days, I struggled a lot with distractions, wandering thoughts. This was primarily because I was not used to silent prayer. I was accustomed to vocalizing my prayer. One spiritual master suggested that I had to discover what worked best for me in fostering the spirit of recollection and meditation. He counseled that I train my sense to focus on Christ, offering to him any thoughts that popped up in my mind during prayer. This worked well for me. When any thoughts came into my mind during my holy hour, I channeled them to the Divine Master Potter to purify them and make them beneficial for my spiritual life.

One evening while praying in the chapel I knelt and closed my eyes firmly. At a certain point, I opened my eyes and gazed at the tabernacle. The sanctuary light caught my attention. It was flickering rapidly. It was burning itself out in a torrent of joy in the divine presence, I thought. I didn't want the light to distract me. But wait a minute, the Spirit moved me to reflect on the significance of the flickering light. I opened my eyes widely, gazing more closely at the sanctuary light. Then I prayed along with its rhythm. As I folded my arms around my chest, another thing drew my attention. It was my pulsating heart that was moving my arms up and down. Hark! This too was saying something to me. Still holding my gaze at the tabernacle, I knelt still and placed my palm against my chest to feel my heartbeat. The beat of my heart was like harmonizing with the flickering light, gently resounding, "Ho-ly . . . ho-ly . . . ho-ly . . ." As I pondered the awesome beat of my heart and the flickering light, I recalled the Psalmist who says that his heart leaps for joy because the Lord is his strength and shield (cf. Psalm 28:7). My heart was leaping for joy. Within a few minutes, the flame started flickering more rapidly and finally went out completely. I thought that human life, like the flickering candlelight, is consumed bit by bit each passing hour. My life burns away gradually. As the last smoke from the candlelight billowed up into the sky, so will my flame, the breath of life, take its leave from my mortal body one day and return to its Maker. My life is created to become a living flame that constantly burns itself out with love in the presence of the Lord. When the last day will come, my life will be completely consumed into the divine life. And then, I'll fly back into the realm of infinite love, into the abode of eternal life.

# The Alligator and the Allegation

It was around 9:00 p.m. Our water system in the community was bad. We ran out of water. Some of the brothers and I gathered some containers and drove to the spring water to fetch water. The spring was about two kilometers away from the community. It was in the woods on the east side of the village. The village had no electricity but we held our flashlights. We drove down to the area. Our brother driver pulled up to the curb of the bushy narrow path. Some of the brothers were afraid of the intense darkness, thinking that dangerous reptiles like snakes might be lurking in the reeds. I led the brothers as we walked about one hundred feet to the rock spring. We made sure we pointed the light well to see that the path was safe to place our feet.

Reaching the fountain, I pointed the flashlight and saw a big alligator on the foot of the rock. The alligator was taking a shower in the spring water, with her toothy jaws wide open. I thought it was a crocodile but a close look revealed her true features that marked the difference. Scared, I called out to the brothers. Some of them who were afraid ran back to the van. Some rushed to see the alligator for themselves. We had nothing to kill it. I kept watching it while the brothers searched for clubs and rocks. Within seconds, three brothers had grabbed heavy sticks and wood planks. Without waiting, we started to pound the alligator with the clubs like an angry mob. It was as though we were striking on a rock. The alligator didn't run. It was flinging her bladelike tail to strike back at us. Each time, the brothers showed their agility, dodging the sharp tail. For several minutes we kept hitting the alligator on the head and the tough body. When it became still, we smashed the head to make sure it was dead. We took it home and prepared it to serve for dinner. It was delicious.

One of the brothers teased me, saying that I had broken the seventh commandment, "Thou shalt not kill." I knew that even though the law against killing is about human beings, we were not supposed to treat God's creation with cruelty but with respect. However, God made animals and gave them to us to serve our needs. He tells us to "kill and eat" (Acts 10:13). I killed the alligator not for fun but for food. This was by no means sinful. I keep in mind my stewardship of the earth and its resources. At the last day, I'll give an account of how I served the Lord with what he entrusted to my care. I always give thanks to the Lord for the gift of the resources of the earth, and I want to respectfully use them not for selfish interest but rather in a way that will benefit my fellow human beings.

## Knocking on the Nub

My former religious community was known for its evangelization apostolate. In line with Christ's commission to reach out to others, we met people right at their homes. We knocked on people's doors to share with them the Gospel of love and of joyful life. As our founder once described it, we knocked on hearts as we sought to help them discover Christ's peace and the consolation of his presence.

I remember an old man we met in the course of our evangelization work in Nigeria. He implored us to pray with his family. His wife was in great distress. She had suffered a heart attack. The woman came into the sitting room, gloomy, and with tears in her eyes. Sitting on a side chair, the woman wiped her tears with a piece of cloth wrapped around her waist. She began to share with us her moving story. We empathized and spoke the word of God to the family. She was heartened up, appreciating that Christ was present in their family and in their lives. After praying, she said she felt like a heavy load was lifted off her heart.

In the course of the apostolate, we met several persons who asked us to pray with their families. That was encouraging to me to learn that despite the challenges of daily living people still strongly trust that Christ is the answer to their every need. I believed that the Divine Master Potter visited them to wipe all tears away from their eyes. God is the true peace that we seek in life. Without him, nothing can make meaning to us. The Lord is our happiness and our peace. He alone can heal the hurting world. "[I]t was our pain that he bore, our sufferings he endured. We thought of him as stricken, struck down by God and afflicted, but he was pierced for our sins, crushed for our iniquity. He bore the punishment that makes us whole, by his wounds we were healed" (Isa 53:4–5).

## The Cock Crow

The bell for the morning prayer went off at 7:15 a.m. The community gathered in the chapel. Soon after we started chanting the Psalms, a big red rooster (cock) came directly to the front door of the chapel and began to crow repeatedly. I wondered what had come over the cock. He crowed again and again, but no one made any effort to chase it out. As if it was not enough, the cock began to emit a cackling sound. Feeling disgusted, two brothers and I got up to chase out the cock. As soon as he saw us approaching the door, the cock ran away. Shortly after we returned to the chapel, he came back to the door and began crowing once again. It was as though he was determined to create a great distraction for us. We could not help smiling as we chant the Psalms. I got up and went to the door the second time. He heard my footsteps and escaped before I got there. I stayed at the door for some time to keep him from coming back. I watched as he roamed about the corner of the chapel waiting for me to go in.

During our lunch that day, we discussed the rooster drama. Some of us had different views about it. One of the brothers remarked that it was a spirit of distraction that entered the rooster. Another brother reasoned that the rooster was interested in worshipping the Lord with us. I looked at it as revealing something to me. God speaks to us in various ways. In the Bible we find that God can use animals to reveal certain things to us. Balaam's donkey shrank against the wall when it saw the angel of the Lord (cf. Num 22:25). In the book of Daniel, all animals were invited to praise the Lord (cf. Dan 3:81). The lions could not kill Daniel because the power of God acted upon them (cf. Daniel 6: 22). It was a dove that communicated to Noah when the flood had receded from the surface of the earth (Gen 8:8). Job enjoins us to receive instruction from the creatures of the earth and the sea (Job 12:7–9). The word of the Lord invites me to learn wisdom from an ant that gathers and stores her food in time (Pro 6:6). Who knows, God might be speaking to me through the rooster to pray more in the spirit, to revere him unceasingly with an undivided heart and mind.

## Thoughts of the Tomb

In the religious community, it was our tradition to have spiritual readings during meal. One afternoon, while the brothers were in the refectory taking lunch, I picked up the *Imitation of Christ* to read for the community. I opened a random page in the book, and what came up was chapter 23 of Book One, which was titled "Thought of Death." The chapter begins thus, "Very quickly your life here on earth will end. Consider then how matters stand with you. A man is here today, and tomorrow he is gone . . . Be always prepared, therefore, so that death will not take you unprepared."

After lunch, one of the brothers asked me with a wry grin: "I'm wondering what made you choose the reading on death this afternoon." I let him know that it was not intentionally chosen. When we returned from house-to-house evangelization in the evening that day, we heard the sad news that a member of our community passed away suddenly. It was painful to us to lose such a beloved community member. On the following day, also during lunch, I decided to complete the reading on the "Thoughts of death." I continued from the paragraph which says, "In the morning imagine that you will not live until night; and when evening comes presume not to promise yourself the next morning. Be therefore always prepared, and live in such a manner that death may never find you unprepared." After lunch, some brothers came to me and said jokingly, "Today, you read the chapter on death again? You read it yesterday, and in the evening we were greeted with the sad news of death. Please stop reading about death so that death will stop coming to us." I tried to clarify that death didn't come to our member because we read about it. Death is a reality and debt that all of us owe in this life.

The passage was reminding us of what Jesus Christ said in the Bible, that we must be prepared always for the unknown last hour of life. Death can strike any of us at any time. "No, it is not my portion," one of the brothers chimed in. "I have not finished the work that the Lord called me to do on earth," the brother added. I laughed and said to him, "You don't even know how much work the Lord wants to accomplish with you. It is for the Lord to determine the nature and the measure of what he has to do with you on earth. Your part is to offer yourself to God without reservation. It is for him to do with you as he deems fit. He alone knows when it will be over with you on earth, when he'll call you back home. You know that the Lord of life warns us to keep watch, for we do not know the time when the last hour of our lives will come (cf. Mar 13:35). We talked at length about death that afternoon.

Little did I know that the enemy's camera and his deadly darts were directed toward me. In the evening of that day, while returning from the evangelization work, we met the messengers of death on the way. Their arrow struck me but a divine hand destroyed its power and guided its movement in my body. I did not return to the community that evening until one month later. What really happened? The following is a testimony of God's amazing grace in my life.

## Ransomed from the Ravenous

By 5:30 p.m. on that fateful day, the evangelization work was over. It was fruitful and all the brothers were in good spirit. We hurried to the place where we parked our van so as to catch up with Vespers (evening prayer) at 6:00 p.m. At about 5:40 p.m., all the eleven brothers were already aboard our Mitsubishi L300 van. It was our traditional period of silence, and so all the brothers endeavored to stay recollected. Some closed their eyes and held their heads down in meditation. Some were reflecting on selected scriptural passages. Some were reading their devotional texts. Still some others prayed their rosaries. It's a fifteen-minute drive from the place of our apostolate to our community. We had hoped to arrive at the community five minutes before evening prayer. Patiently, we galloped along the potholed road. Approaching the road junction which leads to the small town where our community house is situated, some of the brothers noticed that there was a sort of stampede going on around the town.

A young man who was running away for safety recognized our van and wildly waved his hand, signaling us to turn back and take cover. We understood that something sinister was happening up front, but we were not sure what it was. For some reason, we were reluctant to stop immediately. We drove down slowly, intending to find out what the situation was. We sighted a cloud of heavy smoke going up to the sky from around the police station. Some of us feared that "big guys" (gangsters) were in town. Yet it seemed obvious that we were not their target. This notwithstanding, no right-minded person will like to stay in a war zone supposing himself or herself safe simply because he does not belong to any of the warring factions. In this light, we decided not to move forward to be on the safe side. We had barely backed up our van when one of our brothers shouted, "They are coming after us! Please! Please move fast!" Now there was already a feeling of near panic in us. Our hearts raced, our hip joints shook, our knees knocked, and our teeth chattered. Our brother driver reversed the car instantly and drove away at top speed. Reaching the crossroad, he didn't know which way to go. He speeded up the van, taking the same route from where we were returning. We looked back and saw that the big guys were already fast approaching. We broke out in a cold sweat; great fear swept through us.

Who are they? No one was sure yet. But we were convinced that they were up to no good. Their appearance and movement suggested something ominous. In a twinkling, behold, they were just a few feet behind us. All of them, not counting the drivers of their four vehicles, were pointing their guns and grenade launchers at us. It was like soldiers who caught up with their enemy. They were over twenty in number, including two women. Impelled by such frightening sight, all of us burst into ejaculatory prayers: "Blood of Jesus cover us. Mother of peace, pray for us. Archangel Michael, defend us . . ." The intensity and passion of our prayers at that moment was like the event on Pentecost. At an instant, one of the men fired a gun at our vehicle. The heavy bullet hit our van like a volcanic eruption, ripping open its trunk. It passed through the backseats and made its way to the second row of the van's seats. Then it pierced the seat at the left edge where I was sitting. In this apparent helpless situation, our brother driver jammed the brake to bring our van to a stop. In no time, I felt a slight warm sensation around my butt. I stroked my palm against the spot. Lo and behold, my trousers were drenched with blood. "Oh, my Jesus Christ!" I screamed. My brothers saw the blood gushing out from my trousers, and they whined and shrieked more loudly.

As soon as our vehicle stopped, four fierce-looking men dashed out of their vehicles, with their hands flexing on their AK-47 guns ready to open fire. The rest of the gangsters remained in the vehicles, well armed and set against any counterattack. They were in possession of all kinds of sophisticated ammunition. The four men surrounded us, ready to open fire immediately. What stopped them from firing at us? How else would I explain it if not that the Spirit of God stiffened the triggers and held their hands from shooting? We ducked for cover; we made frantic attempt to, at least, shield our heads under the seats. "Identify yourselves!" one of them barked. Some of us shouted at the same time, "We are missionaries," using the term they would understand easily.

On hearing this, the furious men seemed to feel disappointed, like a predator who forcefully pursued an animal but after capturing it discovered that it was not its prey. They lowered their guns. One of them let out a loud sigh and yelled in a pidgin (broken) English, "Why una dey run! Una wan kill una self (why were you running? Do you want to kill yourselves)?" One of them gave a signal and they all dashed swiftly into their vehicles and drove off. Our brothers tried to catch their breath after such a horrific encounter. Seeing me in a pool of blood, one of our brothers screamed, "Brother Clay is dying! Oh god, Brother Clay! Brother Clay! Please drive fast to the hospital!" One of the brothers, who was sitting close to me, held me firmly and covered the wound with his palm to prevent further bleeding. The brothers stormed the heavens with prayer.

Up till this point we were not sure who the big guys were. "Are they a vigilante group or guerillas? Are they a rebel group? Thugs? Assassins? Gangsters?" we wondered. Because they didn't cover their faces, we didn't much suspect that they were armed robbers. The brothers were not so much concerned about knowing who they were as about saving my life. We were rushing along to the hospital without knowing that the guys stopped by a gas station along the way, just a mile ahead. We were in top speed when suddenly two of the men leapt out from the gas station and flagged down our vehicle and pointed their guns at us. "My Jesus, we have run into these guys again!" screamed one of our brothers. The gangsters mounted three grenade launchers on the roadway to scare motorists away. Two of the guys were smoking and strolling around the weapons. The other gangsters were calmly fueling their vehicles at the gas station as though they were in charge of the state. One of the guys ordered us, "Oh, you guys are pursuing us! Surrender your guns now or I blast off your heads." We felt ripples of fear pass through us. "You are wasting my time?" he threatened. One of our brothers courageously pleaded with them almost sobbingly, "Please, we have no guns. Our brother is dying from a bullet wound. We are rushing him to a hospital. Please! Please!"

The man gazed into our van and saw me writhing in pain. He saw the blood that spattered on the seat and the floor. He "pitifully" said to me, "Aboy, noting go do you (young man, nothing will happen to you)." Then he asked me to pull my feet inside the van. I was so completely drained of energy that I could not even drag my legs in. He gently helped me to move my legs inside the van. Then he closed the door of the van. The other man turned to our brother driver and demanded, "Give me the van's key." Our brother quickly handed over the bunch of keys to him. They did not want us to move ahead, perhaps because they feared that we would alert the police to ambush them. He ordered us to stay in the van until they completed their business at the gas station. I was losing much blood. I imagined the possibility of bleeding to death. I felt like death was casting its shadow upon me. I moaned and prayed, "Lord Jesus, is it your will that I die here? Save me now, Lord! Fill me with fresh blood and revive me.

My life is in your hand!" For roughly fifteen minutes, we were under the mercy of those hoodlums.

We could tell that hard drugs had dulled their minds and hardened their hearts. They were on a mission to destroy and their weapons of mass destruction were thirsty for blood. Their voices and movement alone bespoke their inner craving for bloodletting. It was really awful to witness how they threatened people's lives with death-dealing weapons. They were like ravenous lions, but the same God who shut the lions' mouths before Daniel (Dan 2:22) clogged their jaws and enfeebled their claws before us.

Up till this moment, we had not got a clear intimation of who they were. After fueling their vehicles, the group went aboard the vehicles and zoomed off. As they were about to drive off, the one who seized our keys flung it to us. We decided not to continue on the same route to avoid meeting them once again. And so we made a U-turn and continued along the road looking for a nearby hospital or clinic. We stopped at three clinics on the way, but the doctors were not available. We continued searching and praying. At some point, one of the brothers checked my vital signs to see if I would make it to a hospital. But I was still hanging in there. We drove several miles before we eventually arrived at a clinic where a doctor was available. We got there at exactly 7:00 p.m. I was rushed to the emergency section. The doctor and the nurses began to examine and treat me right away.

## The Merciless and the Merciful

"A thief comes only to steal and slaughter and destroy; I came so that they might have life and have it more abundantly" (John 10:10).

It was at the hospital that we discovered that the hooligans were armed robbers. They started out their raid from the very town where I was hospitalized. They attacked three banks. A gunfight with some security officers during the robbery left a number of persons dead and some wounded. Some who were wounded by stray bullets were rushed to different hospitals and clinics for treatment. The armed robbers lost two of their members during the shootout. They carried the bodies of their dead members at the back of their truck. The death of their two members might have so infuriated them that they opened fire on any security officers on whom they set their eyes. When they ran into the police station in the town where our community house was situated, the armed robbers opened fire, shooting indiscriminately. Providentially, the police officers who were on duty that day narrowly escaped certain death. One of the police officers was unfortunately hit by a stray bullet. It was discovered that the bullet lodged in his spinal cord. I don't know what happened to him afterward. The bandits set a police truck on fire and broke into the police cell and released all those who were in detention. When they saw us at a distance, the armed robbers thought that we were security officers who came to intercept them. They ran after us. We are thankful to the Lord who prevented them from crushing our lives with their dangerous weapons. After our encounter with them, we found in our van a finger-sized bullet which pierced through my body.

During my physical examination, the doctor discovered that the bullet bored into my right butt, pulled the ligament around my anal opening, and exited through my left butt. The doctors who examined how the bullet zigzagged its way through my body described it as enigmatic. Ah, they failed to call it by its name: miraculous! It is a miracle! The bullet obeyed the Divine Master Potter and followed the track drawn by him. "They were filled with great awe and said to one another, "Who then is this whom even wind and sea obey (Mar 4:41)?" Yes, the bullet complied with divine command and narrowly missed my vital organs. The blessed Lord is the weapon of my warfare, mighty and awesome in his works. In all situations, God always shows me that he is very involved in my life. The bullet was sent to deliver death, but the Lord of my life saved me and shielded all my delicate organs and bones from the lethal bullet. For over one month, I went through excruciating pains.

The Lord gave me the grace to share in his pain on the cross. In the first two weeks, I felt continuous intense pain from the wound. I hurt day and night, when I sat down, when I stood, when I lay down, and when I walked. I felt a little relieved when I knelt down. I imagined the pain of Job when he groaned, "At night he pierces my bones, my sinews have no rest" (Job 30:17). I was, however, blessed to have the consolation of kindhearted brothers in Christ around me. I can't forget how they tenderly sat beside my bed watching all night as the intravenous fluid in a plastic bag, which was suspended on a pole near my bed, dripped into my veins. They and the compassionate nurse were awake all night looking after me, sharing in my pain. Within one week, the doctor discovered that my wound was deteriorating. He referred me to a specialist in the local teaching hospital. I received intensive care in the hospital for two days. My wound was debrided, cutting off dead tissue from it to hasten the healing process. It was for me a painful procedure. The anesthetic injection didn't work well. After two days in the hospital, I could not stay any longer. The room was overcrowded and stinky. The bathroom and toilet were always messed up. I was very uncomfortable staying there. In compliance to my request, after two days of receiving the needed specialist treatment, I was transferred back to the former clinic where a kind and godly nun nurse dedicatedly and sacrificially took care of the wound.

God also blessed me with many goodhearted friends and caring nurses who showed me every kindness. I remember them with great affection and gratitude. Within a short time, the gaping wound saw a great improvement. After one month in the hospital, I was almost up and about. I know that the pains and sleepless nights that I experienced in those days were part of the process of molding and shaping me into a vessel of the Divine Master Potter. I believe that in him I am forever unstoppable and unconquerable. By the power of his passion and Resurrection, I will forever escape "death."

## The Why of the Wound

As I have already said, the pain of the bullet wound was not easy to bear. I remember asking God, "Why me?" The reply came instantly, "Why not you?" I accepted to carry my own cross following the Lord. One of the essential conditions the Lord gives us for becoming his disciple is carrying one's cross (cf. Mat 16:24). I prayed the Lord to teach me how to make use of my pains for my spiritual interest. I realized that to ask "how to carry the cross" rather than "why should I carry the cross" is to seek God's wisdom and guidance. I understood that the Lord would never explain to me the "why" of the cross. Even if he did, my limited mind couldn't comprehend it.

No human intellect can grasp the whole mystery of divine love, that love sometimes allows his beloved to suffer pains in order to enter deeper into the heart of love. One who suffers with the Lord of love will, at the end, enter into glory with him (Rom 8:17). It is in carrying one's cross that one enters into rest. In suffering with Christ, one finds healing, comfort, and peace. In being a slave of Christ, one gains true freedom and reigns with Christ. It is in waging war against the forces of darkness that the reign of peace bursts forth. All was working for my good. How could I help some people understand that suffering can be meaningful and redemptive if we see Christ in it? Today, I think of many people who are suffering in many ways. Who could bear his or her own pains without the grace of the Lord? In my pain, I was moved to cry out to my Divine Master Potter: "Oh, my Lord, where are you? Did you turn your back on me? Did you intend to leave me in the dark? Remember, you knew me even before you created me, before you planted me in my mother's womb.

"When I was born, my mom cuddled me, but it was you, my Divine Master Potter, who guarded and directed my development and growth. When I grew up and had to fend for myself in some ways, suffering and pain took their toll on me. Fear, distress, sorrow, and trials of life greeted me with their vicious kisses. I looked for relief, but when no voice of comfort was heard, when no soothing hand touched me, my courage started to ebb away. Help, Lord! Hold me, lest I slide down the threshold of desolation and despair. You alone are my consolation. As the darkness of this hour has cast its net on me, I call out to you, my light. Hear me. Come quickly and comfort me. Come and smear my wound with your healing balm. Come with your healing touch, with your holy embrace, and wrap your arms around me. Blow your gentle, healing breeze to cool off the heat of my pain."

Around 4:00 a.m. that morning, I kept silent to listen to the whispering of the Spirit. I could hear the Lord speaking to my heart: "My beloved son. My precious child! Be of good cheer. I am with you. See, I hold you dear in my heart. Be still. Continue to abide in me. Continue to put your trust in me. I am at work in your life. I am with you always. I'll never forsake you." At that moment, I felt a great peace within me. How true the Psalmist says that the Lord is ever near to the brokenhearted and saves those that are crushed in spirit (Ps 34:18). I knew that the Lord is ever faithful and good to me. I recalled the day that the blessed Lord saved me when the water closed over me, ready to sweep me away. I pondered all the many ways the Lord showed me that he was the Lord of my life. I claimed God's promise: "Do not fear, for I have redeemed you; I have called you by name: you are mine. When you pass through waters, I will be with you; through rivers, you shall not be swept away. When you walk through fire, you shall not be burned, nor will flames consume you. For I, the LORD, am your God, the Holy One of Israel, your savior. I give Egypt as ransom for you, Ethiopia and Seba in exchange for you. Because you are precious in my eyes and honored, and I love you, I give people in return for you and nations in exchange for your life" (Isa 43:1b–4).

# Tears of Tenderness

Each year, the brothers in the religious order were allowed to make an annual home visit and spend only two days with their families. It was about a month after visiting home that year that I was shot. I didn't let anyone in the family know of the incident until I visited home. I thought that if word got to Mama she would be very troubled. When I arrived home three months after I sustained the gun wound, I made it known to my family and relatives. It was shocking news to them; however, they praised the Lord for saving my life.

I remember what happened on my home visit earlier before I was shot. My cousin and I were having our dinner in our front room. Shortly after we started eating, Mama dragged her seat close to us. Sitting, she scratched her hair. I understood that it was her usual way of initiating a conversation. So I inquired, "Mama, what is the subject matter today?" She began to recount her strange dream about how she was waving me goodbye as I was setting out for a trip. My cousin cut in and remarked that a mother who gave her son to priesthood bade goodbye to him. My cousin turned to Mama and continued, "You have given your son to the Church. He has been consecrated and set apart for the service of Christ and his Church. You have said farewell to him. Don't expect to have him with you always. He has accepted to go wherever the Church sends him." I thought my cousin gave Mama a good interpretation of her dream. I had no idea at that time that the dream would play out in a different way.

It was exactly a month after the visit that my superior informed me of the intention of the authority of the community to reassign me from our community in Nigeria to our mother house in the New World, where I would serve the needs and evangelization apostolate of the community. That meant that I had to leave my family, country, friends, culture, language, and even traditional food for the sake of the kingdom of God. What a formidable sacrifice! I was in good spirits because I thought that it was providential and a privileged moment of missionary experience, which would, at least in the social sphere, expand the horizons of my knowledge and understanding of the peoples and cultures in that part of the world. I acknowledged that it would be grace-filled, but not without its concomitant challenges and sacrifices.

I completed the immigration paperwork. In my first application, I went to the embassy but the authority did not grant me a visa to travel. To prepare me well for the arduous journey ahead, the Divine Master Potter designed to give me a bitter foretaste of the trials that would face me in the mission. I was at the verge of reapplying for a traveling visa when I sustained the terrible bullet wound. I had to wait for three months to recuperate from the wound. When my wound healed, God opened the way for me. I was granted a visa. It was then that I visited home to let my family know about my travel. I recalled Mama's dream, which seemed to have now become a reality. Now she would say a real goodbye to me.

On the eve of my departure from home, I called my family together and said goodbye to them. Some had great expectations, seeing hope and joy. At the same time, our hearts were struck with a twinge of somberness. There were mixed emotions: the feelings of joy that comes from a fulfilled life, and the sadness that boils in the heart for missing a dearest one. However, such feelings are unavoidably part of being alive. Mama was particularly concerned about when she would see me again. I can still see her sitting on the short old wooden seat, with her arms folded and her eyes noticeably fogged with tears as she gazed at me. I knew for sure that at least five years would go by before I would see my family again. What should I say to her? As I cast my head downward, I tried to hold back my tears. But I didn't succeed doing so. Tears quickly beclouded my eyes and trickled down my cheeks. I quickly wiped my tears away with my left arm. I tried to hide my feelings in order to demonstrate my masculinity. As might be expected, I grew up within an African culture where some people believe that "real" men don't cry. My folks think that it is women who cry because they are more emotional and more tenderhearted than men. I didn't want my cousin to chide me, "Don't cry like a woman." I hung my head to avoid anyone noticing my tearful eyes. I called Mama and said to her in a low voice, "Do you recall the dream you had during my last visit? Perhaps it was a revelation of this reality. It is now the time for you to say 'goodbye' as you had in the dream. I am going for a mission for the Lord. I hope to get back to see you before long. In any case, do not forget that Papa enjoined us to always resign to comply with the will of God. God alone knows what is best for us. Trust the Lord." The encouraging words helped to inspire strength and hope in Mama. The family joined hands in prayer and each of the individuals who were present that evening gave me his or her farewell counsel and good wishes.

On the following day, I set off to return to my religious community. Mama and my little nephew walked me to the bus station at our village square. Mama carried my traveling bag on her head. My nephew carried the other bag, which contained some fruits which Mama bought for me. Mama and I walked side by side. As we walked along the roads, Mama told me some stories about the village. When we arrived at the park, I boarded the bus. Before I could wave my goodbye, Mama was already in tears again. I tried to blink back my tears, for I thought that it was time to say goodbye to move ahead for the mission!

The week before my departure to the New World was for me a time of questioning, concerns, and great uncertainty. Where am I really going? When shall I return home? I wanted to be sure that I made the right choice of leaving home? As I stepped aboard the airplane, I remembered home and friends. But a strong voice came from within: "You are on a noble mission! Do not look back!" I accepted the reality right away. I recalled the words of our blessed Lord, "Amen, I say to you, there is no one who has given up house or brothers or sisters or mother or father or children or lands for my sake and for the sake of the gospel who will not receive a hundred times more now in this present age: houses and brothers and sisters and mothers and children and lands, with persecutions, and eternal life in the age to come" Mark 10:29–30). With these reassuring words and by the grace of God, I didn't look back anymore. Joy and peace flowed from within my heart. Even though the road is rough and narrow, each time the Divine Master Potter calls me by name and says to me again and again, "I have chosen you for this mission. I have designed the way for you. Follow me! I am taking you through the narrow way to life." Yes, Lord, I have abandoned myself to you. Hold me by the hand and walk with me so that I may never grow weary. Steady my feet and guide my steps so that I may never stumble. Light my path and open my eyes so that I may never be blind to your presence wherever I go. Guard my heart and direct my mind so that I may never tire in loving you; touch my mouth and loosen my tongue so that I may never stop praising you. Oh, my Divine Master Potter, set me on fire with your love and consume my life as a savory holocaust .

## Newcomer in the New World

The journey to the New World was long. After an exhausting twelve hours in the air, the chief flight attendant asked us to prepare for landing. I was excited that I would see what the highly esteemed New World looked like. Our airplane had reduced its speed, gradually descending for landing. As I looked out from the airplane window, I could view the city constellated with electric light of all colors. The landing was scary. I thought of cases of plane crash during landing, especially in my country. I was praying my rosary, and that gave me confidence that the Lord was in control. Our plane was almost about to touch down when it abruptly veered up, back to the sky. I had no idea what was going on at that moment. I broke out in cold sweat. I felt like I was passing out. Fright quaked my knees. I looked around and saw that all the passengers were quiet and motionless. They seemed not disturbed. I didn't want them to notice that I was near panic. "Perhaps it is normal way of landing," I reasoned. I tried to hold myself together, praying in my heart. I stood up to use the restroom, but one of the flight attendants blocked me off. "Please no movement now," she ordered. I quietly went back to my seat like a kindergarten student. No one informed us of what was going on. I was upset. I could understand the fear that assailed the disciples when they faced the storm in the sea (Mt 8: 23ff). Like the disciples, the fear so blinded me that I could see only the master who was asleep. I couldn't see the unsleeping Savior. I didn't remember to keep my focus on the unfailing divine pilot, the Holy Spirit. My rapid heart rate was like an urgent appeal for help, "Wake up, Lord, we are perishing." You can see my little faith! Our plane had to perform a "go-around" for over seven minutes. At last, it hit the ground safely at 2:00 a.m. I heaved a sigh of relief. I praised the Lord for granting us a safe journey. Later, I found out that our airplane could not land immediately because the local controller did not give us clearance to land due to air traffic. It was really a horrible experience.

# The Wonderful Woods in the West

The road into the overwhelming wooded solitude
where Br. Clay was groomed for the mission.

I had arrived safely in that celebrated nation, the New World. The technological advancement was apparently evident. I could see the prosperity, the awesomeness of western civilization. I watched with fascination the stunning city, its surpassing physical grandeur. I saw the luxurious structures that dotted the city, high buildings, well-kept ornamental flowers, glittering electric lights of all colors, well-built clean streets, and flashy cars that ply to and fro uninterruptedly. It was really a new world! I didn't stay long in that glamorous city.

As you know, the spirituality of my community calls us to live with our divine spouse in a solitary setting. Before our airplane arrived, two of my brothers in the Lord came to pick me up at the airport. When I came into the waiting room, I saw them as they sat patiently waiting for me. When they saw me, the brothers sprang from their seats and ran toward me. With great excitement, they both threw their arms around me. What a joy for brothers to love one another! Our faces were lit up with heartwarming fraternal affection. With that deep joy in our hearts, we walked along to the park. I could identify our car in the garage. Our battered car stood out in the apparent flaunt of cars in the airport garage. Age had eaten up its luster. It is not surprising to me. Our religious life calls us to live a life of material simplicity. As we drove along, I was stunned by the beauty of the city. I constantly turned my neck and ran my eyes over here and there. Anyone who saw me at that time would know that I was a "JJC" ("Johnny Just Come," a colloquial name we use to describe someone who newly arrived in a particular place). The endless movement of my eyes all over the place would have given me away as a new visitor.

We gradually drove past the city, going into an overwhelmingly wooded countryside. The tall and elegant buildings and the charmingly glittering city lights were gradually disappearing as we rode onto a dense forested road. It was as though I was entering an African jungle. Where are we going? I wondered. Ah, I remembered. Our religious life is the same everywhere. The "desert" is our chosen spot to withdraw for prayer and heart-to-heart with the divine spouse. After a roughly forty-five-minute drive from the airport, we arrived in the heart of intense woods. I looked around and I could hardly see the sky, for the whole area was in overwhelming dense foliage. Branches of trees of all kinds and sizes enveloped the whole property. It was very dark. "No electricity here?" I asked. The brother let me know that they usually turned off outside lights before going to bed in order to save energy.

One of the brothers led the way to the kitchen with his flashlight. He served me some food. It was cold, and so he warmed it up in the microwave. I didn't enjoy the meal. It was sweetened. I was not used to eating sweet food. I didn't bother because I expected a different food than my favorite *garri* and fufu. It would take me a while to make the necessary adjustment in the mission land. I drank juice to hold me until morning. The brother walked me to my hermitage, about 600 feet away from the kitchen. It was a little wooden tent, about 10 by 16 feet in size. The number of the hermitage was seven, which was a very significant number for me. Everywhere was very calm and frightfully solitary. It was a place befitting a pilgrim. The wooden cabin was a constant reminder to me that I am a stranger and alien on earth (cf. Heb 11:13). My hermitage was located on a high ridge overlooking a deep valley stunningly wooded with oak trees of varying sizes.

At daybreak, I was jet-lagged, fatigued due to the long journey from Africa to the New World. Yet I was excited to view the surroundings. I looked through the window. I sighted a number of squirrels. Some were hopping on top of trees. Some were squatted on the ground munching nuts. I noticed that one squirrel was busy hoarding some nuts. It was amazing watching the little animal picking some nuts, making holes on the ground, storing the nuts, and covering them up. Later, I was told that squirrels use the hoarded nuts during winter. At the other end of the valley, I sighted a deer and her two fawns calmly grazing. The deer seemed unafraid. I thought I could hunt as many deer as I want. No, I was no longer in Africa! I had come to a country where law is venerated. Almost everything had a law governing it. The people inquired the legality of whatever they want to do. Unlike my native country, the New World has laws for simple things as hunting and fishing. Anyway, I opened the door and came out of my hermitage. I stood at a high rock to get a better view of the panorama. It was very delightful to behold that serene lushly wooded terrain. The silence of the place spoke to me about an encounter with the divine. It was for me a place where a bride would hear the whispering of her bridegroom. During my days in that holy ground, my heartbeat constantly echoed in harmony with nature, a joyful song of praise to my Divine Master Potter. "Break forth, mountains, into song, forest, with all your trees. For the LORD has redeemed Jacob, shows his glory through Israel" (Isa 44:23b).

The hermitage, where Br. Clay lived for five years. Every day, the Lord spoke in the silence of his heart. "Morning after morning He wakens my ear to hear as disciples do" (Isaiah 50:4b).

# Dance at Dawn

The first Mass that I attended in the New World was quite memorable. One of the hymns that we sang that day was titled, "Come Dance in the Forest." The song triggered a memory of our cultural dance in the village. I wondered why the songwriter invites us for a dance in the forest. Surely a forest isn't a choice place for a dance. We did not dance in the forest. We danced in public places and at homes to entertain people. As I reflected upon the strange invitation to dance in the forest, some thoughts came to my mind. The song invited me for a dance in the Spirit! Since I arrived in the woods just a day before, the Divine Master Potter was calling me to come dance with him in the woods. Of course, it is not the same as my folk dance. I can discern the difference.

My old dance was an "entertainment dance," while this new dance is a "love (agape) dance." The entertainment dance was gratifying while the love dance is transforming. The fun dance was socially exciting while the love dance is spiritually purifying. In our cultural dance, I entered into my people's way of life. In this new love dance, I am absorbed into the life of Christ. The cultural dance was conventional while the love dance is covenantal; it is a nuptial dance, a personal, life-giving relationship. Many people know about entertainment dance but only few understand the surpassing splendor of this love dance. The beauty of our cultural dance was in the beating of percussion and rhythmic body movements. It was focused on appealing to the senses of the spectators. My new love dance is ennobling, life-enriching, and refreshing to the soul, it is not meant to win people's recognition and praise. Not many people like to dance in the Spirit. Agape dance is an encounter that infuses life into the very core of my being and it is attained with passion of the heart and zeal of the soul. My heart, soul, body, and spirit dance for my Lord. The fun dance did not call for self-emptying, sacrificial love. But the love dance compels me to pour out my life in sacrifice for the sake of my beloved. There is no better way to be truly free than to be a slave of the Savior! There is no better way to be truly happy than to do the will of the Divine Master Potter. Oh, entertainment dance, how transitory, how temporal you are! Ah, love dance, how so unceasing! How so refreshing, so soothing, so life-giving! How so beautifully inspiring and so inspiringly beautifying! My soul cannot stop dancing with you, my Lord! A dance with you brings peace of mind and joy of soul. You refresh me with inner joy and breathe in my heart your breath of peace and love. I have tasted this new dance of love. There is nothing to compare with it. It is spiritually inebriating and sweetly consoling. I dance with the "Undivided Three-in-One." The Father pours out his love in my heart, the Son reveals the unbounded love of the Father and invites me to enter into the divine dance, and the Holy Spirit plays the tune of love dance, teaching, empowering, and guiding me to dance well.

Everyone is called to dance with the Lord. The baby John the Baptist blazed a trail of this dance, beginning right from his mother's womb through the desert and ultimately offering his life as an eternal holocaust of love (cf. Luke 1:41). His whole being was made an awesome love dance to the Lord. Both saints and sinners are called to this dance. A harlot danced with her whole being for the Lord and was made holy (cf. Luke 7:37). She poured out her life, spreading everywhere the fragrance of her unreserved love. Her tears welled out, flooding the feet of her divine spouse. By wiping the feet of the Lord with her hair, she was purified by the Blood of the Lamb. The woman afflicted with hemorrhages for twelve years danced the love dance, and she was purified and made whole (cf. Mark 5:25ff). The sick danced with the Lord and were healed. Lepers danced and were cleansed. Come and dance with the Lord. Are you a weakling? Come and you'll be made strong. Are you frustrated? Come and the Lord will give you a cause for hope. Are you abused, rejected, or despised? Come and dance with the Lord, who will care and uphold you.

How do I dance? Well, it is a heart dance. I dance with the tambourine of prayer, with the cymbal of faith, and with the horns of praise. I dance with the harp of charity, with the harmony of faithful service. Every evening, I shout the trumpet of silence before the Lord, listening to what he says to me. Lord, by the grace you have given me, no sufferings, no tribulations, no trials can prevent me from dancing with you. You do not want the glamour of the world to lure me aware from this dance. You invite me to dance with you in the forest. Now push aside from me the noise of the world so that it may not deafen my ears from hearing and relishing the true, sweet melody of the song, and let me soak in the river of your love. You have drawn me into a desert. The skill and strength to dance are yours. Teach me how to dance with you and make my whole life an eternal dance of praise to you.

I can hear you calling me, "Come, my beloved son! Come dance with me in the woods!" Here I am, my Divine Master Potter! I give my life without reservation to dance with you eternally.

## Evangelization Experience

Clay teaches the children about Christ, urging them to direct their
hearts to the divine love. "Train the young in the way they should
go; even when old, they will not swerve from it" (Prov 22:6).

Because of the delay in the approval of my visa, I arrived in the New World three weeks after the seminary had resumed for the academic year. I was asked to wait for another year to begin my studies in the seminary. I joyfully surrendered to the will of God. I spent the period taking language classes and doing door-to-door evangelization. We knocked on several doors each day, braving the humid summer heat and the biting cold of the winter. I met several people of different religious and ideological backgrounds. It was a culture shock for me to see that some of the youths in the New World do not believe in God. Some who were raised Christian had lost their faith to various belief systems, including paganism, agnosticism, Gnosticism, atheism, and secular humanism. Secularism is aggressively spreading like a wildfire because modern culture says "no" to God. Some think that freedom means rejecting God and doing what they want. Some argue that God did not imprint any natural moral law in our minds. For them, what is true is determined by the choices they make as individuals or as a society, and the goodness of an act is measured by what they like. How do we help such people understand that true freedom comes by embracing what is good and true?

I had a remarkable conversation with one woman who claimed to be a Christian but wanted to serve the Lord in her own way. We knocked on her door and waited for a few seconds. A huge lady by the name of Tilli (not real name) answered the door. She was nearly twice my height, and her large body could comfortably enclose three persons of my size. Tilli pulled a face and inquired, in a rather masculine, hollow voice, "What is going on here?" Her facial expression and commanding presence were enough to make a weakling tremble with fear. But the Spirit I received does not make me timid. God gives his followers the grace of proclaiming the good news with temerity, even when threatened. My fellow religious brother and I introduced ourselves as visiting the neighborhood from the Catholic church. Tilli nodded and said in a striking polite manner, "Okay, what can I do for you?" We responded, "Do you have a home church that you like?" "No, I'm not a religious person," she answered. We then asked her if she would share with us what that meant for her. She hesitated a little bit and said, "Well, I don't belong to any church because I don't want to be told what to do." I affirmed her, saying, "It's not easy to live in a way that someone else tells one what to do." Then I asked her if she had a minute to talk with us. "Sure," she kindly replied. She invited us in and offered us seats.

Sitting down, I said to her, "I understand that you don't go to church because you don't want to be told what to do." "Yes," she nodded. "Could you tell us more about this?" Tilli began her story. She told us that she was raised in a Protestant church. When she was a teenager, her parents divorced. She moved out to live with her grandma, who was an active Catholic. She and her grandma attended Catholic church for a long time. She got baptized and received her First Communion in the Catholic church. When she was eighteen, she went to college and came in contact with people of different belief systems and values. In her curiosity, she tried some other religions and ideological groups. She read many books, observed, and learned many things. She said,

"I came to learn more about religion and spirituality. My eyes were opened." She continued, "I describe myself as spiritual but not religious. I don't need to go to church to be spiritual. I don't like any organized religion, especially the Catholic church, which is a law-making institution. I don't want to be in a place like that. The leaders are a bunch of impostors. They don't keep the rules they make, but they want to monitor and control what others do. The priests are pedophiles and money mongers. They are arrogant and egotistic, interpreting the Bible to meet their own selfish agenda. Most of the adherents are naive and sycophantic. I read the Bible and pray always at home. I'm tired of letting spurious pastors and deceitful church leaders tell me what to do."

Tilli said many things that day against the Church. I didn't interrupt her. I didn't get defensive. I felt she needed time to purge her deep-felt animosity against the church. When she kept quiet, I asked her some questions. I found that she had some personal issues and an unfavorable encounter with one church leader. She felt wounded, and so she was transferring her anger against the Church. After discovering Tilli's problem, I asked her, "You said you learned more about religion. Would you like to share with us some important things you learned about organized religion?" Tilli answered, "I have no problem with religious people. I am concerned about overly legislative church, a church that marshals endless laws." I asked if she would like to talk about any particular laws in the Church that she found uncomfortable. She replied, "They are many, including complicated marriage laws, laws that discriminate against gays, abortion law, and what have you." After asking her what she would like to happen in an organized religion, particularly the Catholic church, Tilli remarked that she was not gay but she didn't want a church that judges people or tells them how they should live their lives. "It is a matter between them and God," she added. I tried my best to answer some questions she posed to us. I believe the Holy Spirit will continue to work in her to bring her to the fullness of truth. When I got home that day, I reflected on some of the questions that Tilli raised.

Some people find fault with the Church because one of her leaders didn't treat them well. One thing we have to keep in mind is that Christ himself did not select twelve perfect men as apostles. Judas Iscariot was a cheat, thief, and traitor (John 12:6). The Bible tells us that he sold his Lord Jesus Christ for "thirty pieces of silver." Now does Judas betraying Christ mean that the rest of the apostles are traitors? Does Judas's evil deed discredit the truth of the Gospel which the apostles proclaimed? Does it make the organized early church evil? If one marries a bad spouse, does it mean that the institution of marriage is bad? In all societies, in all institutions of the world, there will always be good and bad people. Regarding the rules in the Church, human beings are social beings. We are not meant to be isolated individualistic beings. We are created to live in a relationship with others. There is no society without rules of some kind. Wherever there is no rule of living, there is no life to live.

We need rules and regulations in society so as to have order, fairness, safety, and freedom. Imagine driving on a complex road network without safety rules. We want to observe the traffic light, signs, and speed limits for our safety and the safety of others. Can a family stay together when everyone does whatever he or she wants? Friends cannot maintain an intimate relationship unless they agree on some ways of living, such as no cheating, no pretending, no lying, no backbiting, no breaking of confidence, no stealing from each other. I have never seen any sports competition without rules and regulations. St. Paul speaks of an athlete who cannot "receive the winner's crown except by competing according to the rules" (2Tim 2:5). Of course, some rules are based on truth while some are not beneficial for the common good and our spiritual life. God wants us to obey not sinful rules but only those that are not contrary to truth. Shadrach, Meshach, and Abednego chose to be martyred rather than to bow down and "worship the golden statue" (Dan 3:18). The law says, "An eye for an eye and a tooth for a tooth," but Christ teaches us not to take revenge but to forgive and bear injuries patiently (cf. Mat 5:38–39).

God gives us reason to ponder and seek truth. Not all truths are known to us without someone teaching us. Christ came to teach us truth (for he himself is Truth) so as to bring us into a relationship with him. The Lord did not teach truth without giving us certain standards to live in truth, for no relationship exists without principles or etiquettes. Christ says, "If you love me, you will keep my commandments" (John 14:15). St. John strongly points out that he or she who claims to love Jesus without keeping his commandments is a liar (1 John 2:4). Didn't Jesus drive out those who did not observe the regulations and purpose of the temple? (cf. Matt 21:12).

If we have rules in living quarters, in business, in sports, in mathematics, in driving, in relationships, in secular institutions, don't we need rules and regulations in the church? Don't we need rules in faith communities, in guiding us into the way of truth and life?

## Laws of Living

Br. Clay at a church in the New World pondering "the Law
of living," "How can the young walk without fault? Only
by keeping" the Lord's "words." (Psalm 119:9).

God gave me freewill and ability to reason and do what is good. I can choose to say or do what is right and good. God made me to grow up to mature man, yet the Divine Master Potter wants me to do the right thing and be childlike in my relationship with him. It is God's will that even as I mature in body and mind I remain docile and obedient to his commands so as to be able to enter the kingdom of heaven (Mt 18:3). To be childlike is to trust and love the Lord with an undivided heart and to obey him joyfully. I find my freedom and peace in following the way of the Lord. The Psalmist tells me that to walk in the right path I must keep God's word, which is "a lamp for my feet, a light for my path" (Psalm 119:105).

How do I know what the Lord wants me to do? There are certain things I can know without being taught. Without someone teaching me, I know that killing a good person who helps me is evil. I don't need to go to school before I can learn that my hand is part of my body. Of course, some truths require instruction before one can understand them well. The law which says "Do not kill" human beings may require some elucidation that human beings include unborn babies right from the first day of conception until death, from the moment s/he begins to develop in a womb until the day s/he is lowered into a tomb. Modernity and social developments bring with them some cultures that are in opposition with Christian faith. People need to have an explanation of the spiritual implications of certain ways of living and lifestyle choices which they passionately and tenaciously embrace.

God didn't call us to a relationship with him without providing us with inspired or trained people to guide us to spiritual life and discipleship. God didn't give us the Scripture without giving us inspired and/or trained scholars and spiritual masters: prophets, priests, catechists, theologians. Christ chose his disciples and commissioned them to go and proclaim the Gospel to all nations. In a word, the Lord entrusted the Church with the authority to instruct us on matters of faith and morals. The Church is not a "law-making institution," as some argue. She is rather our "teacher of truth." The Bible calls the Church "pillar and foundation of truth" (1Tim 3:15). Some people want to interpret the Bible as insolated individuals or based on their own subjective understanding of it. One has to keep in mind that many have read the same Bible and interpreted it in different ways. Some become "eclectic Christians," selecting only some portions of the Bible which they thought served their own ideology or spirituality. God speaks to us through the Bible, and he wants us to understand exactly what he is saying to us. The Ethiopian eunuch could not understand what he was reading from the Scripture (Acts 8:31). It was a trained instructor who explained the scripture to him. Moved by the Spirit, Philip, one of the leaders of the Church, shed light for him on what he was reading from the word of God.

The Church is necessary for leading us to the fullest of truth; otherwise, Christ would not have instituted it with his disciples. I need this divinely authorized "formator of consciences" to analyze for me certain matters and actions in accord with truth and right for my salvation and the salvation of the whole world. Sometimes, God's commands conflict with my values and desires. This is so because our fallen nature oftentimes has its own contrary passions and inclinations. When a certain rule disturbs or challenges me, it may be a sign that I need to work on my ego, my passions, my agenda, my lifestyle choices, and my value system. I who am a disciple of Christ must open myself to be challenged by the Gospel, to be healed by Christ. God's commands are like a bitter medicine to our fallen nature. Most persons don't like taking bitter medicines, but because they want to be cured of an illness they take it. I bear in my body the wounds of sin; hence, the need for the spiritual physician to prescribe the right medicine for my healing. Undoubtedly, some church leaders are not good in instructing and correcting their members to bring them to repentance and acceptance of the truth. They may not be merciful, compassionate, gentle, peace-loving, good listeners, and devout. In any case, the Church is my "Father's house" (John 2:16). It does not belong to any pastor or church leader. Each pastor will come and go but the Church remains. Jesus Christ is the Master and Lord of the Church.

I may not like certain laws or someone who interprets the laws. I may not like the person who puts all kinds of road signs on the highways, yet I obey the law so as to be on the right track, to be safe. I may not like some person who preaches the Gospel or teaches me the rules of Christian life, yet I want to obey what God commands because they are for my good. It is not about the pastors or the bishops or the pope. It is about God, who loves me and calls me to share in his love. It is about my salvation. When one pastor treats me badly, instead of leaving the Church, I have a better option to meet other leaders of the Church or move to another parish. Yet the faith demands that I love every person notwithstanding how the person treats me. I know that the Church is a steward and an interpreter of the commands that come from the Father who loves me so much and wants my good and freedom. The blessed Lord wants me to listen and identify with the Church (cf. Heb 10:25), and be submissive to those in authority as he says, "Obey your leaders and defer to them, for they keep watch over you and will have to give an account, that they may fulfill their task with joy and not with sorrow, for that would be of no advantage to you" (Heb 13:17). Again, it is not easy for our wounded nature to obey someone it does not like. However, it is not nature but grace that moves me to obey the Church. Grace prompts me to overcome my stubbornness and selfish interests. Grace moves me to say "no" to those desires of the flesh that contradict the demands of Christian life. When one encounters Christ, one experiences a transformation that comes from the Holy Spirit, who makes the flesh subject to the spirit. The Lord invites me to live the truth and teach the truth with love, keeping in mind that "mercy triumphs over judgment" (James 2:13). I pray always that the Lord may renew in me the power of his grace to love and passionately desire and strive to do his will all the days of my life.

## Daring the Drug Domain

It was another day of door-to-door evangelization in the New World. One of our brothers in Christ and I were together in that street to share the good news of Christ. We had heard that the street was a dangerous one. Soon we ran into an elderly woman who greeted us, saying, "Be safe, guys." The brother who was with me became worried about our safety in that notorious crime-infested street. He suggested that we leave for another area. Though I was a little bit afraid, I tried to hold back my fear, encouraging the brother to fight his fear with faith. We prayed some ejaculatory prayer and continued our evangelizing in that street. We knocked on the first three doors. Surprisingly, the people we met were receptive and open to listen to us. We had wished that the Lord continue to bless our mission with such pleasant people. But it was a different experience when we got to the fourth door. We knocked but no one answered the door. As I was placing a bulletin on the mail box at the front door, a man forcefully opened the door. He had no shirt on, but he wore short pants. His large body was completely defaced with awful tattoos. He shaved his head bald but his beard was long and shaggy like that of Moses illustrated in my children's Bible. His eyes were evidently sparkling with rage. He wagged his fingers at us, howling, "Nope, nope! Get out of here! Don't ever come here next time or I will blow off your heads." In no time, the brother who was with me hopped across the road. As I slowly stepped off of the porch, I calmly pleaded with the man that we never meant to hurt him. Then, I caught up with the brother who was noticeably shaking with fear. I was happy that he faced the fear with faith. The Spirit urged us on.

Later on, when we got back to the parish we received word that the man who yelled at us called the parish office to apologize to us. He said that he felt terribly disturbed for treating us with such hostility. The brother supposed that the man was under the influence of drugs, and would have opened fire at us were it not for the grace of God. Personally, the man's reaction scared me, but the Spirit helped me to control the fear. Who knows, he might have been under the influence of drugs. Or perhaps he projected onto us his inner turmoil and bitterness. Since we did not speak with the man afterward, we had no basis to make judgment on why he acted the way he did. I prayed that grace may continue to work in his life.

As I reflect on the incident, the first scriptural passage that came to my mind was from St. Paul's letter to the Romans: "Do not be conquered by evil but conquer evil with good" (Rom 12:21). My faith requires that I take no revenge or give room for resentment in my heart. The Lord wants me to bear injuries patiently and with love. Christ was rejected, insulted, and crucified, yet he forgave those who persecuted him (cf. Luke 23:34). St. Stephen prayed that the Lord might forgive those who were stoning him (cf. Acts 7:60). Whatever might have moved the man to berate and threaten us, the best way to preach the Gospel to him at that point is to respond to his rudeness with respect and to answer his aggression with meekness. The Lord used our peaceful, calm response to quench the fire of his rage, and stirred up his heart to feel the heat of guilt and sorrow for his bad attitude.

It was for me a privilege to receive such rejection in the course of the mission. The stories of the early missionaries were stories of opposition, persecution, insults, and sometimes martyrdom. The Church, however, persevered and progressed with love and joy of sharing the Gospel. Christ conquered the world by his love of those who opposed him. When I treat others with love, when I repay evil with good, I am letting love lead and reign in the world. I know that in the past I had talked back to people, responded to some rudely, fought back against those who provoked me. I had retaliated hurt done to me.

I have resolved, by the grace of God, to react wisely, peacefully, and with love to one who attacks me. By his grace, I'll not let my anger control me; I'll strive not to use disrespectful, vengeful words against anyone. Christ has called me to love and exercise love to all, as he had shown us an example to follow. I have come to see my vocation in the world as one of light. I need to radiate the light of faith wherever I am so that those in darkness may see the way to Christ, the way to life. I remind myself daily that Christ is in all persons, and I am to treat them with respect and unconditional love no matter what they do to me.

I have learned that when I return good for evil, when I do not take revenge, when I do not hold a grudge, when I help those in need, I am inviting others to the true life, peace, and freedom in Christ. In this light, every morning I pray for the grace to live in the spirit of love so that the spirit of the flesh may be obedient to the movement of grace. Every night, I do "the Daily Examen," reflecting on all the events of the day to see where and how I had exercised charity or failed to do so.

## Unstoppable Step

When the seminary was about to reopen for the second semester that year, I prayed very devoutly for God's will to prevail. I met with our superior to grant me the privilege to begin my studies. He consulted with the authority of the seminary for the possibility of having me begin studies in the second semester. The rector replied that he was willing to give me a chance to try. When my superior asked if I felt I could catch up with the class, what came to my mind was the words of St. Paul, "I have the strength for everything through him who empowers me" (Phil 4:13). I stayed up all night studying. It was going well in the beginning, but after some time I felt ill with a stomach condition that was painful and troublesome. Nearly all the food was loathsome to me. Some days, I could hardly eat any food without hurting. As time went on, it grew worse and I lost a great deal of weight. I could hardly cope with the heavy study. I feared that if the situation continued that way I might be kicked out of the seminary. How easily fear freezes my faith! I remembered a cake inscription which the founder of our religious community wrote on a cake presented to me on the feast day of my patron saint. It read, "O Clay, your call is to the noblest, the *real* warfare." I realized that my stomach condition and my pounding headache were part of my share in the wounds of Christ. The more I hurt, the more I am plunged deeper into the heart of his Passion. I felt blessed to carry my cross to follow the Lord. Over time, my gnawing stomach pains subsided. However, up till date, the "thorn" is still in my flesh, but as he assured me, the Lord grants me strength to press on at each moment.

## Preaching Practice

Clay serves as the "cross bearer," at the Mass of Installation
in the seminary. "whoever does not take up his cross and
follow after me is not worthy of me" (Mat 10:38).

While in the seminary, I took classes in homiletics, the theology of preaching. When I was preparing my first homily for the class, I asked the Holy Spirit for guidance. Opening my Bible, I was led to the first Book of Samuel, chapter 1. I read about the prayer of Hanna and God's answer with the gift of a son named "Samuel," a name that translates "God hears." It was that very day that I chose "God hears" as the motto for my preaching, and this was covenanted on February 2 that blessed year. My first homily for the class was addressed to the seminarians, and the Gospel was from Matthew. The following is an excerpt of the homily:

## Seeking God in the Desires of Our Hearts (Mt 5:17–37)

All human beings desire. Desire can lead us to God or take us away from him. It can divide our hearts. Our Christian faith calls us to seek the Lord in all things. He is the true happiness that our hearts really desire. Now we know that the passion of the human heart is affected by the wounded nature; hence, sometimes we desire the wrong things. Think about the area of sexual desire. When one is driven by sexual passion, one can commit any form of sexual sin, like adultery.

In many cultures, adultery is understood as evil. Before the advent of Christianity in Africa, my people knew that adultery is bad. A woman who committed adultery has transgressed against the gods and defiled the land. By indulging in adultery, she had acted against right reason. If she is caught, she would never be allowed to relate with her husband until certain sacrifices were offered to appease the gods, and cleanse the land.

The Jews too knew that adultery is bad. The law forbids it, and the penalty is death. The one aim of the Scribes and the Pharisees is to satisfy the demands of the law. But God wills that our religious observance must find harmony between our interior and exterior dispositions. Our Christian faith calls us to this perspective of worship that involves the whole being, soul, mind, heart, body, and strength. Christ teaches us to live in the spirit of the law, rather than only in mere external satisfaction of its letter.

In today's Gospel, Jesus tells us that if we look at a woman lustfully we have committed adultery. So we commit adultery not only by "doing it" but also by "looking it," not by the action, physical contact, but also by our lusting for it. When we allow disordered sexual desire to settle in our hearts, we are also guilty of adultery.

In every age, human beings have to wrestle with the inclination to sin resulting from the fall of Adam. How challenging this is in our age of technology! The enemy is very sly; he builds his temple close to every church. Think about the modern electronic media: Internet, television, newspaper, and what have you. The enemy has taken advantage of them, using them as tools to incite lust in our hearts. Avoiding adultery of the heart becomes a daily struggle, even more so for us seminarians who desire to be celibate and chaste. Jesus gives grace to those who desire sanctity in truth and in spirit! We can escape the trap of the enemy only when we open our hearts for his grace, when we turn to God and learn to rely on the Holy Spirit. He alone can shape our desire. We have to learn to mortify our flesh and control our minds, and not permit them to wander in impure thoughts. When our minds tend to wander away, may we recall that the devil comes "to steal and kill and destroy." May we make an effort to replace any impure thoughts with thoughts about the beauty of our call to sanctity, and stay away from any occasion that may lure us into sin. Ponder the peace we receive from the Lord when we obey the voice of conscience.

As we prepare to receive Jesus in the Eucharist today, may we keep our focus on Christ and remember that we are united with him. We desire and strive to be holy, not necessarily because we want to satisfy the demands of the law, but because of our union with Christ, who is holy. He alone sees the secret of our hearts. In this light, we say "yes" to chastity and mean it, for any desire contrary to it "is from the evil one."

## Letters to the Beloved

Several months had passed after my arrival in the New World. It was a great sacrifice to be away from my native land and dear ones. To make matters more demanding, we had limited permission for keeping in contact with family members, relatives, and friends. Most of them had not heard from me since I left home nearly one year ago. They had waited so long to receive the news of how I was faring in my new station. I was sure that any further delay to communicate to them would be conceived as levity on my side. So one afternoon I picked up my pen and started to write to satisfy their yearning. Because we had not much time for long letters, I endeavored to seize any free time I had to drop a line to some of my friends and relatives. The following are some of the letters I wrote during that period:

❖ To my brothers in the community in Nigeria I wrote:

Dear brothers,

Thank you so much for the letter you had the kindness to send me through our superior. I was so delighted with your beautiful words that I had to read the letter again and again. I had intended writing you individually so as to have room to weave in some friendly jokes as we normally did. I regret that certain constraints have forced me to write to you as a group, hoping that you'll understand. I'm happy to learn that you are doing well, really good news! In any case, we have to keep in mind that our courage and love of our vocation are a sign of God's abundant grace in our lives. We have cooperated with the grace and so now we breathe in the air of courage, love, and perseverance. We boast that "his love compels us."

Some days ago, I recalled these two clichés that sound contradictory: "Absence makes the heart grow fonder," and "Out of mind, out of sight." Which of the sayings is right? Perhaps you may say that either is right depending on one's personality or the context in which it is used. Personally, the former is true in my case. It is now roughly four months since I left you for the New World. Sincerely, I feel as though the period has stretched to four years. Each time that I think back about our days in the community, I wish that I could be lifted up in a flash to where you are, just to see your faces again. You may not understand the degree of this nostalgic sentiment, for it is better experienced than explained. I think that it is practically normal to feel this way since I had been with you for a while and had come to establish the bond of love with you in our Lord Jesus Christ. Now I find myself in a new environment, everything seems different: people, culture, language, climate, and food. However, my consolation is that it is not the end of it all. God willing, we are still going to come together again—maybe either here in the New World (for those who will have the opportunity to join us here soon) or there in Nigeria.

All of the brothers and sisters here are in good state.

We were delighted to have our local superior with us here for a couple of weeks. He was really of a tremendous help to us, especially during our "upkeep," evening chores. Every night, he assisted Br. Goddy in washing plates and cleaning the refectory while we took care of other assigned work. You know we are few in the men's community, so any additional hand is highly valued. As you all know, Br. Samy had his perpetual profession last month. It was indeed a colorful cerebration. Br. Anointed will have the rest of the story for you when he returns to you next week. I have begun my studies in the seminary. New change, isn't it? Brs. Goddy and Samy are pushing ahead in their studies too. Certainly, studying at the seminary is a question of feat. Copious reading assignments are part of its busy academic schedule. We barely have time for personal upkeep and recreation. With courage and trust in God, our victory is assured. Keep us in your prayer as we do for you. All the brothers here send their warm greetings. They too are missing you all.

Again, thank you for your spiritual and moral support during my "bullet wound" ordeal. You all showed your concern and love in various ways— your encouraging words, exciting smiles, your soothing touch, prayerful support, and comforting presence. You gave your time with joy, some days of sleepless night, offering to share in my pain. You were my "hands" and "feet" during those days of trial. Thank you for the many ways you showed me love. Some of those who witnessed your tremendous generous support and affection said, "See how they love one another." This really bore an eloquent testimony of our vocation, which is essentially one of love.

Let me remind you once more that it is a lofty and sublime vocation that we have—a vocation of love. We should not grow weary even in moments of adversity. Rather, we have to strive to embrace our call with passion, being constantly connected to the Lord in prayer and works of mercy. Through this way we fan into flame our original zeal standing on solid ground to resist all worldly attractions that tend to take our minds away from our vocation. "Try to enter, Jesus tells us, "through the narrow gate." Ours is truly a narrow way to life. So do not look back, for we are confident of the one who calls us. And since he is leading us, he is the way, the truth, and the life. We move forward, following him without looking back. The Lord leads, and we follow. We join you in celebrating our recent list of progresses attained in Nigeria: the deaconate ordination of our two brothers (Godwill and Hope). Please extend my special congratulatory message to them; I sing for new postulants our traditional welcome song: "you are welcome in the name of the Lord . . ." The brothers in my batch who are in seminary (Brs. Akanso and Obidinso), may God grant you the wisdom to excel in your studies, and most importantly, the grace to deepen ever more in your relationship with the Lord. Our father founder expressed his appreciations for our newly completed hermitages. He described it as "superb." We are grateful to our able superior for being the brain behind this, and for his fatherly and unrelenting efforts to keep things in shape. All the brothers here join me in sending their warm regards to you all.

In union of prayer and love!
Br. Clay

❖ To my beloved friend, I wrote:

Dearest Nwachi,

So late a letter! You have waited a long time to hear from me. My apologies for not writing you earlier. The delay is not without some reason. Permit me to clarify this question in this letter, and it is my hope that my words will meet this goal. Obviously, one of the features of the western world is its development in the area of communication media. Now that I am stationed here in the New World, it is natural for people to think that I have the facilities readily within my reach, and thus I should be in a better position to reach out to my friends and relatives in the developing world. When this expectation is not met, it may be considered as a kind of levity or self-absorption on my side. You may not have thought so, but even if you have I should not place the blame on you. It is natural to think in this direction, especially when it involves a dear friend with whom one had maintained an intimate relationship.

One of the many sacrifices we make in our religious community is limited use of modern technology. It is disconcerting to some people to learn that we do not have personal cell phones. We are not allowed to make use of our private email accounts. We have limited contact with people outside the context of our religious community. I didn't intentionally keep you *incommunicado* for so long a time. It is really a big sacrifice to miss the company of a wonderful friend that you are. I do remember you always, especially in the exciting days we spent together. Hope the Lord will grant us the grace to meet again to share our joy in our blessed Lord in whose love I have become a slave.

On your part, whenever you have time, please write me and keep me informed of the progress you make in your business and other matters in your life. I have heard the news of the many ways that the Lord has blessed you. I rejoice with you, praying that your future may be filled with abundant blessings beyond your imagination. I urge you to strive daily to renew your faith and love of the Lord through unceasing prayer and good works. St. Paul puts it well for you, "Whatever you do, do from the heart, as for the Lord and not for others, knowing that you will receive from the Lord the due payment of the inheritance; be slaves of the Lord Christ" (Col 3:23–24).

Know that you have a permanent place in my prayer, and I ask that you pray for me too. I am not sure when next I'll see your face again; I pray and yearn that it will not be too long. May the blessed Lord continue to fill your heart with his enduring peace and joy! Stay blessed until we meet again.

Affectionately yours,
Br. Clay

❖ Before I left home for the New World, two of my brothers in the Lord and I paid a visit to my brother's family. I wrote to my sister-in-law to thank her for her hospitality and also to acquaint her with how I was progressing in the New World:

Dear Ugodiya,

I have the pleasure to write you this letter. I would have written earlier but for some reason I was not able to do so. I ask that you receive this letter in a spirit of love and forgiveness. I hope that all of you are in good state. I believe that whoever rests his/her faith in the Lord is always in safe hands. We may experience some adverse circumstances, but we are rest assured that all work together for our good.

I really appreciate the overwhelming gesture of hospitality you showed my friends last time we visited the family at the new residence. The brothers who accompanied me to the new home expressed their heartfelt joy and appreciation for your loving kindness and generosity to them. They really enjoyed the delicious dinner. Most especially, they were intrigued by your cheerfulness and welcoming spirit. They yearned for another opportunity to visit with you. You wouldn't believe this: one of the brothers said that if he could find a woman like you, he would consider marrying. We couldn't help laughing when he said this, for we thought that he didn't know what he was saying. We considered it as a joke, though the remark was good testimony to your goodwill and generous heart. I have been with you for a while, and I can testify that yours was never a dissembling attitude, but one that came directly from the heart. Your virtuous character strikingly reflects the faith and love you have for the Lord. Keep up with that spirit!

I hope my little niece is doing well in school. Please do well to get them to study at home. Try to put in time sitting with them to educate and direct them. Embrace it as your responsibility to raise them not only in mind but also in morals. They will bring you joy tomorrow if today you make the sacrifice of spending quality time with them to raise them in the discipline that comes from the fear of God. I always recall the deepest affection we shared in the family. I feel joyful when I think of the love we shared together as a family. At the same time, my heart hurts because I miss all of you. Remembering that at least five years would go by before I'll see you again brings tears to my eyes. I wish I could turn the hands of the clock forward so that the years would elapse quickly so that I can come home. I wish I could fly on the wings of the wind just to be with you even for a minute. This sentiment unavoidably springs up from my inmost being as a sign of my profound affection for all of you. God made us that way: to love and to share, to live and to care.

Though I am not present where you are at this moment, rest assured I'm with you in spirit. My being away from the family is one of the biggest sacrifices that I have to make for my love for the Lord. It is the Lord who called me to serve him in a mission land, and as a sign of my love for him I accept it with joyful resignation. It is not easy, but true love goes with sacrifice, and to make a sacrifice is a way of giving and receiving love and life. My consolation is that I'm on the right path, on the way of love, the way of life. Remember that you all share in the graces that come with this sacrificial love which has taken me away from you.

I had some difficulty adjusting to this foreign land in the first five months after my arrival. Now it seems I'm getting acclimatized. As it was the case with some of the slaves of Christ who served before us, I have got my own share of the suffering of Christ. I have been frequently ill since I arrived here, but it has not deterred me from doing all I needed to do. So it is nothing to worry about. Even amid the pain, each morning God refreshes me with his strength enough to complete the task of each moment. His river of grace does not run dry in my heart. My courage is that his promise will prevail in our lives. The pains and hardships that I experience at this present are a makeup of his suffering. His victory will unfailingly be our victory. "And the victory that conquers the world is our faith" (1John 5:4b).

Hopefully, in the near future, I shall be with you. Know that my prayer is with you. Do well to extend my warm affection to all in the family, to our relatives and friends.

Stay blessed!
Br. Clay

❖ I received a letter from a brother in the Lord. After some period of probation, his community decided to ordain him to the priesthood. I wrote in reply to his letter and also to rejoice with him for his ordination scheduled to take place within two months from the time this letter was composed. I also acknowledge his kindness to me.

Dear Br. Ndidi,

It was humbling to receive the letter you had the kindness to send to me. I'm pleased for the trust you placed in me to get the stuff you requested. I spoke to our Superior about it and he permitted me to get it for you. I found some extra one from our common supply. I am glad to send the two to you. Hope you will find them useful. I'll try to see the possibility of sending it to you whenever we have someone traveling to Nigeria.

I was more than happy when I heard that your ordination is scheduled for May. It is hard to believe that the long-awaited day has come at last. It is a day to celebrate God's grace and your spirit of dedication, hard work, and patience. Delay, as they say, is never denial. Wait a minute! No, you were not delayed. On the contrary, all fall into the divine plan so that the victory will be relayed. The Divine Master Designer has used the time that some considered as delay to rejuvenate and reconfigure you for the great work entrusted to you. Now you are set to begin a new chapter of your life. God has refined you in a special way for the holy service. Why not pour out the sweet fragrance of your life into the sacred service? You have been called to lay down your life for others. *I bu uko-chukwu ebebe* (You are a priest forever)!

You have shown that you are not a fainthearted person who gives up when life seems uncomfortable. Rather, you have faithfully persevered and joyfully walked with the Lord bearing the pain of your own cross. A person of faith

202 | Rev. L. C. M. Ibeh

does not solve a temporal problem by giving up. You did not lose hope; instead, you faced and overcame the hurdle with an imperturbable self-possession and doggedness. Now the trophy is yours! Hold it firmly. It is a special treasure and authority for the mission. Priesthood, as you know, is not a title one receives but a "configuration to Christ." It is not a seal outside oneself but an interior transformation, a permanent mark in the soul. The call comes with the sword, the shield, and the breastplate that you need to embark on spiritual warfare for the Kingdom of Kingdoms. You are a great soldier of Christ. You have all it takes to be a hero for the Lord. A Christian hero is not necessarily a person of great physical strength, but rather primarily a person of interior strength. The Lord's grace will always be sufficient for you. I am really inspired by your unwavering faith and total surrender to God's will. Congratulations and thank you for cooperating with grace!

I remember all the many ways you showed me great love during the time I was shot. I cannot forget that long night that you kept vigil as you sat beside me watching the drip flow slowly into my vein. I felt all your soothing touches and heard your words of consolation as I groaned and sighed in pain. I appreciate all your kindness more than I can say. What more do we expect from a consecrated servant of God than to have the heart of "the Good Shepherd"!

My graduation from Philosophy is scheduled for next month. God willing, by August, I'll begin my studies in theology—still a long, narrow way to trod! I ask you to do me one more favor: pray for me that God's will may continue to prevail in my life.

May the blessed Lord renew your zeal and use you as a fiery instrument for renewing the face of the world.

Your brother in Christ,
Br. Clay

❖ Another brother wrote me a letter. The following is a reply to his letter:

Dear Br. Nduka,

I was very happy to hear from you. I was deprived of the pleasure of sending this reply earlier. Father Sentis left a day before your letter arrived.

Please bear with me for this belated reply. Your letter was exciting to me partly because it acquainted me of some important news that I had longed to hear, and partly because it was punctuated with your great zeal and enthusiasm to do the will of God. It is my hope that my words will not smother this fire in you.

Some of the brothers who wrote to me remarked that I was blessed to be in the New World. I agree with them. However, I'm not blessed because I am in this mission land. I'm rather blessed because the Lord is in me. I ask that you don't consider yourself less favored because you are not with us in this foreign land. Do not be tempted to put off your happiness, thinking that you will be happy when . . . My happiness is not located in a particular place or in a given thing. I have discovered it within me. It is a Person, Jesus Christ, who lives in me. Nothing gives true happiness except a living relationship with Jesus Christ.

Some who thought that they would be happy when they travel abroad, or when they attain this or that, or when they come to this holy ground, have felt so disappointed that they sank into gloom. If you can show me a truly peaceful and joyful heart, I'll show you a heart that has joyfully surrendered itself to the will of God.

God called you to the religious life, and he alone has the road map. He is taking you somewhere where he wants you to serve him and his people. Please don't be tempted to spend your time searching for where life will be easy for you. No place is a land of happiness on earth. Happiness is within you. It is not outside yourself. Christ, who comes to make his dwelling in you, is your happiness. Without Christ in one's heart, no power, no position, no prerogative can bring lasting happiness. Again, don't spend your time anxiously trying to know exactly where the Lord is taking you. You may not be able to know it. He wants you to always take a leap of faith. Listen to the whispering of the Spirit. Believe that the master of the vineyard is trustworthy. Be rather concerned to spend each moment of your life to pray, to love, to share, to serve, and to rejoice in Christ. Does it sound simple? Perhaps, but in reality it is not practically easy. It is not easy to be a true Christian; it is not easy to be a devout religious.

If your religious life is always comfortable to you, it may be a sign that you have not have found your true vocation. If the road to your religious life is straight, you have most probably missed the way. If everything is going your way, you may need to try another way. If everybody likes you, you may have to consult your spiritual director. Always remember that Christ calls us to carry our cross and follow him; yet the good news is that he gives us sufficient grace to carry them and walk with him through the narrow way. So do not give up, my dear brother. You are specially chosen for this mission. With the eyes of faith, fix your gaze on him who died for you, and cling to him. Can't you see the Lord who holds you by your hand, leading you to the way? Look well into yourself with the eyes of faith, and you'll see him who lives in you. He'll never forsake you. Follow him!

I would love to learn more of the challenges and progress you make in the community.

Your brother in Christ,
Br. Clay

❖ It was a feast day of one of our brothers in the community. I wrote to him a note of compliment for his celebration.

Dear Br. Onye-ije,

How blessed in the solitude are the feet of he who shares the Good News! I see your feet hasten to bring good tidings to the poor. I see your heart burning with zeal for the task of sharing the Gospel. I hear your mind chime the hymn of silence. I listen to your heart resound the symphony of recollection. I hear your voice announce the saving words.

Today we join you to celebrate the feast of your patron saint. It is another moment of grace, of joy, and of love and service. You are a man of joy. Your joy jolts my heart to rejoice, and your fervor for the Gospel sets me to shout, "Alleluia!" You are a brother who loves others. You love the Lord. Jesus is your love, and your love is the joy of your heart. I'm blessed to be one of your spiritual brothers, and it is edifying and inspiring that you have chosen to offer your life in service of the Lord. I pray that the Spirit of joy may continue to fill your heart with endless peace in his presence.

Blessed feast day, my dear brother!

❖ Our superior and founder celebrated the anniversary of his priestly ordination. I wrote to him a note of gratitude.

Dear Father Sanctus,

It's time to celebrate you, dear Father! Yours is a celebration of victimhood, a jubilation for a gift of sacrificial love. It is beautiful to celebrate one who has a grateful heart, a heart consumed with love. A heart that offers itself as an "eternal hymn" of praise to its Creator is a heart worth celebrating. Father, yours is a thankful heart! You love the Lord and opened your heart with love to others. Now love so overflows that many around your table sate their thirst from the fountain of love. Your heart welcomed and embraced the bidding of wisdom. Now wisdom abides and blossoms in your heart, and many are directed to the path to life through your counsel.

Fifty years ago, you were anointed and commissioned to preach the Gospel, yet the word remains ever fresh, ever powerful, and ever moving, and the powerful images you use in your preaching are like flowers of elegance. You have sown the seed, and it is spreading, blooming, and bearing much fruit. You have lit the light and it is brightening and flaming. Ah! you are a humble "instrument" in renewing the face of the earth. I am blessed and thankful to God for the privilege he granted me to be counted as one of the children of your wonderful spiritual family. Through you, God has built a precious home for us. Even though it is not a "rich" one to satisfy the choices of the world, it contains a lasting precious treasure that cannot be found in any popular markets of the world.

We are grateful to God for the gift of your life. We pray that you may be sustained and strengthened with grace. And may the Lord grant you more fruitful years of labor in his sacred vineyard! Blessed anniversary!

Blessed anniversary!
Br. Clay

❖ When I arrived in the New World, God blessed me with a wonderful spiritual director. He was a special tool who the Lord used to direct and steady my feet in the slippery slope of life in the New World. The man of God wrote me a number of times. The following is a reply to one of his letters he sent me:

Dear Father West,

I received your exciting letter during the beginning of our mid-semester exam. Today, as the arduous work of preparing for exam is over, I'm writing this letter to express my appreciation for your heartwarming message. Your message reached me at the time I needed it. While we may not count on dreams, I'm compelled to accept that my last dream that I had a day before I received your letter was significant to me. What I can remember in that dream was that I visited you, and seeing that your arms were healing, we threw our arms around each other. The dream was in my mind that morning when I received your letter from my mailbox. I could not believe it: you wrote with your sore arm! I had yearned for the day you would invite me to meet with you at Regina Cleri. I anxiously opened the letter.

Your message worked in an amazing way in boosting my strength and refreshing my mind for the paper I had that morning, yet your fatherly and loving words left me in "joyful" tears. I don't know when that "day" will come when I'll meet with you again; however, I trust that our blessed Lord is at work in your life. This is my consolation: "For it is he who has torn, but he will heal us; he has struck down, but he will bind our wounds" (Hos. 6:1).

You have a permanent place in my prayers, and I also entrust myself to your fatherly blessing. While awaiting the day of our thanksgiving to God for the healing and our reunion, I pray God to grant you the grace to bear the pains of this moment, and may he use them for the sanctification of the world.

Your son in Christ,
Br. Clay

❖ Ijelu lived about a block away from our community in Nigeria. Before I left home, he and I talked about the necessity of having his marriage blessed in the church. A few months after my departure, I received word that he wedded in the church. I wrote to congratulate him:

Dear Ijelu,

I was very happy to learn that at last you have allowed yourself to be moved by grace. Very exciting! I'm sure your devout parents were overjoyed witnessing your wedding for which they had yearned. Truly it is not only delightful to your family but also to your friends and people of goodwill, and above all, the saints in heaven. The heavens are rejoicing today because of you. Through the sacrament, God has poured upon your life grace upon grace. I thank you most sincerely for this positive step toward spiritual growth. I wish I was present to share the joy and blessings of the memorable event. All the same, I was there in spirit. I lift up your family in my daily prayer, trusting that God's choicest blessings may overflow in your family.

Please keep in mind that the grace you received requires that you nurture it in your heart. You are called to open wide the door of your heart for love. I do not know a better way of reminding you of the nature of this love than the eloquent words of St. Paul: "Love is patient, love is kind. It is not jealous, [love] is not pompous, it is not inflated, it is not rude, it does not seek its own interests, it is not quick-tempered, it does not brood over injury, it does not rejoice over wrongdoing but rejoices with the truth. It bears all things, believes all things, hopes all things, endures all things. Love never fails" (1Cor 13:4–8a).

You have received the Spirit who transforms one's heart and makes it submissive to God. How else does the spirit manifest his presence in our lives if not to make us love without measure? Love your wife, love your children, love your parents, love all in your family, love all your neighbors! The God of love has chosen you in the family. So cling to him and you'll always speak the language of love and do the works of love. In so doing, love will ever be your happiness and peace.

I ask that you remember me in your prayer as I progress in my seminary studies. It is my hope that at last God will bless all our efforts. I remember the excuses you used to give me for not being able to pray. Strive now to avoid anything that will keep you from praying constantly. If one cannot pray well, one can never love fully. The moment we begin to grow lax in prayer, the river of love begins to recede in our hearts. Please beg God to grant you the grace to pray without ceasing so as to love without quitting.

May the love of Christ be your peace!
Br. Clay

❖ My brother in Christ and I were going on a trip to another state that evening. We had driven several hours and it was past nightfall. We wanted to stop over in the nearby chaplaincy to pass the night there. It was around 10:00 p.m. We could not see anyone to ask for help when we arrived there. We had parked our car at the front of the chapel preparing to rest our heads in our car for a few hours. Suddenly, we saw a young woman walking in haste to the chapel to pray. We ran after her. She was a "God-send" who directed us to the friary to meet with the friars. I wrote to her afterward to thank her for her help.

My dear Allison,

Thank you so much for your help last week. The Lord sent you on our way. What a great blessing you were to us! I'm glad and grateful to have met with you, my dear sister in the Lord. Rightly do I call you my sister; you know that a spiritual relationship is more powerful and more enduring than a blood tie. St. Paul reminds us that we are one in Christ our Lord (Gal. 3:28). How beautiful it is to realize the splendor and privilege of our vocation as brothers and sisters, children of the kingdom!

Our meeting was really providential. We met at the right spot: in the chapel, which reminds us that our bodies are the temple of the Holy Spirit. I was really moved that you have the habit of spending time alone with the Lord, especially in the sacred place. As I was praying yesterday, I heard the Spirit speaking to my heart that you are a chosen instrument of God. I'm not sure of the exact nature this will take in your calling in life, but I'm confident that if you continue to dispose yourself to him God will definitely make this clear to you in time. Your part is simply to follow him in truth and in spirit, and he will do with you whatever he wills. Be reminded that we are in a spiritual warfare. The world is hurting. Some people have missed their way to life. God needs those who are willing to work with him, those on fire with love and zeal for the mission of saving souls. My dear sister, we cannot be victorious without drawing strength from the Holy Spirit. God breathes his Spirit into us to vivify us and inspire us. When we open ourselves to him, the Spirit comes to refine us, to work in us, for us, and through us. I pray that this year's celebration of Pentecost may bring a release of fresh anointing and power of the Holy Spirit in your life.

If there is anything to pray about, please don't hesitate to inform me. I ask that you keep me in your prayer, as I do for you.

Gratefully your brother in Christ,
Br. Clay

## The Force of Faith

I was gradually adjusting to the culture of the New World. At a certain point, I found that one thing was threatening my stay. My immigration paper was nearing expiration. Things were not working out as we expected. The other day, the lawyer told me that I was on the verge of deportation. According to him, my exceeding a specific number of days in the country would result in barring me from reentering the New World. This situation occupied my mind and gave me great distress. I could hardly concentrate in my studies. The lawyer suggested that I leave the country and come back after renewing my visa. This was an option that was too risky because some who tried it were unable to return to the country. I rejected it in the spirit. We stormed heaven with prayer begging for divine intervention. The Lord promised that he would go before me to level the mountains (Isaiah 45:2). I sent all the possible paperwork as the immigration authority had requested. I stayed still waiting for the Lord's will in faith and in hope. The community prayed for me. My family and friends joined in prayer. After a couple of months, I received a letter. It was from the department. I was anxious to open it to know its content, yet I was resigned to the will of God. Opening the letter, I found that it was a notification that I had been granted a permanent stay in the New World. What a marvel! I jumped up euphorically, feeling overjoyed for such an amazing grace.

## The Drill of Delay

I had been in the religious community for eight years. I loved the religious life, particularly its spirit of prayer garnished by simplicity of life. However, I felt the Lord calling me to a more active life. I didn't disclose this to my superior earlier. I thought of the high expectation that the authorities of the community had of me. They had often expressed to me and to other people their confidence in me that I would persevere in the life. So I felt like one under obligation. For a long time, I kept within me the inner voice summoning me over to a mission outside the community.

Apart from the foiled immigration threat, one other "giant" surfaced. It was at the time my Diaconal ordination was drawing near. I was in high spirits, warming up for the sacred office. About three months to the ordination, a terrible vocation "tornado" hit our community once again. One-third of our priests were swept away from the community. Some left our community and joined other religious orders while some others entered diocesan vocation. It was a great trial time for our community. This brought some degree of erosion of harmony in the entire community; trust gave way to distrust, solidarity broke into suspicion, unity collapsed into dissension. Word got around. People were asking questions as to why the priests left the community.

Tension heightened among the members. We kept vigil, fasting and praying for God's will. I knew the Lord was in control of the whole reality, for nothing escaped his wisdom and power. In accord with his plan for my life, the Divine Master Potter permitted that I suffer the trial of holding over my Ordination to the diaconate. I kept still waiting upon the Lord. I knew it was a special moment of grace. The hope and yearning of my heart, the pain of seeming delay, the discomfort of a "long" waiting were all part of the whole drama of the divine operation in my life. God is using them to shape and refashion me for his glory. The Spirit urged me to remain patient, trusting in his faithfulness. I believed that it would not be too long before the dawn of God's blessings breaks forth in my life. I was hopeful that someday I would tell the tale of my triumph.

## The Vicious Voice

You may recall the snake that wriggled into the Garden of Eden. The old serpent entered the holy ground to destroy the order of things. It was the spirit of contradiction. He urged Eve to defy the command of the Lord so as to become like God (Gen 3:4–5). The insidious voice of the ancient snake has not ceased in our time. One evening, the voice of the serpent came my way, saying: "You have suffered enough for this mission. Surely you are forcing yourself into a wrong vocation." I answered the negative voice, "Surely I'm responding to my true vocation. The sufferings are part of the process. They are a positive sign of the reality of my call."

The following day, my former schoolmate Ojionu called me on phone. She inquired if I had been ordained to the priesthood. I said, "Not yet." Then she asked if I had other plans than vocation to priesthood. I responded that the vocation to priesthood was not my own plan but God's. I was simply responding to his plan for my life. The Lord has not asked me to pursue any other plans. She reacted in a strange way, flaring up as though I touched her sore spot. She yelled, "I'm sure there must be something wrong with you. Stop deceiving yourself! If you have not been ordained by now, it means that your formators have discovered something wrong about you. I'll say it again: stop deceiving yourself! I suspect that you are not a 'normal' man."

She said many nasty things against me that morning. For the sake of decency, it is better not to divulge them here. I knew Ojionu as a nice and devout student. We were together in the same Catholic ministries on the campus. We prayed together, worshipped together, and drank the precious blood from the same cup.

It was strange to hear such vulgar, abusive words from her. Well, I didn't think she had become a bad person. I sensed that she was not herself. Something definitely went wrong with her. She was projecting her inner anger, bitterness, and resentment. It was a spirit of contradiction that spoke through her. Sometimes, the enemy uses even one's close friend or loved one to force one into the fire of fury and frenzy. It takes discernment to identify when a negative spirit speaks in a person. I didn't want to be defensive at the venom of her words. Rather, I remained silent and patient to allow her to purge her body of the negative emotions. When she stopped, I simply replied, "I deserve to hear what you have just said to me." She asked, "Why do you think you deserve it?" I said, "You know very well that I deserve it. Don't you?" She sighed and hung up on me. I knew that the words were directed by the enemy to disrupt my peace of mind. But how could mere words rob me of the precious peace that the Lord had given to me? Bad words can hurt depending on how I think about them. I didn't want to let the power of negativity destroy my missionary activity. I would not let it get in my way to weaken my faith and control my vision. I pushed back the arrow of bad words with the breastplate of faith and love. Love is an elixir to purge out the poisons of negative emotions; it cures the crushing pain of hurting words. Love is a gift of grace more powerful than the wound of our falling nature!

## Carefully Created

Apparently, Ojionu uttered harsh, hurting words. But I didn't let those negative words cause me to disbelieve the truth that the Lord beautifully and wonderfully created me: "You formed my inmost being; you knit me in my mother's womb. I praise you, so wonderfully you made me; wonderful are your works! My very self you knew; my bones were not hidden from you, When I was being made in secret, fashioned as in the depths of the earth" (Psalm 139:13–15).

In the Bible, we see that Job's three friends who came to give him sympathy lacked the wisdom of the Spirit (Cf. Job 2:11). They thought Job was under God's curse, that the divine justice befell him as a result of his iniquity. But their diagnosis of his condition was far from the reality. Job wasn't suffering because of his sins. Rather, God permitted it to refine and demonstrate Job's unconditional faith and love for his Creator and to show forth the divine bountiful love and power to deliver those who trust in him. I don't cite Job's case because I am in any way on par with his righteousness. I affirm with Job that no person on earth can stand justified before God (Job 9:2). Yet, God's love for us is more powerful than our human weaknesses and brokenness. If the Lord visits us with his justice, all the human race would be swept away in the flood of wrath just within a second. I made reference to Job because sometimes some tend to think that one suffers due to one's sins.

The truth is that both the righteous and the bad have their own share of suffering on earth. Many a time, the good ones drink more of the cup of sufferings. This is a mystery. But people of faith trust that in all circumstances the Lord is present and ever working for the good of those who love him. His love will never fail me as long as I remain in him, acknowledging my sins and sincerely turning away from them to follow the Lord. At the end, the Lord will vindicate his people.

I'm confident that the Divine Master Potter will, at the end of my ordeal, show forth his good plans for my life. Those who embarrass me now will embrace me at the end. Those who sneer at me will sing with me in thanksgiving to God. Those who question God's plan in my life will at last give the answer by themselves. Those who are ignorant of God's work in my life will understand it in time. Those who are insensitive to the movement of the Spirit will feel the vibration and warmth of the fire of love. Those who doubt God's presence in my trials will dance with me the dance of triumph. On the dawn of victory, the eyes of those who are blind in faith will be open to see the miracle of love. The ears of those who are spiritually deaf will be open to hear the melody of miracles. Yes, they will see it; they will hear it; they will feel it; they will understand it; they will believe it and turn to the Divine Master Potter. Yes, I deserve whatever I am going through at this moment because the Lord allows all for my good. Who am I to argue with the Lord? Do I, mere clay, have any right to question the work of the Divine Master Potter in my life? What guts do I have to ask the Lord, "What are you doing?" or, "What you are making has no handles" (Isa 45:9).

I believe that the Lord does all things well. I believe that I'll surely fly over all the hurdles in my life. Whenever any obstacle shows up, God gives me the strength to stand firm in faith. Without his grace, I would have fallen into the devouring jaws of impatience and frustration. Were it not his love, the raging wave of despair would have swallowed me up. My victory is assured in Christ!

## Faith Foils Fear

Naturally, distress comes with unfulfilled hopes and expectations. I remember one day in my anguish lamenting like Job, "For to me sighing comes more readily than food; my groans well forth like water" (Job 3:24). Within this time, I experienced deeply my human weakness. I discovered the fragility of my faith. I spent some time glumly thinking of the bleakness, the hardship, and the setbacks that I had faced in my vocation. Even though I had no doubt that God was with me, I felt as one isolated and abandoned. How I needed an increase in faith!

I had a flashback about what happened sometime when I was still a toddler. Papa and I were together in our sitting room that afternoon. I sat on the floor playing with my toys while Papa was on his wooden armchair listening to his radio. Soon, our she-goat appeared at the front door and stood still gazing at me. It nearly scared me to death. I crawled toward Papa screaming for rescue. Papa waved at me saying, "Don't be afraid; it will not harm you. I'm with you." I was not certain of my safety staying close to the goat. I screamed even louder. Papa picked me up. I wrapped my arms around his neck. Feeling safe and confident, I stared at the goat from the height of Papa's shoulder. Then I began muttering my rebuke against the goat.

Certain challenges in life had threatened me like the goat. On occasion, my faith was no stronger than that of my infantile trust in Papa. I knew the Lord was with me at the moment of trial, just as Papa was with me at the time the goat came into the room, yet I was not sure of my safety without feeling his protecting, consoling arms. I was not very sure he was on guard. I wanted tangible proof that the force of his presence was bigger and more powerful than my fear. I wanted a more concrete sign of his readiness and ability to save me. I felt secure when Papa lifted me up and carried me on his shoulder. When I was no more a kid, some situations still caused me to feel a sense of dread. How I needed to mature in faith! No matter the storm in my life, the Lord offered me the spirit of transformation to turn my fear into faith and my anxiety into serenity. I have taken hold of the promises of the Lord. I can never sink into the swamp of fear and worries. I remember the Spirit spoke to me when I was preparing to come to the New World: "You will face many trials, but rest assured, I'm with you always." The Lord's unfailing presence in my life is my consolation.

That year, despite the uncertainty of my ordination, I attended the canonical retreat for men preparing for diaconal ordination. It was a five-day retreat. It was for me a time to reinforce my spiritual and emotional life to press ahead with the mission. On the first day of the retreat, I asked the Lord, "My sweet Savior, how do you want me to serve you?" The response came, "Keep your eyes fixed on me and follow my leading. Then you will discover the plans I have for your life." I asked the Lord how I could see the plans in the midst of the darkness of the moment. The Spirit led me to Psalm 42:6, "Why are you downcast, my soul; why do you groan within me? Wait for God, for I shall again praise him, my savior and my God."

In confirmation of that revelation, one of the Psalms for the day's Office of Morning Prayer (week 2, Monday after Epiphany) was the same Psalm 42. I kept still in prayer. The Lord said to me, "You are here not primarily to be healed of your pain but to be helped in discovering the divine plan, to be transformed into an instrument for healing." I reflected upon the passion of Christ: God did not send Christ to the world to spare him the humiliation, agony, and death on the cross. The Father allowed his beloved Son to experience the pains and death so that he might forever crush the sting of death in the lives of his children. I believed that I was a veritable tool who needed to be purified, formed, and shaped for this mission. My Divine Master Potter, do with me whatever you will.

## Harvest of Hope

"Those who sow in tears will reap with cries of joy. Those who go forth weeping, carrying sacks of seed, will return with cries of joy, carrying their bundled sheaves" (Ps 126:5–6).

One afternoon during the retreat, I was in prayer before the Blessed Sacrament. The Spirit showed me some words which I could not visualize completely. But I could recognize a boldly written word, which read "harvest." I tried to return to prayer in order to read the complete sentence, but all seemed to have disappeared. I couldn't see the words anymore. I told my spiritual director about this. "Return there and ask the Lord to make it clear to you," he said to me. I did as he said, but could not see the sign. I got up at 3:00 a.m. for prayer. In my prayer at that hour of mercy, the word came to me, "A harvest of hope." What was the Lord telling me about this? Well, I know that hope is the trust that my future is in the hands of the Lord. Hope helps me to see the unsleeping Lord in the midst of the storm. Hope opens the door of peace even when situations seem horrible and unpromising. It generates in my heart the joy of the Lord. It keeps me focused and present in the divine presence at each moment without being troubled about what tomorrow will bring to me. Hope brings into my heart the confidence that it is the Lord who designs and disposes the events of my life. Still it was not very clear to me about the harvest of hope. I still sensed within me some twinge of curiosity to know my life's road map, to know exactly where the Lord is leading me. I was ignorant that I did not need to know about my future, but rather to trust that the Lord is taking me in a new direction, to follow trustingly the Lord's leading wherever he would take me. What is the significance of the words "harvest of hope"? I would discover that in the course of my journey of life. "But those who harvest shall eat, and praise the Lord; those who gather shall drink in my holy courts" (Isaiah 62:9).

## Casting for a Catch

The Divine Master Potter has an amazing way of working out his plans for the good of his beloved. Sometimes when I count on how things would go for me, the Lord turned them around and disposed them in a fashion perfectly accordant with his holy will. Imagine someone confidently traveling on a long narrow route only to hit a dead end. This was how I felt when my diaconal ordination was held back. It was as though I had reached an impasse in my vocation journey. I could hear loud and clear the tolling bell of *"Nunc dimittis,"* not in the sense of the fulfillment of God's promise of salvation (as Simon proclaimed in Luke 2), it was rather in a negative sense of it, like a lamentation of a defeated team. The bright sky of my life seemed to have given way to sudden overcast, with tornado-like dark clouds billowing from all corners. I could hear the enemy booing at me. Some monstrous feet were ruffling in an ostensible victory parade. I could hear the rumbling sound of their rallying trumpet. It was like the atmosphere resonated with fiendish frenzied anthem. I could perceive the rhythm of fright pounding in my heart. I could sense the wave of hopelessness and misery rolling in from all sides to overwhelm me. Like Peter, I felt I had toiled through the darkness of the night without fruit.

Nevertheless, there was still an ounce of faith in me. I prayed with many tears calling on the Lord, my hope and my salvation. At some point, I realized that I looked at the whole reality from a carnal perspective. I viewed it with my mere human eyes, listened to it with my mere human ears, evaluated it based on my limited human reasoning system, and felt it on a mere human level. The Spirit used my humble faith, "as small as a mustard seed," to pull down the strongholds of apprehension and topple the mountain of trepidation. My eyes of faith were opened, and I saw that it was the time for the harvest of hope. I could see the streak of dawn and hear the drum of victory. The keeper of the vineyard (cf. Isaiah 27:3) had provided plenteous harvest for me. From the depth of the ocean, fishes had heard the voice of the divine and clustered at my net. I could hear the Lord asking me to cast my net into the deep water for a catch (Luke 5:4).

## Turning to be Transplanted

"See, I am doing something new! Now it springs forth, do you not perceive it? In the wilderness I make a way, in the wasteland, rivers" (Isa 43:19).

One evening our superior summoned a meeting of all the brothers in the community. He asked that if any of us had any doubt or question about his vocation in life he should not hesitate to let him know about it. The superior spoke to us with the tenderness of a loving father to his beloved children. I knew I had some doubt but I was diffident to disclose to him my interior struggle. I had shared this inner struggle with my spiritual director. I had prayed about it. One evening, the Spirit moved me to bring it to the superior's attention. He wasn't expecting to hear that from me. He seemed to have regretted asking us to do so. He said many things, trying to talk me into staying with the community. I let him know that my struggles with vocation were not recent developments, but that I had suffered them since I entered religious life. I thought that the formation I received daily and the years I spent in the life would help me to discern and adjust to the life. I made it known to him because he asked us to do so. He faulted me for keeping such feeling within myself for such a long time (eight years). Then I said to him that I was willing to continue with the life if he wanted me to do so. He thought it wouldn't be the best idea to have me continuing in the life that I wasn't sure I was called to live. After a specific time period, he called me and suggested that I take some time out to discern to see if diocesan vocation was something I would be interested to respond to. He stressed kindly that the community door was always open to have me back or to support me in the vocation. That was really encouraging to me.

It was clear to me that time had come for the "Lord of the harvest" to transplant his little plant to its proper soil. The Lord alone knew the right soil for all his seedlings. It is the Lord who transplanted his servant

St. Anthony of Padua from the Augustinian community to the soil of the Franciscan Order. The same Lord of the harvest called St. Boniface from the monastic setting to the "mission field" to bring those whose souls were thirsty to the living fountain. Because he couldn't hold within him the fire of zeal for the holy mission burning in his heart, with the permission of his superior, St. Boniface set off to the wider, outside world to bring God's people to a saving encounter with Christ.

I couldn't hold within my heart the flame of fervor to be a more active missionary, the ardor to reach out to those in most need, and the passion to bring the consolation of Christ to those who are hurting. I prayed for the Lord's direction. Friends and relatives prayed for the Spirit to lead me to the proper mission field. The church prayed for my continuous openness to the movement of the Holy Spirit.

## The Combat Camp

It had become clear to me that the divine plan for my vocation itinerary was leading me to another direction. I felt the fire down within me to make a right turn to meet God's people in the heart of warfare. Yes, the Spirit was leading me to the more active task, to the diocesan priestly ministry. Taking the step out from that most "meritorious" of vocations—the contemplative life—to the diocesan pastoral ministry was not an easy move. It was a hard turn to make. However, as I have said, I knew that it was not about my personal plans but a divine design for my life; it wasn't about my choice, but the choosing of the Lord of the vineyard. It wasn't about me but about my Creator. It wasn't about my vision, but about the mission which the Lord entrusted to me. It wasn't about my agenda, but the order of the divine sender. It was about the Lord's mission and mandate. It was not motivated by any personal interest, as some thought. I had spent quality time in discerning the call.

I was concerned about the challenges of the priestly ministry in the modern world. You know, being a priest in today's western world is like being a soldier on guard duty at the enemy territory. Even so, I believe that the Lord in me is greater than the forces of the world (see 1John 4:4). The Lord assured me, as he did St. Paul, that his grace is sufficient for me and would be made even more manifest in my moments of weakness. The

Divine Master Potter had fashioned and polished me like an arrow through the austere desert of religious life, and held me as his tool for the sacred task of bringing his light to the dark recesses of the world. It has pleased the Lord to call me to become a "contemplative" active missionary disciple.

The blessed Lord has showered upon me grace upon grace to truly live as a pilgrim in the "pilgrim valley," to live a life of material simplicity in a land streaming with material prosperity. Like St. Paul, I have learned to "live in humble circumstances; I know also how to live with abundance. In every circumstance and in all things I have learned the secret of being well fed and of going hungry, of living in abundance and of being in need" (Phil 4:12).

The Lord transformed my heart to desire to do what is good, to live in the Spirit while journeying through the city of the flesh, to seek not the ungodly gaiety of the world or her gold and glory. I have been trained to keep my soul constantly open to breathe Christ's peace in the atmosphere polluted with the poisonous air of chaos and hostility, to embrace interior recollection in the city where noise and dissipation are prevalent, to set aside quality time for prayer amid the challenging busyness of daily living in the world charged with the technological "weapon of mass distraction." My pastoral charity is for all persons, without distinction of color, race, or language, yet with a special interest to the most vulnerable, the powerless, the neediest of our brothers and sisters. The Lord, who has called me to the mission, is my portion forever. I'll serve him with every fiber of my being, with all my heart, with all my soul, with all mind, with all my body, and with all strength. In him alone I glory, for nothing gives me lasting happiness except to do his will. He has lavished his love upon me, and I joyfully repay him with my life, with faithful love.

## The Christian Counsels

One of the fears my superior had about my going into diocesan vocation was the busyness of diocesan priestly ministry, which can drown prayer life. A priest who doesn't pray is like a disconnected power cable that cannot transmit currents. Christ is the power source of life. Prayer connects me to the Lord. St. Paul reminds me to pray without ceasing in order that I may stay spiritually alive, always recharged and reinforced for the journey to eternal union with the Lord.

Some persons asked me about what I would do with the vows I took as a religious. I believe that as a Christian the "Evangelical Counsels"—the vows of poverty, chastity, and obedience, which I took in the religious community—were not meant only for religious life alone but also for Christian life. They are primarily a bedrock of Christian spirituality. Christ wants all Christians to be obedient to authorities, to embrace purity of life, and to live lives of simplicity. People of faith are called to live the counsels though in accord with one's vocation or state in life. A celibate priest, for example, is called to abstain from any form of sexual relationship for life. Married couples live a chaste life in exclusive sexual relationship with their spouses. I didn't take the vows temporally but perpetually. I'm called to live them in every place and at all time. In my diocesan vocation, I vehemently reject any spirit of impurity, unholy disobedience to authority, and vainglory.

I prayed the Lord to make known to me the diocese to which he called me to serve. I wondered how the Lord would make it clear to me: would he speak to me in a dream? Or through a human being? Or through an angel? Well, I knew that the Lord does not play riddles on his beloved. He communicates things clearly to those who listen and obey him.

The Lord sent me his holy servant to direct me to the right place. I ran into the rector of our seminary one morning. He invited me into his office and we began a pleasant conversation. After letting him know of my intention to discern a diocesan vocation, he asked whether I had any particular diocese in mind. I said "no." With a cheerful look, he said to me, "I have a place for you in the diocese of St. Augustine." The diocese is in a relatively distant state from the seminary. Even though I didn't have any clue about the diocese, I knew right away that it was an answer to my prayer. God had called me to go to the place that was unknown to me. It was a journey of faith.

A few days later, the rector recommended me to the bishop, who invited me and sent me a flight ticket for a discernment meeting. On May 11 of that memorable year, after my final exam I set out for the Flowerland. I arrived in the evening that day after a safe flight. I met with the bishop and the vocation team. After an extensive interview, I was accepted as a seminarian for the diocese. A new beginning!

You, my Lord, sent me forth on this mission. You willed it. I come to serve your holy will. I open my heart to you, my Divine Master Potter. Change my heart and set it on fire with zeal and love for your people.

## Carrying my Cross

"Whenever the vessel of clay he was making turned out badly in his hand, he tried again, making another vessel of whatever sort he pleased" (Jer 18:4).

I had completed my third year theology before I transitioned to the diocese. The journey was not an easy one. The Lord willed to do some reconstruction and renewal in my life. How tough the narrow way! I had hoped that my bishop would grant me the grace to complete my studies in the former seminary, but he chose a different seminary for me.

In my former seminary, I was pursuing two master's degrees: master of divinity and master of arts (theology). I had already defended my thesis and had a few months to complete my course works to obtain the degrees. Now the new seminary offered only one master's degree, and they wouldn't transfer all my course credit hours. This meant that I would lose one master's degree and the authority of the latter seminary would have me spend two additional years before graduation. This didn't bother me, for the mission is not measured by the number of academic degrees but by the degree of love. And so with joy and enthusiasm I left for the seminary.

After a four-and-a-half-hour drive, I arrived at the seminary on the ninth day of August that blessed year. It was on Sunday evening. The faculty gave us a warm welcome. We had our dinner together. After the meal, I walked along the hallway leading to my assigned room. The academic dean caught up with me and introduced himself. "Hi, Clay!" he greeted with a beaming smile. He continued, "I'm glad you are here. Let me know if you need anything. We have evaluated your records and found that you did excellently well. So we decided to place you in the third year." Hearing this, I missed my breath and stood aghast. I thought he mistook me for someone else. I replied to him, "I have already completed my third year in my former seminary." He felt disappointed that I wasn't enthused by their decision. "Well, it is our policy that we do not transfer all credit hours. And most importantly, for a student to qualify to receive our master's degree in divinity and to have our recommendations for ordination, he must have spent at least two years in our seminary. I am sorry that your diocese did not communicate this to you earlier. Don't worry about this now, we shall talk about it later." With a heavy heart, I left for the chapel for my holy hour. I thought of the challenging demands of repeating the year, the strains and rigor of spending two more years in the seminary. I knew that my mind was not settled for quiet time in the chapel.

I returned to my room. Entering there, I knelt and prayed a short prayer: "My Divine Master Potter, I am disturbed by this news. Breathe into me your breath of peace of mind." Immediately a gentle, calming voice came to me: "Do you want it to go your way, or do you want to follow my plans for your life?" The question hit home, taking me back to Jeremiah 18, which says, "Whenever the vessel of clay he was making turned out badly in his hand, he tried again, making another vessel of whatever sort he pleased . . . Can I not do to you . . . as this potter has done?" (Jer 18:4, 5). I prostrated myself and pleaded with my Lord, "Yes, Lord, you are the potter. I resign to your holy will. Let your will be done in my life." At that moment, it was like a heavy load was lifted off of my heart. I felt a profound peace within me. A flood of strength rushed within my veins. I knew right away that it was the Holy Spirit who came into me in a powerful way. Feeling inspirited and heartened, I grabbed my breviary and Bible and left for the chapel.

In the morning, the rector called me. He spoke to me with warmth and comfort, giving his apologies for not explaining the matter earlier before my arrival. His words struck me deeply: "If you consider the cross along the way, you may be discouraged. Think about what the Lord who brought you here wants to do with you." I knew that it was a confirmation of the message I received in prayer. Oh, how human nature abhors suffering! I forgot about true life through the cross. Like Peter, who out of natural affection and tinge of self-love wanted the Christ without the cross, the hero without the piercing arrow, the savior without the scar, the conqueror of death without dying (cf. Matt 16:22). The impulsive apostle reasoned that the Messiah's suffering would cause him suffering, his arrest would expose him to the enemy, his death would bring to him great loss, for he had left everything to follow the Messiah. Peter wanted to save himself from such predicaments. Like Peter I wanted to flee from my own share of the cup of suffering. I forgot that in following the Lord a cross is inevitable; I couldn't escape from carrying my own cross! How the fallen nature beckons me to glory without the goading of pain! But the holy grace teaches me that for me to be a disciple of Christ I must willingly carry my own cross and follow the Lord (cf. Matt 11:28). Nature wanted me to choose the easy route. I judged the reality according to the human point of view, according to temporal consideration and interest. But the logic of love is far different. Love bids me to sacrifice, to self-renunciation, to self-giving, to carrying my cross and following the Lord. I follow your example, Lord! You are the Christ who saves me by laying down your life, who conquers my enemies by offering yourself to be crushed. You are the Savior who sets me free by giving yourself to be nailed to the cross, the deliverer who delivers me by dying, the king who reigns in my soul by accepting the crown of thorns. May your will be forever done in my life!

## A Farewell to the Family

When I was transferred to the seminary, I wrote a farewell letter to my beloved former seminary community. The following is a copy of the letter.

Dear Seminary Community,

I write this email to you with mixed feelings. Firstly, it is with a joyful heart that I email to let you know that after some time of discernment I have been accepted as a seminarian for the diocese of Saint Augustine. Secondly, my joy is mingled with tears because I'll surely miss all of you. My bishop indicated to me that I would be completing my theology at the seminary in Flowerland.

It is really hard for me to say goodbye to you all, having been together with some of you for over four years now. I feel bountifully blessed to have passed through Glen Seminary. I think of the seminary faculty's supportive relationship, guidance, and dedicated service. I recall my classmates' gentlemanliness, diligence, and care for one another. I remember the spirit of fraternal love, devotedness, and fervency that were some of the characteristics of the seminarians in general. I cannot forget in a hurry the dedication and generous service of the entire staff at the seminary. Apparently, life in my formal religious community inevitably kept me back from fraternizing more fully with most of the students, especially the new ones. Even so, in one way or another, you all have made a lasting impression on my life. Most significantly, you have taught me how to love in a sacrificial way. I wish I had the opportunity to meet you individually before my departure, just to say thank you and farewell. Who knows, sometime in the future God may grant me the grace to meet you again. In any case, let us be close in heart; I ask that you lift me up in prayer so that my heart may continually resign to the will of God in my life. On my part, rest assured, my prayer is with you. As St. Paul enjoins us, let us "encourage one another and build one another up, as indeed you do" (1Thess 5:11).

Once again, accept my grateful appreciations, and goodbye!

Your brother in Christ,
Clay

## The Local's Letter

❖ In my diocese, seminarians have a tradition of writing letters to our bishop. At the end of each semester, each seminarian writes to acquaint the bishop with the state of things, how he is faring in the formation and discernment process. The following is a copy of my first letter to my bishop after my first semester in the new seminary.

Dear Bishop,

It is with great joy that I write you this letter. I am grateful to the Lord for the grace of being chosen as one of your spiritual children in this diocese. I appreciate all of the many ways you have given me a warm welcome and support.

When I arrived in your diocese over seven months ago, I was told that I would serve for the summer at Christ the King Catholic Parish, Sunville. Natural impulses stirred certain concern in me, and I thought about the type of persons I would meet there. Would they be receptive to foreigners? At the same time, I felt the inner confidence and zeal that no matter the kind of people I would encounter there the Spirit would guide me in serving Christ in them with dedication and love. So I went there with interior strength and ardor. Providentially, the Lord gave me the consolation of meeting a devout, Spirit-filled faith community. The members of the parish received me with open arms and drew me right away into the life of the parish. This attitude of theirs was for me an eloquent testimony of their profound faith and love for the Lord and the Church. Obviously their wholehearted reception fostered my smooth transition and quick adjustment to the diocesan mission. I am grateful to them.

I should also mention the beautiful relationship I enjoyed with the priests in the parish. It is interesting to note that we had three continents represented in the rectory: America (Fr. Bill), Asia (Frs. Larry and Sean), and Africa (myself). Our pastor Fr. Bill generously took the lead in making the rectory a home for all. We lived in a spirit of fraternal love and care. My heart continued to sing the words of the Psalmist: "How good and how pleasant it is when brothers dwell together as one!" (Psalm 133: 1). It was really a grace-filled time of learning and growth.

I was involved in various activities in the parish. As I mentioned to you before, I went door to door with the Legion of Mary on Wednesdays and Saturdays. As you are aware, knocking on doors is the main apostolate of my former religious community. I found it exciting to continue this mission of reaching out to others with the Good News of Jesus Christ. On Fridays, I helped in serving the poor for the St. Vincent de Paul Society. I also did home visitation with some of the members. It was inspiring to see for myself the excellent work of mercy that St. Vincent de Paul Society offers, particularly, providing material support to many of our brothers and sisters who are in need. I also attended meetings with some other groups within and outside the parish, including the Cursillo Men's Prayer Group, the Men's Faith Sharing Group, the RCIA, the Scripture Study Group, and the That Man Is You.

The months flew by very quickly. Before I knew it, the summer was over. I set forth for the seminary in August. I had an exciting experience the first day I arrived. Shortly after my arrival that day, I ran into one of the authorities of the seminary. He informed me that I had been placed in the third year. I responded "okay." Yet, I knew within my heart that the news somehow dispirited me. Naturally, I weighed the demands of repeating the year and the intellectual and physical rigor. Ah, how weak I am! I went into my room and prayed. Listening to the Spirit, I heard clearly from the depth of my soul the still voice say to me, "Do you want it to go your way? Or do you want it to go in accord with my plan for your life?" Immediately, I felt like one who was jolted from a deep slumber. I responded, "No, Lord! I want to follow your way." Then I remembered the paradox of Christian life: the way of the "cross" is the way to true life. I accepted it; I embraced it with joyful resignation. Since then, I have been at profound peace and my joy continues to increase daily. I am thankful to the Lord for bringing me here in the seminary. The Spirit continues to work in my life, using the seminary community in shaping and molding me as he sees fit for the sacred mission.

I am grateful for the gift of my brother seminarians, particularly those from our diocese. They have touched my life with their characteristic fraternity. I am blessed to be among them!

Reflecting on my vocation journey so far, I am strongly convinced that the Lord had been preparing me to serve him and his church in your beautiful diocese. Not long ago I shared with my friend that I am a little plant in the Lord's garden. Our Lord Jesus Christ is the divine gardener who alone knows the proper soil for each person. He has transplanted me into your diocesan soil. I am at peace, praying for the continuous outpouring of divine grace to enable me to take unshakable root, to grow, blossom, and bear good fruits without ceasing. Yes, it is the Lord that calls, and thanks to his grace I was able to respond to his invitation. I pray daily that the Holy Spirit may continue to lead the way, for I have no power of my own.

I ask that you continue to give us your blessings. By God's grace I will keep faith with you, serving in obedience, dedication, and sacrificial love.

If there are any other matters I have not mentioned that you would like me to address, I would be glad to speak about them when I meet with you within a few days.

Your son in Christ,
Clay

# Don't Worry About Words

A year after my arrival in the diocese, some friends contacted me to inquire whether I had been ordained to the priesthood. When some of them learned that the ordination wasn't held at the time they expected, they said many negative things. One asked me to come back to the country and get married for I was almost "overdue" for it. The other said that I had wasted my life pursuing a "position" that wasn't likely to be realized. Still another said that I was fighting tooth and nail to wear the "collar," which many, who had felt disgusted wearing it, stripped it off. Were they really expressing their genuine concern and love for me? I didn't read their minds, and so I wouldn't judge their motives based on my perception. I do not blame them anyway. They didn't know God's plan for my life. They couldn't perceive the fire of zeal for the mission flaming within the center of my being, which I couldn't control. I knew that people are different. I know that they can think, understand, act, and say things differently. I know that in one thing people can think or say different things or act upon it in different ways. With regard to what people say, one's words may be good or bad, false or true, harsh or pleasant, discouraging or uplifting, insulting or respectful, corrupting or edifying. Whatever the case may be, I have an option in what is said to me. I can either allow myself to be controlled by the words, or I can choose to control my thoughts about what has been said to me. We know that words have no hands and feet, but they can be very powerful to grab, crush, and hurl a giant into hell, into endless misery. True, words have power to build or to destroy depending on how much I allow them to act upon me. If I am generous and someone calls me selfish, does it mean that I am selfish? No, but the words can influence me to begin to act selfishly. Negative words do not come from a good spirit but from the spirit of contradiction. They don't build up but rather aim at disturbing and harming, at getting a person to think and act negatively, to change from what one is doing to what they want one to do.

I know that the Lord has called me to a mission of love and of light, of encouraging the weak, of proclaiming the saving Gospel to all. Those called to the mission of love have the spirit of light. They see and hear and love with the heart. They see and hear what human beings cannot perceive with their sense organs. Those led by the Spirit do not allow the sword of negative words to pierce through their hearts. They do not expose their hearts to the spirit of darkness. They do not give away their thoughts to be rocked by the storm of negative words. When one is driven by the flesh, those words will drive one, but when one is driven by the Spirit, the Spirit will drive away words that are not for one's spiritual interest. As a person of faith, I respond to adverse words, not according to the flesh but by the Spirit.

I answer negative words with positive attitude, discouraging words with hope, insulting words with respect, hateful words with love. By the grace of God, I refuse to allow human words to take me captive, to pierce me with the spear of anger, to bind me with the bond of bitterness. I resist giving words a chance to throw me into the prison of gloom. Let people say whatever they want to say; let them do whatever they want to do. I'll continue to cling to him who is my heart's desire. I'll continue to wait upon him who is at work in my life. I'll continue to stay with him. No negative words or actions against me can drive me away from the peaceful and joyful life in the Divine Master Potter.

## The Movement of Mercy

As part of our formation program in the new seminary, we had a spiritual pastoral ministry training program, learning how to minister to the sick and those with special needs. I had a great experience in the training. The following is my reflection on my encounter with one particular patient over the summer.

That afternoon, I was on call at the Memo Hospital. The medical team paged me. I went to the emergency room and met the team attending to a patient named Lily (not real name). Lily is eighty-one years old. She is an active Catholic. I first talked with Lily's daughter, who brought her mother to the hospital. Lily took ill with fever and heart pain three days before they rushed her to the emergency room. After running some tests, the doctor explained that her heart was not functioning properly. She needed a pacemaker. With confidence and prayerful spirit, I approached Lily after the doctor and her medical team had completed their examination. I introduced myself as a chaplain.

Scared, Lily almost shouted with a wobbly voice, "No, no! I am not dying! I am not dying . . ." I answered her that I came to her because I found that she was not dying. Feeling reassured, she affirmed, "Okay, I am not dying. I have things to live for . . ." As I interviewed her, I saw that Lily was afraid for her life. Her hands and feet were shaking, her heart was racing, and her breathing was labored. Lily was scared that she might die of her illness. She told me that she couldn't control the fear within her. I felt compassion for her. I thought about how best to help her get over her anxiety and fear, and regain courage and confidence to face the reality of her sickness. After praying over her, she said that she felt better, yet she clung firmly to my arm. I stayed beside her for a while because she needed my presence. She said to me, "When you introduced yourself as a chaplain, I didn't intend to be mean or nasty to you. I thought that you were a priest who came to give me last rites."

I understood Lily, and my heart was moved for her. I knew that she was afraid of dying. At the same time, I was surprised that Lily, who was an active Catholic, misunderstood the significance of the sacrament of anointing. How many Catholics are poorly catechized! After she recovered, I helped Lily to understand that anointing of the sick was not only administered to those who are actively dying. It is given to those who are sick to bring physical, and most importantly, spiritual healing to them, as St. James exhorts the Church to do (cf. James 5:14–15).

I know that wherever people hurt, wherever people suffer, Christ is present with them. The Lord was always moved with great compassion when he met someone hurting, when he met the sick and the suffering. He never hesitated to heal the maladies of body and soul of those who encountered him. The Lord invites me to continue this mission of bringing his love and healing to the hurting, to console the sorrowful, to care for the castaway, and to visit the sick. Christ wants me to be his visible presence to my neighbors, to weep with those who weep and to rejoice with those who rejoice (Rom 12:15). So whenever I visit the sick, I always keep in mind the words of Christ, "I was sick, and you visited me" (Mt 25:36). Reflecting on my encounter with Lily, I saw grace at work in her. She loved the Lord. It was a consolation to me knowing that my presence, prayer, and passionate concern meant a lot for her. The Lord calls me to be a missionary after his compassionate heart, a servant of his merciful love. I may not be able to solve the problems of the sick and the suffering, but my love and care can help them find healing. My encounter with Lily really taught me how much the sick needed a caring heart, a soothing touch, and a consoling presence. Now when I visit the sick and the homebound I keep in mind that I was not just there to do my "job" of bringing Holy Communion but to bring Christ's healing presence and care to them. I pray constantly that the Lord may grant me the grace to live the spirit of mercy.

## A Flight over the Fence

Clay on a pilgrimage to Mexico, visited the historic
Pyramid of the Moon and the Pyramid of the Sun.

The Basilica of Our Lady of Guadalupe, Mexico

Our tour guide in blue jacket recounts the fascinating
story of the apparition of Our Lady of Guadalupe.

A magnificent statue of Our Lady of Guadalupe.

Clay with his fellow pilgrims walks uphill to visit the chapel at the top of Tepeyac hill in Mexico.

❖ After spending one year in the seminary, I was assigned to the vibrant parish community at Palm Side for a pastoral year (internship). In early February that year, I had the privilege of making a pilgrimage to Mexico, visiting the shrine of Our Lady of Guadalupe. I wrote the following reflection on the holy journey:

At a time when the government was building a "wall," God made a way! I didn't dream of going to Mexico. I wasn't planning to go on a pilgrimage to Guadalupe. It was an outpouring of generosity of Cemy and Rilly (not their real names), a devout couple who were graced with tenderness of heart and kindness. They have shown me unbounded hospitality, opening their hearts, their arms, and their doors for me. Once in a while, I spend my day off at their lovely home in Palm Side. One particular evening, they had invited me over for dinner. Rilly prepared a delicious dinner as usual. I had just devoured the meal and was still licking my lips when Rilly cleared her voice and said in her natural soft voice, "Clay," would you like to go with us to Guadalupe?" I thought that there was a place in Flowerland that was called by such a name. "Where is Guadalupe?" I inquired. "Our Lady of Guadalupe in Mexico!" Cemy replied. With a sense of excitement and wonder, I stood still for a while. Like the prophet, my heart was filled with delightful joy when they said to me, "Come let us go to the mountain of the Lord" (Micah 4:2). "How would we go to Mexico? Your government is building a border wall," I said jokingly. "No, we are flying over the wall," Cemy replied humorously. I thought it was an inspired reply. The divine finger had drawn the itinerary of our journey to Mexico. We would indeed fly over all obstacles. Nothing would hold us back. Who and what could hinder what the Lord had decreed? "For the Lord of hosts has purposed, and who will annul it? His hand is stretched out, and who will turn it back?" (Isa 14:27, *RSV*). My kindhearted pastor didn't hesitate to give his permission. Within a short time, Cemy had got our paperwork ready for the pilgrimage.

I had read the story of St. Juan Diego and the apparition of Our Lady of Guadalupe. Some devout souls have shared their exciting experiences of visiting Guadalupe. The Lord had granted me an opportunity to visit and see for myself what I had read and heard about the apparition.

Some thought I was going to Mexico for vacation. No, I was rather going there as an expression of my vocation as a missionary. I wasn't going for fun but for faith. I wasn't going to Guadalupe to be entertained, but to give thanks to the blessed Lord for the gift of his blessed Mother. My journey to Mexico wasn't for leisure but as a measure against spiritual slumber. I wasn't going to work in Mexico, but to walk with the Lord and the blessed Lady.

I spoke with a friend on the phone and he made a sarcastic remark that I didn't need to travel far to be with the Lord. True, Jesus is everywhere. He's with me always. However, going on pilgrimage is significant to me for some reason. The journey from my home to the sacred shrine serves as a symbolic reminder of my pilgrimage here on earth. I have no lasting city in this world. I'm a pilgrim and my eternal home is in heaven. Visiting that holy ground where the blessed Lady appeared and gave the world a visible gift of her love and presence would inspire and foster in my heart a more intense spiritual fervor and growth. Remember that Jesus journeyed to Jerusalem for a pilgrimage (cf. Luke 2:41–42). He went into the wilderness to spend a quality time alone with his Father (Mt 4:1ff).

I drew my theme for the pilgrimage from St. Paul's exhortation to Timothy: "[I] remind you to stir into flame the gift of God that you have ..." (2Tim 1:6). The journey to the sacred city will afford me the opportunity to ponder and pray for a fresh touch of the Spirit. I begged the Lord to rekindle in me the fire of fervent faith, to refill me with genuine joy, and to renew in me the spirit of indefatigable diligence to love and serve him without growing weary. Regardless of how humble my gifts may seem, I pray always that the Lord may grant me the grace to put them to work for his greater glory.

On Thursday morning, February 2, we set out for Mexico. It was on the Feast of the Presentation of the Lord. I begged the blessed Mother who presented her Son in the temple to present to him all those who were making the pilgrimage and also those who had asked me to pray for them. That morning, four of us rode in Cemy's car to the airport. Approaching the city, Orlando, we discovered that the traffic was heavy and we were running late. After much delay, we arrived at the airport about twenty minutes before our flight's departure time. Our hearts remarkably raced as we feared that we might miss our flight. We dragged our luggage along as our feet hurried down the hall for check in. I prayed silently that the Lord might keep the plane for us. We boarded the plane just a few minutes before the plane's door was closed for takeoff, thanks be to the Holy Spirit. Soon after we were seated, our flight departed. After three hours in the air, we landed in Mexico City; it was a smooth and safe journey. Some other pilgrims had arrived from different states in the United States. There were twenty of us altogether. Our tour guide picked us up in a shuttle bus to the hotel.

When I entered my assigned hotel room, I couldn't figure out how to turn on the light. I looked around for someone to help. Soon a young woman ambled along the hallway. She was a housekeeper. She didn't understand English. Since I don't speak Spanish, I made up a sign language to communicate with her. She smiled, nodding her understanding. I led her to the room and she taught me to place my room key card into a slot on the wall. She was such a kind and joyful woman.

I learned from her that love is a language of its own. Everyone understands it. When communication is difficult, speak love and you'll experience a miracle of "tongues." The housekeeper cared for others and passionately served with love. Lovingly, she opened her heart for me; patiently, she listened to me; caringly, she understood my question; readily and willingly, she helped me. Our differences in language, color, and nationality weren't a barrier to her service of love. "There is neither Jew nor Greek, there is neither slave nor free, there is neither male nor female; for you are all one in Christ Jesus" (Gal 3:28).

In my hotel room was mounted a giant television. I resolved not to turn it on. Note that television is by no means a bad thing, yet blessed and truly free is one who knows when to turn it off so as to pray and to listen to the Lord. I decided not to use it at that period of pilgrimage as a measure to mortify the senses. Of course, I didn't go to Mexico for television but for "theo-vision." I went there to see and relish the awesome visible manifestation of the eternal reality. I went there to get away from the crowd in order to recharge spiritually. In this light, I wanted to avoid anything that would create an occasion for dissipation. You can understand the constant struggle between the desires of the flesh and the prompting of spirit. Even so, grace always triumphs in the lives of those who sincerely seek the Savior. Without his grace, my frail flesh would slide me into spiritual slops.

On the second day of our pilgrimage, I woke up in the middle of the night praying the Holy Spirit to renew our strength. At 6:30 a.m., we had breakfast and set out for the shrine of Our Lady of Guadalupe. When we arrived at the holy ground, we saw only a few people. But as the day progressed, people trickled in, and before noon there was a sea of heads at the large property of the shrine. Many youths and older folks swarmed the street into the holy ground for prayer and/or sightseeing. It was exciting to watch some pilgrims walk on their knees as a form of penance. Oh yes, to those who love the Lord and appreciate his unbounded love, no sacrifice is too much. It was interesting to hear from our tour guide that the shrine is the second most visited Catholic shrine in the world after Vatican City, which takes the top position in pilgrimage ranking. After celebrating Mass at the Basilica of Our Lady of Guadalupe, we viewed the miraculous "Tilma" on which Our Lady of Guadalupe left the ageless, awe-inspiring imprint of her image.

We left the shrine in the afternoon. After nearly a forty-five-minute drive, we made it to the temple of Quetzalcoatl, the location of the famous Pyramid of the Sun and the Pyramid of the Moon. I stood speechless as I gazed at the spectacular architecture of the pyramids built before the invention of modern technology. I climbed the two pyramids which were over two hundred feet high. I could see the fire of faith in the hearts of the Aztecs, the ancient Indians of Mexico, who labored to erect the enormous pyramids. They had no doubt that human beings were created to worship their Creator. They knew that they needed the divine in their lives. But like a blind person seeking a lost treasure, the pagan Aztecs groped in the darkness, searching for the true God with every fiber of their being. Nothing could stop them from constructing and dedicating the terrific temple to their gods. They worked faithfully as a community, with a spirit of collaboration, solidarity, and devotion. As a result, they were able to leave on the sands of time such an astonishing, monumental symbol of their faith.

The legacy of the Aztecs' religiosity taught me something about faith. Though they didn't know the true God, the Aztecs worshipped their gods with all fervor of faith, with their whole hearts, minds, souls, and powers. Unlike the Aztecs, I'm graced to live in the age of Divine Revelation. God has revealed himself to me, especially through the gift of his beloved Son, Jesus Christ. I have been blessed to be a Christian, to witness numerous apparitions, signs, and wonders. The Lord calls me personally to build, not necessarily pyramids made of stones and metals, but a spiritual one, a pyramid of faith.

We see in the Bible that Christ chides his disciples for their lack of firm faith. The Lord has assured me that if I have faith I can move mountains;

yes, I can do more incredible things than the Aztecs did (Mt 21:21). Is there any better pyramid that the faithful can build in today's world than to love one another, to care for and share our resources with one another, to work for justice and peace? I pray that all nations of the world may not be like the cursed cities in the Bible (Chorazin, Bethsaida, Sodom, and Gomorrah) who didn't turn from their evil ways after their "time of visitation." Think about this: if the primitive Aztecs were blessed with the miracles which the Lord performs in our time, they might have converted and accepted the true God. May the Lord have mercy upon us and help the world overcome her unbelief.

On the third day, we visited the tomb of Blessed Miguel Pro, who was martyred during the anti-Catholic crusade in Mexico. After celebrating Mass at that beautiful parish named the Holy Family Church, we viewed and prayed before the first- and second-class relics of the saint.

As we walked out of the church, I pondered in silence the day's Gospel reading that struck me deeply. It was from the Gospel of Mark, where Christ instructs his disciples, "Come away by yourselves to a deserted place and rest a while" (Mar 6:31). I reflected on the true way to rest; that is, to stay with the Lord. I pondered how my busy life sometimes tends to prevent me from spending quality time alone with the Lord. I thought that no car runs continuously without refilling. A bee can't sting twice without returning to its beehive to recharge itself. In the same way, I need some time to withdraw in order to renew my spiritual strength from the divine power source. It is not possible for a Christian to have an effective, deep spiritual life without spending time alone with the Lord. The pilgrimage was an opportunity for me to disengage with the pressures of daily living so as to engage more deeply with God.

On the fourth day, we visited the state of Puebla, about two hours' drive away from Mexico City. The road to the state was a lovely hilly terrain, naturally decorated with high mountains. Our bus gently navigated the high land which our tour guide described as "over ten thousand feet above sea level." We visited the historic St. Michael Church, located in the countryside of Puebla. It was the site of the miraculous apparition of Archangel Michael to Diego Lazaro in the year 1631. We celebrated Mass at the parish chapel. It was fascinating to see a busy open-air markets near the church. The villagers were selling a variety of stuff ranging from cooked food, fresh fruits, and vegetables, to utensils and clothes. It really brought memories of my childhood and my village market in Nigeria, where I used to peddle my handmade baskets. We spent the rest of the day sightseeing in the beautiful city of Puebla.

On the fifth day, we returned to the Basilica of Our Lady of Guadalupe. After Mass and private prayer, the bus took us to some of the memorable churches in Mexico City. As we walked down the bustling street, I saw a young woman and her little daughter, who was about five years old, selling some handmade woven baskets on the sidewalk. The daughter was weaving a new basket while the mom was attending to customers. I watched with delight the little girl's marvelous dexterity in weaving. I shook her hands, complimenting her amazing skill. She shyly glanced at me and gave me an innocent smile. My heart was moved with compassion. I reached for my wallet and gave her a little money I had to encourage her effort. She accepted it, and with her face brilliantly beaming with joy she said to me in Spanish, "*Gracias, señor* (Thank you, sir)." She handed the little money to her mother. Obviously overjoyed, the mother fondly addressed her, "*Mi amor* (My love)." What a touching gesture of love! See how devoted, loving, and supportive they were of each other! As we walked away, thoughts of the woman and her little daughter stayed in my mind. Poverty might have denied the little girl education, but surely not elation. Their state of impoverishment might have robbed her of the treasures and pleasures that some of her mates enjoyed, but obviously peace and thanksgiving never run dry in her heart. In her world plagued with poverty, the woman had taught her daughter to be faithful, to be joyful, and to be productive and hopeful. While some parents teach their children to beg, she taught her daughter to give. While some train their children in ways of vice, to lie, to cheat, to flirt, to hate, the young mother instructed her daughter in virtue, to embrace discipline, to work hard, to be just and honest, and to contribute with her skill in building up a just society.

Our pilgrimage to Mexico came to an end on the sixth day. Our bus arrived early in the morning. We bade farewell to our fellow pilgrims and left for the airport at 5:15 a.m. We arrived home safely. Ah, what a journey so joyfully inspiring and so spiritually refreshing! What a pilgrimage so peacefully triumphant!

## Finding Happiness in Sadness

One afternoon during my pastoral year I received an email from the vocation office informing me that the bishop had scheduled my diaconal ordination for November that year. The joy of my heart knew no bounds. I thought that the appointed time, the long-awaited time had finally come! My long struggle was not in vain, blessed be the name of the Lord! I bemoaned the past times that beset me with great anxiety while I awaited the realization of the vocation. I remembered the gloomy times of exhausting hard work and setbacks. Ah, how limited my human eyes that failed to see the rays of victory twinkling in the midst of the future.

Then I thought how time passes quickly. I also pondered how life flies very rapidly too. I recalled that each passing time brings either sadness or happiness. Each passing time can be tough and distressing for some individuals, while on the other hand full of joy and delight for some others. Some who rejoice at a given time wish such a time would go on forever. In their moment of grief, some people wish the world would end at once. Sometimes, people rejoice because they used their time very well. Sometimes some suffer afflictions because they chose to live recklessly and irresponsibly. Still some meet with adversities even though they use their time well. So both good and bad people suffer in this world. No matter the circumstances they face in life, people of faith are confident that the Lord is at work in their lives. They rejoice and give all glory to God. They understand and live the demand of charity: to share with their neighbors' sorrows or joys (cf. Rom 12:15).

I know that sometimes God permits one to experience hardship in order that one may learn humility, to open one's eyes to realize that one is not yet "home." St. Paul reminds me "that all creation is groaning in labor pains even until now; and not only that, but we ourselves, who have the first fruits of the Spirit, we also groan within ourselves as we wait for adoption, the redemption of our bodies" (Rom 8:22–23). Neither suffering nor sensible delight can separate me from the love of my Lord. I pray that my sweet Savior may save those who sink into a cesspit of depression and despair and those who find no meaning in life because of their affliction and misery. I know that sorrow with Christ will in time turn into endless bliss. Joy without Jesus Christ swiftly turns into sorrow. When time brings me sorrow, it is the Lord alone who can console me and wipe away all my tears. When I meet with failure, it is he alone who can turn things around to grant me success. When the turn of events delivers privation in my life, it is the Lord who can satisfy all my needs and quench my thirst in the fountain of life. In warfare, my victory is assured in his holy name. His promises are true. I prayed to the Lord to grant me the grace to persevere in faith till the end.

I prayed that the Lord might make each passing time truly joyful for me as I seek to do his will at all times. No matter what life brings to me, the Lord is my joy! When the Lord permits that I sow in tears, I trust that at last I "will reap with cries of joy" (Psa 126:5). I pray that each passing time may spur my heart to grow ever more in love for the Lord and to savor more fully Christ's abiding peace and joy both in the time of sadness and the time of happiness.

## A Heartfelt Farewell

❖ At the end of my pastoral year at Palm Side, I wrote a farewell letter to the parish to express my grateful appreciation for their wonderful hospitality and generosity.

Some parishioners in the New World celebrate
their call to be "the light of the world."

Some years ago, when my mom was expecting a baby, people inquired when she was due. When the baby boy was finally born, questions and expectations changed. Some people asked whether he came into the world healthy and whether Mom was safe from the ordeal of delivery. They also wondered what the future held for him. As time went by, the baby progressed through stages of growth and development; from the moment he was born, Clay began his life's journey on earth replete with constant movement and developments until the last "bus stop," when his spirit will take its leave and return to its divine source, God.

In August last year, my life's journey brought me to Mother Seton Parish for a pastoral year. Some people asked how long I would serve in the parish. "One year with hard labor," I would say humorously. The one-year countdown began on August 8, the day I started the internship. Days slid by, and before I knew it, the last month of my internship arrived. How true it is that time flies!

It's time to say goodbye to you! Yet, it's hard for me to do so, for you have touched my life in a very profound way! My heart hurts, my mind is whirling, and it can't stop thinking about you; it can't erase the memories of your care and generosity. My eyes are fogged with tears, because my heart is engulfed with mixed feelings: the feeling of joy that comes from an experience of a warm relationship, and on the other hand, the feeling of sadness that comes from missing a dearest one. The two emotions which now well up within my heart are by no means in conflict. They are naturally normal impulses of a soul journeying through the world of many goodbyes.

In the course of my life, I have bid countless goodbyes. Some years ago, I said farewell to my beloved schoolmates and teachers in elementary school, high school, and college. I bade goodbye to my colleagues, close friends, and relatives. Over ten years ago, I broke down with tears saying "goodnight" to my loving dad as his body was lowered into the grave. That was really the most painful parting of my life, for I knew I would never see him again in this life. In the evening when I set out for the New World, my mom and my siblings walked me to the park and gave me an emotional goodbye. It's been over six years since I last saw them. I thought that by now I would be used to the pain of saying goodbye to loved ones. No, my tearful goodbye to all of you in this parish is a reality check to my inability to overcome this feeling.

I could imagine how St. Paul and his brothers and sisters in Christ in Ephesus felt when he was expressing his heartfelt farewell to them: "They were all weeping loudly as they threw their arms around Paul and kissed him, for they were deeply distressed that he had said that they would never see his face again. Then they escorted him to the ship" (Act 20:37–38).

I can't thank all of you enough for all the many ways you have shown me great love. I'm grateful to our pastor, Fr. Kaston, for his kindness, his affable personality, and his dynamic leadership. He received me with open arms as his "brother" and mentee. I thank the two amazing parochial vicars, Fr. Ruma and Fr. Xima, for their humble disposition and captivating fraternal spirit. As you know, we have three continents represented in the rectory: America (Fr. Kaston), Asia (Fr. Ruma and Fr. Xima), and Africa (myself). No wonder a friend calls the rectory "IHOP," International House of Priests, even though I'm not yet a priest. Fr. Kaston, generously took the lead in making the rectory a home for all. We have evidently lived together with the fraternal spirit which Christ asks of his disciples. My heart continued to sing the words of the Psalmist: "Behold, how good and pleasant it is when brothers dwell in unity" (Psalm 133:1).

I'm grateful to Fr. Well who has served as my spiritual director during this internship. He devotedly helped me to improve and grow in my faith experience. I have enjoyed a supportive relationship with Fr. Ginus. I also thank Fr. Roys for his delightful humor which always put a smile in my heart. I have the blessing of working closely with the rectory staff since my arrival in this parish. All of them have worked collaboratively to make the rectory office a place where community relationship and efficiency meet, where faith is expressed through love, dedication, and service. How could I not praise such wonderful women who give me excellent examples of living the faith? "Charm is deceptive and beauty fleeting; the woman who fears the Lord is to be praised. Give her a reward of her labors, and let her works praise her at the city gates" (Pro 31:30–31).

Our parochial school is very vibrant. The students are very loving, obedient, faithful, smart, and disciplined. Whenever I attend the Wednesday school Mass, I always felt as though I was worshipping with angels. It is amazing to note that the students, including those in kindergarten, are very attentive and participative in the liturgy. They have learned to be reverent at church. In Africa, when a child is well-behaved, people ask who her/his parents are. In the case of the students in this parish, I thank their devoted teachers who always work very hard to educate and nurture the children in the discipline and morals that come from the fear of God.

I am truly blessed with the privilege to serve you at this spirit-filled faith community. I wish this paper would be enough to mention your names individually. However, know that I appreciate you for the many ways you have shown me great support for my vocation. You have indeed made a lasting impression in my life. You have taught me how to live by way of your fervent faith, your spirit of hospitality, your generous gifts, your many hearty hugs, smiles, words of cheer, and your sincere supplication and sacrifice for vocation in our diocese. You didn't accept me because of what I would do for you but because of what the Lord has done for you. You didn't support me because you wanted me to thank you; no, you did so because it was a way for you to express your thanksgiving to God. You didn't welcome me because I deserved it, but because the Lord demands it of you, to welcome strangers. Christ in you is the secret of your splendor and service of charity. It is beautiful and encouraging to see in this parish people of different cultures and languages come together, work and worship together, speaking one language of faith.

In early February this year, I had the privilege of making a pilgrimage to Mexico, visiting the shrine of Our Lady of Guadalupe. I'm grateful to the couple who generously sponsored the pilgrimage. It was an unforgettable experience!

Truly it has been a grace-filled year for me, a time of learning and growth experience. Since coming to the parish, I have been involved in various activities. I love the door-to-door evangelization with the Legion of Mary. We made many contacts with fallen-away Catholics, people of different faiths and beliefs, and nonbelievers. We were passionate to plant the seed of faith in their hearts, trusting that God alone causes it to germinate, to blossom and bear fruits. In addition to doing the rounds of the homebound, I conducted the weekly communion service at the two assisted-living facilities, namely Laguus and Palm-City. Some of the people whom I met in those places have taught me to be always grateful to God at all times, to serve his people from the heart, with merciful love, pure joy, patient humility, and sincere respect and care for all. I believe that God put them on my path to strengthen my feeble faith.

I take solace in the hope that this may not be my last goodbye to you. Hopefully, I'll meet you again. Who knows, the Lord may grant me the grace to serve you in this parish in my future priestly ministry. In any case, let us be close in heart; I ask that you lift me up in prayer so that my heart may continually resign to the will of God in my life. On my part, rest assured, my prayer is with you. As St. Paul enjoins us, let us "encourage one another and build one another up, as indeed you do" (1Thess 5:11).

Please mark your calendar: my diaconal ordination is scheduled for November 18 this year. I invite all of you to come join me in the great celebration of my ordination at the Mary's Parish, Flowerland. I ask that you continue to pray for me so that the Lord may prepare, protect, and present me to his church as a refined, faithful instrument of his grace and mercy. "One thing I ask of the Lord; this I seek: to dwell in the Lord's house all the days of my life, to gaze on the Lord's beauty, to visit his temple" (Psa 27:4).

As the famous scholar Shakespeare once said, "All's well that ends well." Yes, my stay at Mother Seton has ended well! It's a victory of faith shared in love and hope renewed in faith. As forward movement is an inevitable part of life's journey, I'm going forth to the other side of the "mission field" on which the Lord sends me.

May we stay close in spirit, praying fervently, working diligently, serving lovingly, sharing generously, and keeping our eyes firmly fixed on Christ as we journey together to our eternal home. I pray that the Holy Spirit may sustain and strengthen you with grace and fill your hearts and minds with his peace and joy.

Thank you and goodbye!
Clay

# Wedding Day!

Clay celebrates his ordination to the priesthood. "Those who sow in tears will reap with cries of joy. Those who go forth weeping, carrying sacks of seed, will return with cries of joy, carrying their bundled sheaves" (Psalm 126:5-6).

"Nations shall behold your vindication, and all kings your glory; You shall be called by a new name bestowed by the mouth of the LORD. You shall be a glorious crown in the hand of the LORD, a royal diadem in the hand of your God. No more shall you be called 'Forsaken,' nor your land called 'Desolate,' But you shall be called 'My Delight' . . . For the LORD delights in you . . ." (Isa 62:2–4).

The eve of my ordination was a busy one. I had rehearsed the Mass liturgy a thousand times in preparation for my first Mass. Some members of my family and friends had arrived from Nigeria and from other places within and outside the New World. Phone calls were coming in myriads. Gifts and congratulatory messages were pouring in like a torrent of rain.

Some people praised me as though I achieved the ordination by my power. Some applauded me as if I had earned a doctorate degree. I wish they could simply shake my hand and praise God who, out of his abundant grace, called and consecrated me for the mission. I wish they would just say, "Thank God for what he has done for you." Nevertheless, I know that they didn't mean to ascribe the glory to me; they thought that it was fitting to thank me for being open to the movement of grace. They showed me great love and gave me much support. I appreciated all their prayers and good wishes. I'm grateful for all the treasures they spent in generous giving. Indeed, their hearts were full of love; hence, they couldn't stop giving; they couldn't stop caring; they couldn't stop serving. The more the Lord filled them with his love, the more they shared it joyfully.

On that Saturday morning, my brother deacon and I processed solemnly into the magnificent cathedral, a very beautiful church adorned with the finest architectural design. As I processed along the aisle, I stole a subtle sideways glance to the pews. I could see a sea of heads, many people from different races, colors, cultures and faith backgrounds. All eyes were on the two of us who were the ordinands. To prevent the spirit of distraction, I prayed in my heart, asking the Holy Spirit to turn my thoughts into prayer. I pondered that the "assembly of all the saints," not only the living but also countless angels and saints in heaven, were present celebrating with us on this sacred event of our ordination. Certainly, the blessed Mother Mary was present in a special way. I could hear Christ commending me to her, "Woman, behold your son."

The processional hymn was an inspirational song from Dan Schutte:

"[H]ere I am Lord, is it I, Lord?
I have heard you calling in the night.
I will go Lord, if you lead me.
I will hold your people in my heart."

The voice of the choir resonated inspiringly through the church. I had heard this song time and again; it was my favorite song. Even so, there was a sense of fresh sweetness that came from the song. I felt such a sublime emotion as though I was lifted up to the third heavens. The two of us who were to be ordained sat excitedly at the front pews, each with his family. It was our wedding day!

During the Litany of the Saints, two of us lay prostrate on the majestic marble of the magnificent cathedral. Then, the bishop laid his holy hands upon us. As soon as he placed his hands on my head, I felt the vibration of an inflow of the Holy Spirit. An indescribable peace and warmth surged into my soul like a gentle refreshing breeze. I could sense that something extraordinary had permeated into my very soul, enwrapping me completely. I could sense the power of the Holy Spirit moving all over me; I could feel the transformation take place. Then the bishop prayed the prayer for ordination. My heart was filled with joy beyond all telling. I felt as though I had mounted wings, like an eagle soaring high in the beautiful blue sky.

After dressing in the new priestly vestments, then came the time for anointing. I had waited longingly for this part. I knelt before the bishop, stretching out palms to him. He poured chrism on my palms, rubbing it hard. I felt goose bumps run over me from head to toe. It was as though my heart was pumping oil, transporting it through my veins. I could sense my body and my soul drenched with the oil of anointing. I could see the walls of the church and the roof dripping with the holy oil as raindrops in the woods; I could perceive a spring of anointing, like a fountain gushing out from the floor where I knelt before the bishop. As a thirsty ground absorbs water, so my soul soaked up the anointing.

The prayer he said as he anointed me was very powerful: "The Father anointed our Lord Jesus Christ through the power of the Holy Spirit. May Jesus preserve you to sanctify the Christian people and to offer sacrifice to God." As the bishop uttered the words, I could hear Christ reading the scroll about his prophetic anointing with the Holy Spirit: "The Spirit of the Lord is upon me, because he has anointed me to bring glad tidings to the poor. He has sent me to proclaim liberty to captives and recovery of sight to the blind, to let the oppressed go free, and to proclaim a year acceptable to the Lord" (Luke 4:18–19).

I thought of my long vocation journey. I couldn't hold back my joyful tears as they streamed down my face. I knew I had been configured forever with Christ, sealed with the indelible brand of the divine. My heart explodes with joy as I think of this unmerited mercy. I praised the Lord for granting me the consolation of the ordination. Like a bride, Christ has handed me over to his holy church to serve him in his people and to serve his people in him. I have been configured into Christ forever. My desire for the holy vocation has been fulfilled! The long night has at last given way to a joyful dawn. At long last, God's wonderful plan for my life has prevailed. Now, the Divine Master Potter has equipped and commissioned me for the holy service, to bring the good news of salvation to the "poor." Amen, alleluia! *A buru lam uko-Chukwu ebebe n'usoro nke Melkizedeki* (I am a priest forever in the order of Melchizedek)!

# Holy Honeymoon

I have joyfully responded to the call to a celibate state, and this means that I'll remain unmarried and chaste all the days of my life. I'll not have natural children of my own, but I'll have plenty of spiritual children. The children of God will be my children; they will be my mothers, my fathers, my brothers, and my sisters. Their family will be my family; their community will be my community. I desire and strive daily to be faithful to this radical call, trusting that his grace and mercy will see me through.

It is a great privilege for me to be among the few who are chosen to be a "sign" of the life to come. For, as Christ says, "At the resurrection they neither marry nor are given in marriage but are like the angels in heaven" (Mt 22:30).

The vocation to priesthood is a kind of marriage. When a priest is newly ordained, he is filled with sublime joy, passionate zeal, and love for the Church, just as a spouse in a honeymoon loves his or her partner. During honeymoon, a couple focuses wholly on each other in a more heart-to-heart bonding. Their bodies are connected, their minds are united, their souls are knit together, their strength is refreshed in mutual self-giving love; their hearts desire one thing: an endless intimate companionship, for the beloved is treasured beyond all price.

In this light, as a newly ordained priest I want to speak of my own honeymoon. I want to talk about what is bubbling over in my heart. After many years of hard labor, studying, praying, discerning, and persevering, the Church has granted me the grace of ordination. Thinking about this grace brings to my heart an overwhelming joy!

In this spirit of joyous elation, I thought of the fact that some had felt the same excitement but over time foiled it. Their honeymoon did not last long and they flung away their "nuptial" ring and trampled under feet their "wedding" garb.

How long will my honeymoon last? How long will my vocation to priesthood endure? Well, I know it is not by my own power. My courage rests in the assurance that the grace of the vocation is with me. The Holy Spirit will not abandon me. "Now I know the LORD gives victory to his anointed. He will answer him from the holy heavens with a strong arm that brings victory" (Psalm 20:7). I have wholeheartedly said my definitive "yes" to the Lord's call. I have sincerely resolved never to retract it. I believe that my Lord designed this sacred path before he created me. He called me, chose me, and consecrated me even before my mother conceived of me. He has clothed me in sacred garment, girding me with an unbreakable cord. He imprints his seal of ownership on me and poured upon my heart his Holy Spirit (2 Cor 1:22). The Lord has set me on fire which no created power can put out. The joy of my honeymoon will stretch on to eternity.

I understand that the journey is not going to be all smooth and calm. The journey of life in this world is exposed to many roadblocks and adversities. There will be moments of storms, times of war and sorrow. I know there will be tempests that will rock me, waves that will threaten to sweep over me; there will be ups and downs through the road, hard and challenging times. Time will come when it will seem that my beloved Lord turns away from me, when "the master of the vineyard" will permit that I receive humiliation rather than honor, rejection rather than recognition, pain rather than pleasure. At that time, the demands of love (sacrifice and service) will beckon to me. When that time comes, I pray that the Lord may protect me from despair. Whatever the Lord permits me to experience along the way, I know he walks with me. I'll keep my eyes fixed on him, for his grace is always enough for me. Thomas à Kempis reminds me that "a valiant lover stands his ground in temptations and yields not to the crafty persuasions of the enemy."

I have learned the secret of peace and joy. I have learned the key to victory. Life is not in my hand but in the Lord's. When things do not go my way, I praise God and pray for the grace to always accept God's way. I have learned that prayer is to my soul what breathing is to my body. To stay alive and faithful in the sacred service, I need to breathe in prayer, drink prayer, eat prayer, and allow prayer to consume me. I must cultivate and savor constant communion with the Lord. I take comfort in God's merciful love, in his unfailing protection, as I consciously seek every moment to live in his holy presence. I ask for the grace not to stay in slumber like the disciples who were with Christ in the garden of sorrow. The Lord cautions them to watch and pray so that they might not fall into the waiting hands of the enemy (Mt 26:41). When the Lord permits that I fall sick, I will praise God and pray for healing. When the Lord allows that I meet with rejection, humiliation, or persecution, I will praise God and pray for his protection. When I am confused, I pray for the Spirit of clarity of vision. When the Lord permits that I grieve, I will praise him and pray for his consolation. When I fail, I will sincerely confess my sins, pray for the grace to learn from my mistakes, and move forward in faith and hope.

I pray you, Lord, wrap me in your arms and protect me from the snares of the world. You may strip me of all comforts, but I beg you do not take away your love from me. Your love is better than life (Psalm 63:3). To have you is to have all things. I will pour out my life in the service of your Gospel, even though this is less than a drop in the ocean compared to your boundless love. May I never substitute pure love of you for any created things. May I seek nothing more than what is eternal, nothing more than what is pleasing to you, nothing more than what leads me to you. May I cling to you rather than to the world, for the string of the world's love will collapse, but you are ever strong, ever faithful, and ever abiding in love. I loathe the worldly attractions and distractions that tend to divide my heart. Lord, set me on fire with love for you, and may no created force put out its flame. Speak to the fire within me so that it may blaze ever more intensely until it consumes every fiber of my being. You have invited me to die with you so that I may rise with you.

I know that certain impulses in me have refused to die and they will not die until a day after I die. Ah, I have to live with them as long as I endure in this pilgrim's valley. Those desires are a legacy which nature bequeathed on the progeny of Adam and Eve. They are not evil in themselves, yet they are like sparks flying out into the straw house. They need to be guarded; otherwise, they will set the heart on fire. When the crowd of cares hems in, when cloud of confusion billows up, when the tempest of temptation swirls around me, when the sword of desire pushes to divide my heart, the Holy Spirit pours upon me the grace to prevail over them.

Each morning, I ask for the grace to channel all my strength to the service of God. I preach the Gospel "in season and out of season." I find time to play. When I pray, I beg the Lord to grant me the strength to choose the good so as to stay faithful to him. I seek counsel from holy men of God to guide me to stay on the right path. When I preach, I share with others, either by words or deeds, the joy of Christ which wells up in my heart. Sometimes, I take a walk or jog along the wooded path in the neighborhood. The lush trees, blooming grasses along the path, and the beautiful blue sky speak to me about God.

Sometimes I ponder the amazing love of some holy men and women who encountered God and left us an example of firm faith to follow. I think of Abraham who walked by faith and found peace in the journey of life. Despite the bleakness of the way, he obeyed the divine command and journeyed to the unknown land which the Lord promised him (cf Gen 12). Job remained true to himself in spite of the terrible trial of his life. He confidently said, "I know my redeemer lives" (Job 19:25). St. Paul suffered greatly for Christ, yet he rejoiced always. He was whipped, shipwrecked, imprisoned, stoned, and rejected. He labored day and night without sleep. He was wracked with hunger and thirst, yet he rejoiced because Christ is his strength (2Cor 11:23ff). Imitating the faithful, I have resolved to resign to the mystery of God's love. I have tasted the Lord and seen that he is good (Psalm 34:8).

I will cling to my Lord with all my soul, body, mind, heart. My body may grow weak, but my heart will grow ever stronger in your love. Age may slow down the sharpness of my mind, but I will never forget you, for your word abides in me. My eyes may grow dim but your Spirit will illumine my way and direct my faith vision. You are my way; you are my true happiness. You are always faithful and will not abandon me. You are the secret of my perpetual peace, a key to the door of endless honeymoon.

## Hands to Heaven!

Today, the blessed Lord has consecrated me in truth for the mission of his love. He has anointed me and sent me on this mission so sublime, a mission so radiantly graceful and so profoundly transforming. Rejoice, my soul, for the privilege of being called to the sacred harvest! I've been called to a radical mission; it's a journey that leads to Jerusalem, a road to death, but a death which turns into a wellspring of life. Oh yeah, to be called to the priesthood is to be called to die so that others may live. Yet, I know that whoever risks his life in charity to offer others the life of Christ is truly alive. I have the happiness for the privilege of being one of the few that are chosen for this holy mission. My hand is now set "to the plow," no turning back. I offer myself without reservation, for it is the passionate love for his holy mission that urges me on. By the power of the grace operative in my life I can't hold back giving all, for I am confident that in giving myself totally and in dying with him I become truly and fully alive. The glory of priesthood is in the victimhood, in self-emptying, in self-offering, in identifying with the joys and sorrows of others, just as Christ did.

## Early in Life

The vocation to the priesthood was a fire that the Lord enkindled in my heart early in life. Like a wet wood, the Lord gave me some time to dry up the moisture within me so as to flame up with the fire of the Holy Spirit. Each passing day the fire in my heart blazed with greater intensity. I'm the Lord's Clay! The Lord is my Divine Master Potter who continues to shape and smoothen the rough edges of his vessel. He is the divine architect who designed the itinerary of the mission. As the wise guide, the Lord took me through a vocation detour: through colleges and jobs outside the seminary. When the time came, "the Lord of the harvest" properly set me en route. After many years of great struggle and sweat, here I am today joyfully celebrating the fulfillment of holy vocation. So great a privilege! So profoundly a sublime grace to become a priest at last! I'm not late in this ministry, for no one whom you call to work in your sacred vineyard begins late, but only those who are dead.

## All Glory to God

Clay's long night has at last given way to a joyful dawn.

I am a witness to his transforming encounter! The Divine Master Potter has chosen, molded, and shaped me into his tool; I'm a vessel of his healing balm. He has poured into me his sacred oil. He dips his finger into my life and smears the healing oil on his people to heal, to set free, to bless, to consecrate, to inspire, to enlighten, and to reclaim them from the power of the world.

When Christ anoints you, you can't stop proclaiming the saving Gospel; when he touches you, you can't stop blazing. When he finds room in your heart, you can't stop rejoicing. When he satiates your soul with his wine, you can't stop loving. When he intubates you with his Spirit, when he breathes his life-giving air into your lungs, you can't stop breathing life. When he feeds you with his word, you can't stop savoring his sweetness.

My heart will always rejoice in you, Lord; my soul will always praise you. You have hushed all fears that rocked my heart; You have renewed my strength. You have taken away all my worries and calmed my throbbing heart; my heart will forever sing your praise, my peace. You have consoled me and wiped away all my many tears; I'll forever exalt you, my mighty comforter. You have led me safely through the stormy sea; I'll exalt you, my faithful companion. You spoke to my life and my long night gave way to radiant dawn; I'll forever cling to you, my divine light. May my whole life be a holocaust of praise to you, my salvation. Together with all your saints, my heart will eternally sing the triumphal song of those who have conquered the world.

Clay's victory comes from the triumph of the Cross. It is a victory of faith shared in love, hope renewed in faith, and love expressed in sacrifice.

"Not to us, LORD, not to us but to your name give glory because of your mercy and faithfulness" (Psalm 115:1).

The Divine Potter continues to mold and shape his Clay into a vessel of his grace.

Printed in the United States
by Bookmasters

Printed in the United States
By Bookmasters